Published by the
House of the Wannsee Conference
Memorial and Educational Site

Liebe Mutti!

POSTCARDS FROM THERESIENSTADT 1943–1944

with artworks by
Inbar Chotzen

MEMORIAL AND
EDUCATIONAL SITE
**HOUSE OF THE
WANNSEE CONFERENCE**

CONTENT

THE MEMORY

Klaus Hillenbrand

Preserving the memory of people who suffered under the Nazis is not the sole responsibility of those active in the fields of historical research, politics, memorial sites or civil society. This task, above all, falls on the families whose loved ones were taken from them.

Some survivors or their descendants have documented the lives of the persecuted in books, while others have made films or videos about the fate of their relatives, with actors portraying the murdered victims, and there are those who have written poetry or music in memory of their beloved family members. Some have painted or created sculptures and monuments; others have developed photo series and installations or have allow themselves to be interviewed. There is a near-infinite number of different ways to remember and each is unique.

A summer scene set in nature. A young woman dressed in white sits in the grass while her companion stands in the background. The colours of the painting are vibrant; brushstrokes are applied purposefully. The image radiates peace and beauty. There are no barbed wire fences and no barracks. The painting embraces life rather than death. Nevertheless, it is also a reminder of the depicted, who were tortured by the Nazis. The work was painted by the artist Inbar Chotzen, who never had the chance to meet her relatives. As an Israeli artist and descendant of persecuted people, Inbar Chotzen has found her own way of remembering, using an artistic approach that integrates the preserved visual memory in the form of photographs and postcards from her lost Berlin family.

How easy it is to write 'visual memory preserved in the form of photographs and postcards.' In truth, however, this is not easy but incredibly difficult. In her art, Inbar Chotzen seeks to directly confront the legacy of a family, i.e., the parents, four sons and their wives, all of whom suffered under the terror of the National Socialists because they were Jewish. Their family name was also Chotzen.

Inbar Chotzen's immediate family was able to emigrate from Germany to what was then the British Mandate of Palestine, now the State of Israel, thereby escaping the Shoah. The artist recalls that the persecution was not discussed in her family when she was a child. As they were starting over far from Germany, the survivors stayed silent about the life they had left behind in Berlin and the fate of those family members who had been unable to flee and fell victim to the Holocaust. These included three brothers from a different branch of the Chotzen family: Hugo-Kurt, known as Bubi, Erich, and Ullrich Chotzen. Hugo-Kurt's wife, Lisa, Erich's wife, Ilse, and the father, Josef Chotzen, also died. The only family members to survive were the son Joseph, known as Eppi, his mother Elsa, who came from a Christian family, and Ullrich's wife, Ruth.

Until a few years ago, these images had yet to concern Inbar Chotzen, as she knew nothing about the family's history. In 2015, she and her husband decided to go on holiday to Berlin. Before they left, she checked online to see whether there were any traces of her relatives in Berlin. She knew that her immediate family with the unusual name of 'Chotzen' had fled from the German capital to Palestine during the Nazi era. She was unaware, however, that there had been another branch of the family, descended from a brother of her great-grandfather. She was all the more astonished when her online search for 'Chotzen' and 'Berlin' turned up a computer screen full of results. Who could these people have been?

This, however, was no mystery in Berlin. The House of the Wannsee Conference Memorial and Educational Site had received the family archive from this side of the Chotzen family through a testamentary donation. The memorial had asked the historian Barbara Schieb to examine the collection. Years after she informed Inbar Chotzen that most of these family members had been murdered by the Nazis. Inbar Chotzen visited the house at Johannisberger Strasse 3, where the Chotzen family had lived. 'I saw five stumbling stones there. That was an incredible moment,' she says.

The deep shock Inbar Chotzen experienced upon seeing these stumbling stones demonstrated that the survivor generation was not the only one to be personally affected by the Shoah. It continues to deeply affect the victims' children and grandchildren as well. It is a wound in the collective memory of Jewish families that will not heal – not 80 years later and probably not 200 years later.

The Chotzen family archive includes numerous photographs because the sons were avid amateur photographers. 'Seeing the people in these photos really helped me connect with them, especially as an artist. I started drawing sketches of the photos. This has been my way of understanding who these people were. I remember that my first sketch was based on a photo of nearly the entire family. I wrote the appropriate name under each figure. That's how I got to know them. Their faces became familiar to me,' Inbar Chotzen noted.

The sketches became the basis for a larger project. 'I never decided to turn all this into art. It just happened.' Over many years, the artist has created an entire body of work.

Through Inbar Chotzen's paintings, these nearly-forgotten people have reappeared. In her work, however, the artist does not portray the family members during their time of suffering, when they had to perform humiliating forced labour in Berlin or were imprisoned in the Theresienstadt ghetto. In her paintings, we see them as happy people, playing sports and enjoying nature. These are optimistic images that suggest a peaceful life – or at least a few brief mo-

ments of joy when the Jews were able to evade the hardship of everyday life under the Nazi regime.
With their rich colours, the paintings contradict the viewer's expectation of grey doom. They show us that the persecuted Jews in Germany were not just victims, not just objects of oppression, but also living people, who enjoyed happiness and who, for as long as it was possible, tried to shape their lives according to their own desires. We know from one son's written testimony that, despite everything, they remained optimistic about the future and refused to be dragged down by their circumstances. Many Jews turned to sporting activities in the 1930s as a way to escape the growing misery of everyday life under the Nazi regime. After they were banned from non-Jewish sports clubs, they could still join Jewish clubs. With each passing year, however, such opportunities also became fewer.
The images show the reality behind the obvious. Although the topic is about the Shoah, these images address a truth that differs from the one most viewers expect. At the same time, they preserve the dignity of those depicted.
These are not imagined situations that ascribe a happy life to the people who were murdered shortly thereafter or who managed to survive. Eppi, Hugo-Kurt, Erich, Ullrich, Božka, Lisa, Ilse, Ruth and the parents, Josef and Elsa, really did live happy lives. The young men continued to play sports at their club as long as they could. They took excursions into the Berlin countryside and paddled across the Brandenburg lakes. They took pictures of themselves. Inbar Chotzen closely modelled her paintings on these photo motifs. The painting of a couple in a summer landscape is one such example.
And yet there is a break in the presentation. In one painting, the mother, Elsa, is seen in a blue dress. The lower half of the picture is covered by two words written in large letters: 'Liebe Mutti!' It sounds so harmless, an endearing form of address, not even worth mentioning. Not worth mentioning?
In October 1941, the Nazis began deporting German Jews to German-occupied Eastern Europe. Jews who were allowed to remain in Berlin had to do slave labour: some people, including members of the Chotzen family, were forced to work as early as 1938. The father, Josef Chotzen, died in January 1942 at the age of 58 as a consequence of the hard labour he had to do. That same year, the SS deported one of the sons, Erich, along with his wife, Ilse, to the Riga ghetto in German-occupied Latvia, where they were murdered the same year. Hugo-Kurt and Ullrich were also deported with their wives, Lisa and Ruth, in the summer of 1943. They arrived at the Theresienstadt ghetto, a former military fortress where tens of thousands of Jews were crammed together, where food was far too scarce and medicine barely available; where there were not enough beds and it was freezing cold in winter. The only thing that was plentiful was forced labour. Furthermore, trains left

Theresienstadt regularly for Auschwitz in the east, where nearly all the prisoners were murdered.
Unlike in the concentration camps, prisoners in Theresienstadt were allowed to correspond with their relatives according to strict rules and heavy censorship. The inmates could send a postcard every four to six weeks. They were also allowed to receive food parcels from home and confirm that on a preprinted postcard.
The Chotzens took advantage of this. A total of 369 messages from Theresienstadt have been preserved in the family archive, a unique collection that shows how the deportees communicated with their relatives. The sons sent postcards to their mother, Elsa Chotzen, who remained in Berlin; they were mostly addressed to 'Liebe Mutti'. There it is again, the inscription on Inbar Chotzen's painting of the mother.
This painting is a bridge to the artist's other paintings, which contrast the Chotzen family's good life in their homeland with their miserable existence in Nazi captivity. They, too, are based on scenes from the family photographs. Here, however, Inbar Chotzen added a new element: the postcards that the deportees sent to their mother from Theresienstadt.
On their postcards, the deportees were not allowed to mention anything about the terrible circumstances of their daily life. They also did not want their messages to cause 'Mutti' – Elsa Chotzen – any more anxiety than she already had or give her cause to worry about them. They thus sent optimistic messages and

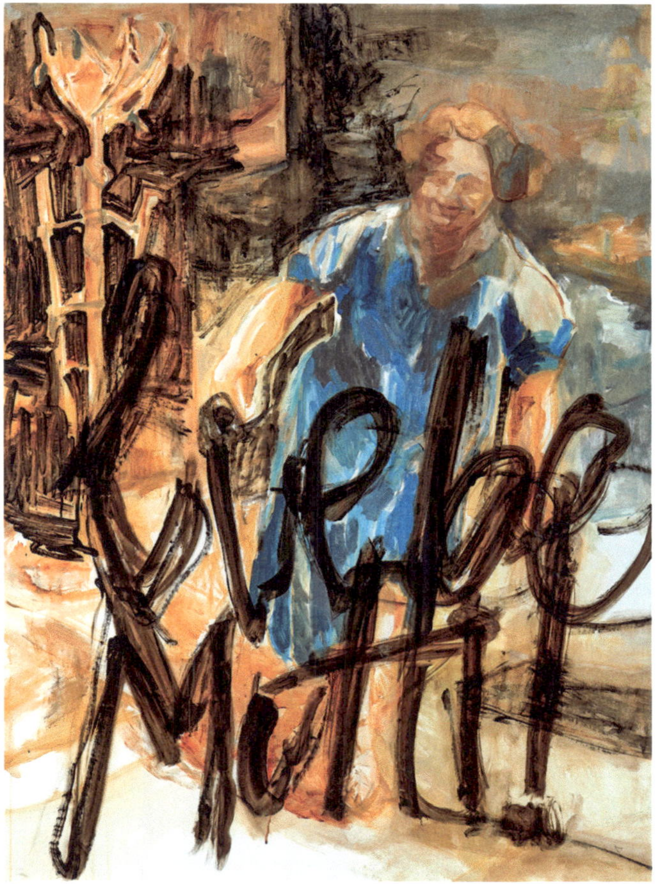

Inbar Chotzen:
Liebe Mutti!
Oil on canvas,
2019

described an imaginary Theresienstadt in golden colours, far removed from reality, but reminiscent of their earlier, happier life. On one of their first cards, they pretended they were on a holiday and transformed their deportation into a delightful journey through Saxon Switzerland. Once they arrived in Theresienstadt, they wrote that it was 'always fine' and that 'swimming, football, cabaret, music and theatre are our diversions.' 'Coffee and cake' are served on birthdays and there are 'lots of nice presents.' The work seemed to be interesting, the neighbours were friendly, life was good. It would be a mistake to call this a delusion. In their misery, these people created an idealised image of their lives. Maybe they derived strength from this image. It was certainly meant to reassure those back home.

On their cards, the deportees also repeatedly expressed their heartfelt thanks for the food parcels that 'Mutti' sent. This contradicted the constructed image of their captivity in a land of plenty. It was rare that the cruel reality seeped through in the messages.

Elsa Chotzen, her son Joseph (Eppi) and his girlfriend Božka, who all remained in Berlin, were not fooled by the messages on the cards. These messages, however, were an extremely important sign of life. As long as the cards kept coming, they knew that the others were still alive.

Inbar Chotzen worked for many years as a graphic designer and this influenced her artwork: the paintings are compositions made from parts of the scanned postcards in combination with the brush and ink drawings that she created based on the family photos. They convey the two levels of meaning in the lives of the deportees – their former good life and the memory that grew out of it, which was manifested in the messages they wrote on postcards to 'Liebe Mutti'. Or, as Inbar Chotzen explains: 'It's a confrontation between Theresienstadt and their former life. They wrote about sports and about how they would make it through because they were athletic and how they could swim and watch theatre in Theresienstadt. It's heartbreaking to know what happened to these people behind the walls of Theresienstadt.'

We see a drawing of three boys playing ball, dressed in white shorts, black jerseys and red socks. Then we see the text beginning with 'My dear mum' on a postcard from Theresienstadt that Ullrich sent to his mother, Elsa, on 31 July 1943. The victims' brief moments of reprieve are confronted with the cruelty of daily life in the ghetto.

More than a year later, life in Theresienstadt ended for the deported members of the Chotzen family. The greetings sent on cards to Berlin stopped. On 29 September 1944, Ullrich and his brother Hugo-Kurt, known as Bubi, were taken on a transport to Auschwitz. Ullrich's wife, Ruth, followed a week later. Three days after that, Lisa Chotzen was also forced to board a train to Auschwitz.

Auschwitz was not their last place of suffering. Ullrich Chotzen died on 23 December 1944 in the Landshut subcamp of the Dachau concentration camp. He was 24 years old. Hugo-Kurt also died there on 20 February 1945. He was 29 years old. Lisa Chotzen, née

Scheurenberg, died in the Bergen-Belsen concentration camp. The exact date is unknown. She was 23 or 24 years old. Ruth Chotzen survived.

No, Inbar Chotzen's paintings cannot bring them back to life, but the art invokes the memory of the Chotzen family. The artist says that the photos left behind show them as a completely normal family, just like the people who live near Johannisberger Strasse 3 in Berlin today: 'I painted them playing sports in the neighbourhood, at the same places where people do this today.' Inbar Chotzen says that her connection to the branch of the Chotzen family that was murdered has brought her closer to the cultural roots of her existence. 'This sense of belonging is strong and rewarding,' she says.

With her pictures, the artist hopes to create an encounter between the viewer and her lost family. Her mission is to tell the story of her family, to whom she, through her paintings, has become so close.

THE HISTORY OF A FAMILY

Ruth Preusse

We come to know a family here. Although most of the mail sent from Theresienstadt was written by four individuals – two Chotzen sons and their wives – their sparse censored words vividly convey an impression of this close-knit family and its members. In her art, Inbar Chotzen exposes the underlying significance of their correspondence. Her drawings and prints, the historical photographs and brief words written on postcards, acquaint us with the loving home the parents, Josef and Elsa, created for their four sons in Berlin-Wilmersdorf. We learn the nicknames of Joseph, Hugo-Kurt, Erich and Ullrich and hear about their hobbies and dreams for the future. We feel the warmth with which their girlfriends and future wives were welcomed into the family. *'They lived for one another,'* Ruth Weinstein, the sole survivor of the deported family members, says in a documentary film from 2004.[1] Who were these people?

The mother, Elsa Arndt, grew up in a Protestant family in Cottbus. She met Josef Chotzen through her work. The two fell in love, but Josef's father was opposed to their relationship: he was a cantor and kosher butcher and Jewish traditions were important to him. Even after Joseph, their first child, was born in 1907, Josef's father still refused to accept his son's marriage. In the early years, when Josef's parents were trying to gain a foothold in Berlin, the young boy lived with his maternal grandparents. In a memoir written many decades later, this son, Joseph, who everyone called Eppi, wrote that his mother

> *'fought for years to get his parents to consent to the marriage: Through her perseverance, she finally won not only the respect but also the love of the entire family.'*[2]

The wedding finally took place on 22 April 1914 after Elsa converted to Judaism. The small family soon moved from Prenzlauer Berg to a flat in a building at Johannisberger Strasse 4 in Wilmersdorf, where the young couple ran a linen business.

Their second son, Hugo-Kurt, was born in 1915. He was named after his father's brother, Hugo, who was killed in action in World War I. He would have been Inbar Chotzen's great-grandfather. Everyone called the child Bubi. The next son, Erich, was born in early 1917. That summer, Josef, the father, was called up to serve in World War I. This would later have consequences under the Nazis: In 1935, Josef was awarded the 'Cross of Honour for War Participants', which meant that both he and his sons were temporarily protected from deportation. In 1920, after the birth of their fourth son, Ullrich, called Ulli, the family of six moved into a larger ground-floor flat at Johannisberger Strasse 3,

1 'Chronik eines verordneten Todes – die Vernichtung einer deutschen Familie', director: Sönke El Bitar and Gorch Pieken, 2004

2 Eppi Chotzen: [Die „Endlösung" hat uns eingeholt], Erinnerungen, probably written between 1983 and 1985, unpublished, GHWK, Chotzen Family Archive

the address on the postcards sent from Theresienstadt twenty-three years later.

The Chotzen family felt the economic strain of the 1920s. They had to close their linen business and Josef took a job with a textile company as department manager and purchasing agent in 1929. The eldest son, Eppi, completed secondary school, began a commercial apprenticeship in 1924 and later worked for the renowned Michels Silk House. Although they were not wealthy, the family had a steady income in the early 1930s. Religion played a subordinate role in their everyday lives, and they celebrated both Jewish and Christian holidays.

Over the years, Josef, soon supported by his sons, documented the family's life in photographs, which were pasted into photo albums with comments. The images show the Chotzens travelling, attending sporting events and at home in the flat in Johannisberger Strasse. They also convey the family's closeness, humour and joie de vivre. **Fig. 1–3**

As children, Eppi, Bubi, Erich and Ulli's lives revolved around sport. They were members of the nearby sport club, 'Berliner Sport-Verein 1892' (BSV) and played on the hockey, handball and football teams. The family was well-known and popular in the neighbourhood. In his memoirs, Eppi wrote that they felt at home there. Before the Nazis came to power, there interactions with their neighbours had not *'even a hint of hostility or dislike'.* On summer weekends, the Chotzens often went to Wernsdorf next to Lake Krossin, where a local merchant rented out simple weekend cottages. The family spent their time there sunbathing, swimming and paddling in their

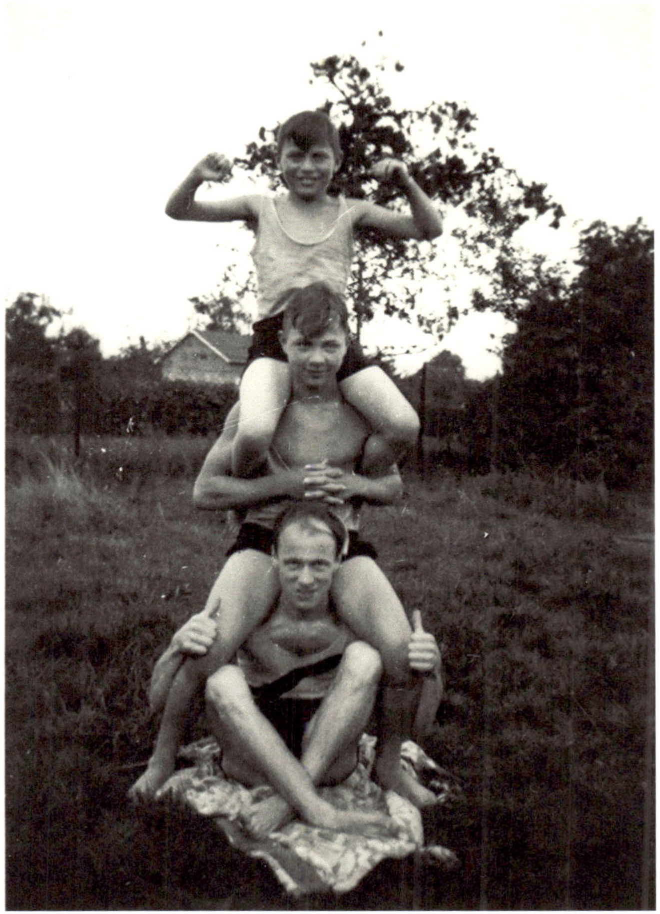

Fig. 1 Eppi, Erich and Ulli in Kaulsdorf, early 1930s, from the children's photo album (1929–1937)

Fig. 2 Left: Ulli, Erich, Bubi and Eppi, caption: 'Papas Siegesallee 1933', from the children's photo album (1929–1937)

Fig. 3 Right: Bubi, Ulli, Eppi and Erich on the BSV sports field, from Eppi's photo album (1935–1938)

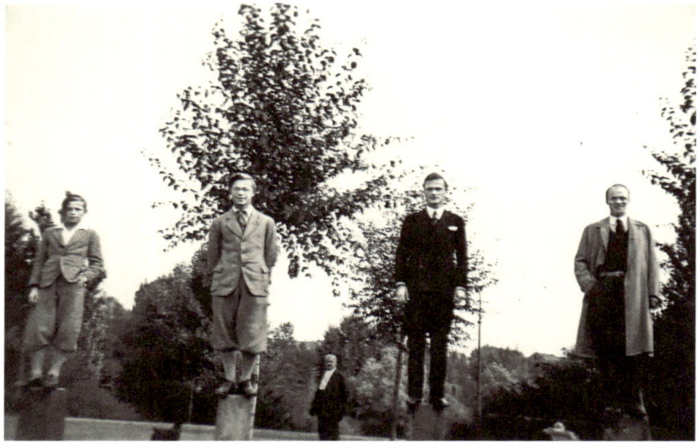

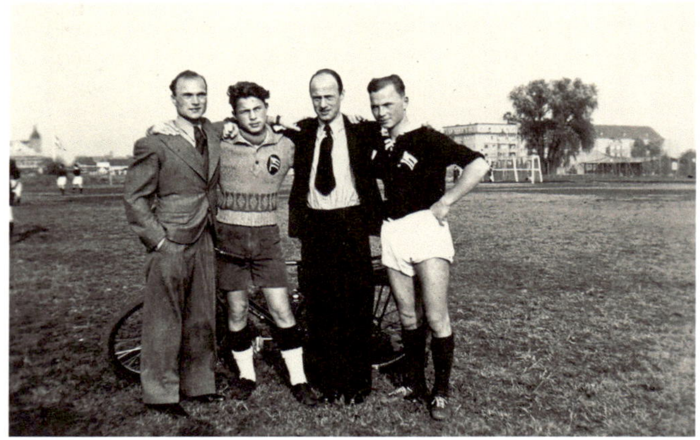

own canoe. They also enjoyed making music together. Since 1928, Eppi had been in a relationship with Božka, who was born in Czechoslovakia, and she quickly became part of the family.

In 1933, the Nazis came to power, and the party's antisemitic ideology turned the Chotzens into outsiders. It threatened their everyday lives, their economic livelihood and all their plans for the future. Over time, the Chotzens became utterly excluded from society.

The careers of Josef and his four sons followed a similar trajectory: Josef was harassed at work for antisemitic reasons and dismissed in 1936. The certificate issued by the Mitex company to its senior employee stated that Josef Chotzen was an 'extremely conscientious and dependable employee.' It noted that he had been dismissed as part of the process of 'Aryanising the business.' Joseph, who until then had been the family's main breadwinner, was now 53 years old and had developed health problems from the stress and mistreatment he'd experienced over the last few years. Henceforth he was only able to find poorly paid temporary jobs.

Eppi, the eldest son, was politically active and had joined the German Communist Party in 1929. In February 1933, when Eppi was 25 years old, his employer insisted he resign as a consequence of his trade union activities. This is when he decided to go underground and join the resistance. For a few months he hid in a room on Lake Krossin that Božka had rented under her name. When he heard the Gestapo was looking for him, he turned himself in to avoid endangering his family. He did not feel his underground activities were having much effect anyway. In July 1933, he was sent to the notorious 'Columbia House' in Berlin-Kreuzberg for about two weeks. He was interrogated several times, but not because of his political commitment: a former work colleague had denounced him for being critical of the Nazis. Božka, who worked as a housekeeper at the Danish embassy, used her connections to get Eppi released. Thereafter, he only found short-term employment as a labourer.

It had been Bubi's dream to teach sports, but instead he ended up following in his father's footsteps and trained to work in the textile industry. He was 18 years old when the Nazis came to power and his life was all about sports. Jewish athletes were excluded from most clubs in 1933, but the Chotzens were able to stay in the BSV club until 1937. Then, overnight, they were told they were no longer wanted there. Bubi lost his job the following year when the Jewish owners of the Berglas weaving mill were forced to sell their business.

Sixteen-year-old Erich hoped to complete his secondary school exams and go to university. He had attended the Heinrich-von-Kleist-Realgymnasium and was a good student. However, in the summer of 1933, his teachers urged him to drop out at the end of the school year. They argued that, as a Jew, his chances of being admitted to university were slim. He started an apprenticeship at the textile company Blum & Co., but had to switch jobs twice when his work place was 'Aryanised'. He ended up taking a job as a sales clerk and never received his qualification certificate.

Ulli, the youngest, attended the building trade school in Kurfürstenstrasse in 1933, where he studied civil engineering and well construction. He gained practical experience at the Rutzen well construction company. After being denied the opportunity to take the final examination for his apprenticeship, he was classified as an 'unskilled worker' and the Rutzen company was 'Aryanised'. His professional future was thus destroyed.

After the family's linen business closed, Elsa became a full-time housewife. By staying well-organised and keeping track of the household budget in a 'Haushaltsbuch', she tried to provide for her five industrious men and make their daily lives as pleasant as possible. **Fig. 4–5**

What the Chotzens experienced during this time followed a pre-determined plan: Beginning in 1933, Jews were systematically pushed out of the labour market. In December 1938, a decree was passed allowing unemployed Jews to be used for forced labour. Since all four brothers and their father had lost their low-paid temporary jobs that year, they were forced to do menial labour – on farms, in factories, clearing snow and collecting rubbish. Photographs of them at work do not reveal their lack of freedom or the humiliating circumstances in which they found themselves. Instead, the dominating impression is one of people striving to lead self-determined lives. Bubi added

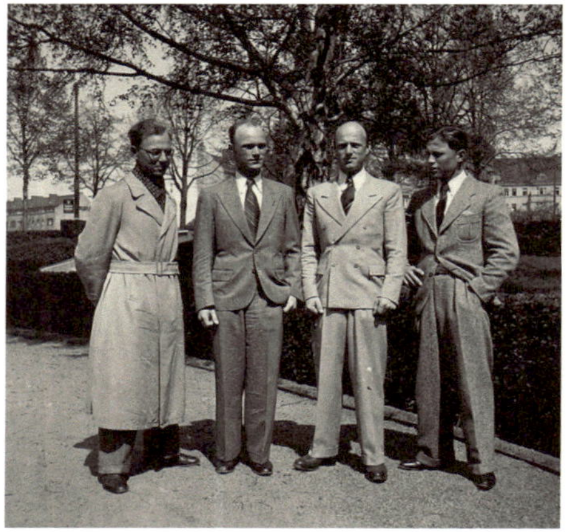

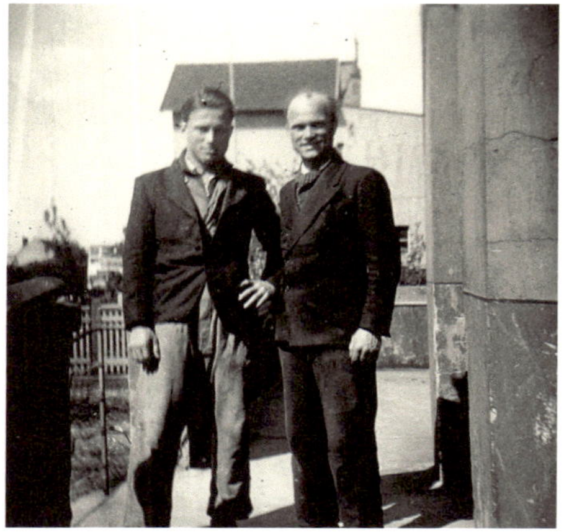

Fig. 4 Erich, Bubi, Eppi and Ulli, late 1930s, from Eppi's pocket album

Fig. 5 Ulli and Bubi during forced labour, c. 1940, from Eppi's pocket album

a sarcastic comment to a photo in his album that showed him working as a rubbish collector: 'Berlin is being cleansed by the Jews!'

The atmosphere in their neighbourhood had also changed. The Chotzens' Jewishness was suddenly an issue. Eppi vividly described this change in his memoirs:

> *'It was more than astonishing how an icy wall had already surrounded us. Communication with our surroundings very quickly diminished until there was suddenly a marked silence. Only occasionally would someone try to discreetly greet us.'*

On the night of the pogrom on 9 November 1938 and the following day, stones were thrown at the windows of their ground-floor apartment. They knew that their upstairs neighbour had instigated the attack, but they had no way of defending themselves.

The situation was exacerbated by the 'yellow star' decree introduced in September 1941. The entire family, excluding Elsa, was required to wear the star. Elsa had been forced to leave the Jewish community and was now classified as 'Aryan'. Eppi later described how this felt:

> *'It was no doubt confusing to see four blond, athletic men wearing the Jewish star as they marched to work. These marches took place often. This did not fit with the Stürmer image with its slander and lies about Jews.'*

The Chotzens faced these attacks from the state and society with courage. The family actively sought ways to maintain control over their own lives. After the painful experience of being expelled from their sports club, which had been like a second home to the sons, they joined the 'Jewish Sports Association 1933' (JSG 33) with the same enthusiasm as before. This club was part of the association 'Sportbund Schild' of the 'Reich Federation of Jewish Front-Line Soldiers'. After the November pogrom of 1938, this club was also banned and the 'Reich Federation' was dissolved. Shortly thereafter, acquaintances took the brothers to the Zionist training site 'Gut Winkel' in Brandenburg, where Jews were given training in preparation for their emigration to Palestine. It also gave the Chotzen boys a chance to play team sports, compete in competitions and attend parties together – until the Nazis closed the grounds down in June 1941.

Bubi met his future wife, Lisa Scheurenberg, at JSG 33. They both shared a passion for sport. Photographs show how they circumvented many antisemitic bans on multiple occasions. Prohibited from using public pools, they swam in the lakes around Berlin. Instead of visiting parks, they sunbathed on the roof of the house that Scheurenbergs were forced to move into as part of the antisemitic housing policy. The last pictures in Bubi's photo album are dated 22 June 1941, the day Germany invaded the Soviet Union. They show the couple taking an illegal stroll to the Brandenburg Gate: Jews were no longer allowed to enter the city centre. Shortly thereafter, Jews were prohibited from owning cameras. Pictures of the family from 1942 exist, but they were all taken indoors. **Fig. 6–8**

Erich also fell in love. He met Ilse Schwarz in 1938. Ilse's sister Ruth, who had managed to emigrate to England in 1939 and work there as a domestic servant, survived the war. Their father, Josef Schwarz, died in 1940. After his death, the mother and daughter became very close.

Ulli probably met his future wife in 1938, too. Ruth Cohn had been forced to leave her apprenticeship as an office clerk and was performing forced labour in a mica factory in Kreuzberg. They met through acquaintances and soon Ruth was spending more time at the flat in Johannisberger Strasse than at her own home. She wanted to spend what little free time she had with Ulli since she worked day shifts and he often worked nights. She always felt welcomed at Elsa's. The young people made music together and listened to records. This let them forget, however briefly, that they were no longer allowed to socialise outside the home.

The brothers made several attempts to emigrate. Between the summer of 1937 and April 1939, Elsa recorded regular payments in her 'Haushaltsbuch' under the heading 'Israel'. It is unclear why they ended this investment. Money may have been tight or perhaps they realised that the chances of receiving a visa for Palestine in the current political climate were low. Eppi wrote in his memoirs:

> *'I know with certainty from Bubi that he had by then made repeated efforts to flee abroad. He simply did not succeed. The rest of us had also tried different ways; we had filed applications, filled out forms, visited offices, attended language and other emigration courses, such as at the Jewish community centre. I recall that at one point we even tried desperately to emigrate to Argentina as a "whole family". It was a project to bring large families with young people to the country. We were four brothers with young wives. But that didn't work out either, after we had been put off over and over again!'*

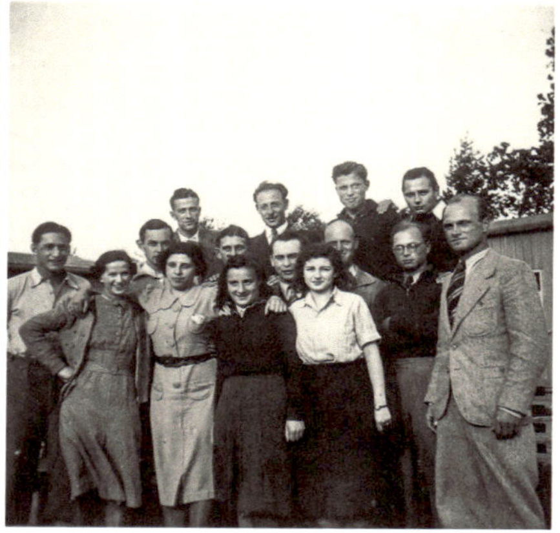

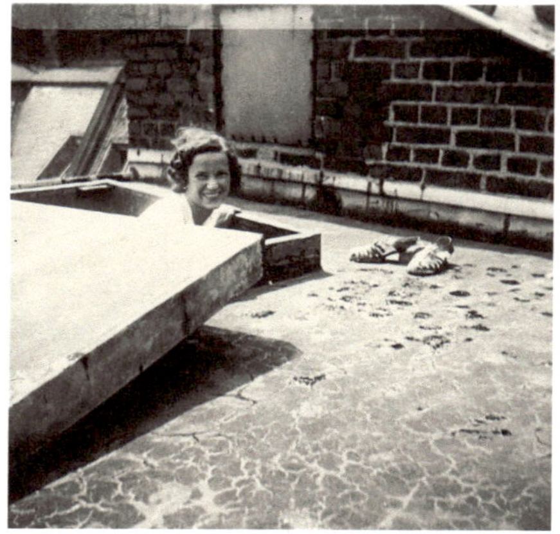

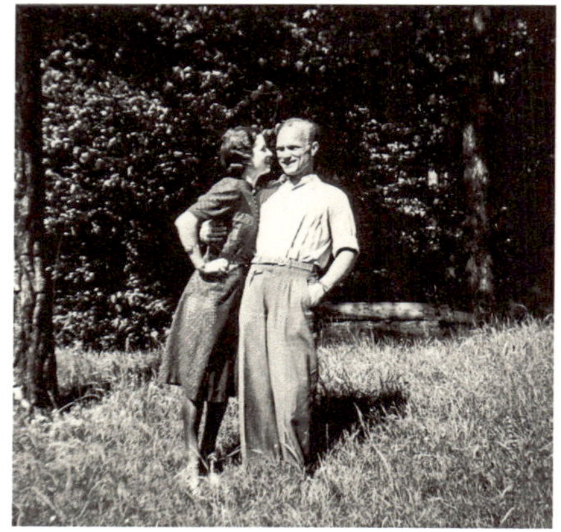

Fig. 6 Group photo taken at Gut Winkel: Lisa stands 2nd from left; Bubi stands at the far right, next to Erich and Eppi, with Ulli behind him, between 1939 and 1941, from Bubi's photo album (1936–1941)

Fig. 7 Lisa exiting the hatch on the roof of the building at Elsässer Strasse, probably 1941, from Bubi's photo album (1936–1941)

Fig. 8 Lisa and Bubi, late 1930s, from Bubi's photo album (1936–1941)

Under a picture of the four brothers, Erich wrote in his photo album: *'There is only a light cool breeze here, but the day when we will be blown to the winds does not seem far off. It will then be time to bid farewell to everything that the photos in this book have captured. What we take with us from our family home: May it always connect us and enable us to build a new, valuable life in the outside world!'* They also explored the possibility of joining a resistance group, but ultimately ruled it out as too dangerous for the whole family.

The systematic deportation of Jews from the German Reich 'to the East' began on 18 October 1941. An emigration stop for Jews followed shortly thereafter. Eppi was the first to receive a 'notice to vacate', but his employer issued him a life-saving certificate stating that the forced labour he was performing in the armaments industry was 'crucial to the war effort.' Thanks to this status, his name was removed from the deportation list. Henceforth the entire family lived in constant fear that a deportation order might come for any one of them at any time.

Believing that their own 'half-Jewish' status could maybe protect them, within a few weeks at the end of the year, three of the brothers, Bubi, Erich and Ulli, married their girlfriends. They were unaware that following the Wannsee Conference on 20 January 1942 at the latest, the status of 'Geltungsjuden', was no different than that of a 'full Jew'.

Erich, the first of the sons to wed, married Ilse on 7 November 1941. Their wedding ceremony was the only one held in the synagogue. The young couple moved in with his widowed mother-in-law at Hohenstaufenstrasse 56 in Schöneberg. Bubi and Lisa married on 18 November 1941. They temporarily subletted rooms in the flat of an elderly woman in the same building in which the Scheurenbergs lived. Ulli and Ruth married on 1 December 1941 and lived in the Chotzen family flat in Wilmersdorf. **Fig. 9–11**

Before the Nazis came to power, Eppi and Božka, who was not Jewish, decided to postpone getting married. Eppi feared that if they were to marry, his political activities might create problems for his girlfriend. After the 'racial laws' were introduced, marriages between a Jew and a non-Jew were no longer allowed. Eppi and Božka married in June 1945, just weeks after the war ended.

The family's brutal demise began in 1942: in January 1942, Erich's mother-in-law, Käthe Schwarz, received an order to report for deportation. The young couple volunteered to accompany her on her journey. Three days before the appointed day, Erich wrote a farewell letter to his family. He did not know where they were being taken or what awaited them:

> *'My Dears, Berlin, d. 16.1.42*
> *Especially you, dear Mum and Dad.*
> *I must write you a few lines to somehow say goodbye and offer comfort. I fear on paper it won't even look close to how I feel. In fact, I don't even know if it's possible to describe it at all. I cannot, that's for sure. No – I can't find the words. So only briefly: I have to cause you, dear mother, such deep sorrow, especially at such a moment, and yet I can't help it, as much as I love you.'*

'At such a moment' is a reference to Josef's acute health condition. He had developed erysipelas, a severe skin disease, in his leg as a result of the hard labour he had been forced to do. The father was in constant pain and his condition continued to deteriorate.

On 19 January, just two months after their wedding, Erich, Ilse and Ilse's mother were deported from the Berlin-Grunewald Station to the Riga ghetto. Before they departed, Elsa gave her daughter-in-law a necklace with a pendant containing a photo of her engagement to Erich. In Latvia, the couple were separated; Ilse was assigned to clean up after a group of German soldiers. One of them let her use his field post number to send letters to Berlin. To get her messages through the military censorship, she signed them with the soldier's name, Adolf. In the second half of 1942, the Chotzens in Berlin received eight letters, which they answered and sent parcels. One of the letters contained the shocking news that Erich had died on 25 March 1942. He had never seen his wife again after arriving in Riga. The cause of his death is unclear: He either drowned while rafting logs on the River Düna or fell into the water and caught pneumonia, which was left untreated. At some point, the Chotzens in Berlin lost contact with their daughter-

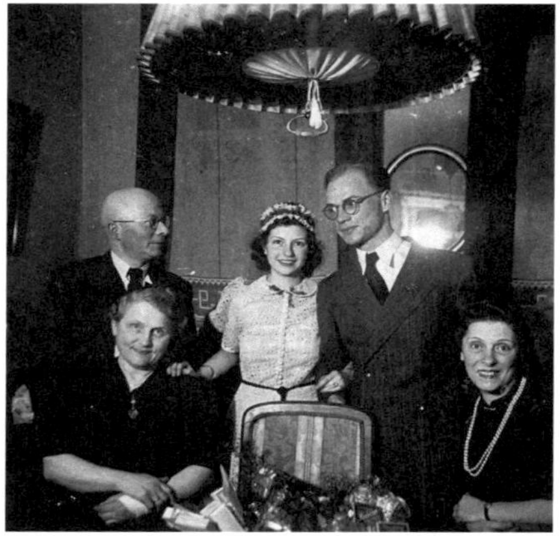

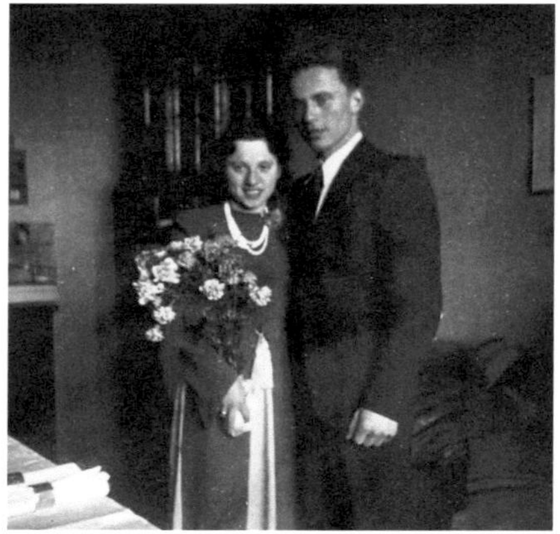

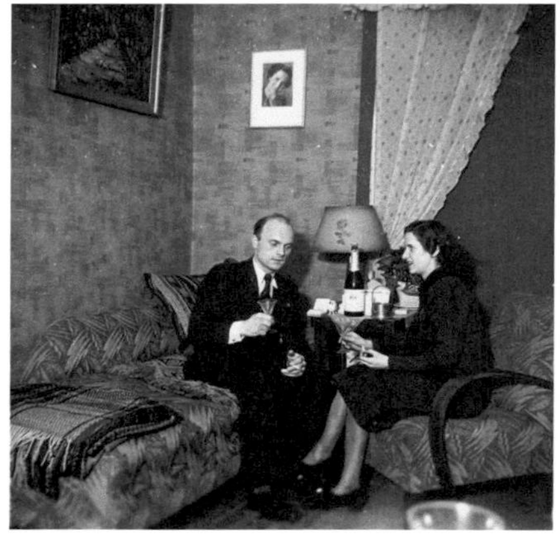

Fig. 9 Erich and Ilse's wedding picture with Elsa, Josef and Käthe Schwarz, 7 November 1941, from Eppi's pocket album

Fig. 10 Ruth and Ulli's wedding picture, 1 December 1941, from Eppi's pocket album

Fig. 11 Bubi and Lisa, probably at one of the previous weddings, late 1941, from Eppi's pocket album

in-law. Ilse and Käthe Schwarz also died in Riga under unknown circumstances.

Elsa was deeply affected by the news of her son's death – it was the second loss she had suffered in a very short time: Her husband, aged 58, died in the Jewish Hospital just a few days after Erich and Ilse's deportation on 27 January 1942. In his memoirs, Eppi draws a connection between these events, noting that the deportation was *'a major blow for my father in this situation.'* Josef was buried in the Jewish cemetery in Weißensee.

In her compensation case after the war, the mother, Elsa, stated that she had developed serious health issues in 1942: Insomnia, heart problems, and uncontrollable sobbing. She constantly worried about her sons and daughters-in-law. At the same time, she found the strength and courage to confront the Gestapo and succeeded in getting the Chotzen name removed from deportation lists several times. Eppi wrote that his mother had to *'eat humble pie over and over again … She begged for Bubi's release six times.'* Bubi, Lisa and Ruth were detained during the 'Fabrikaktion', a Berlin-wide wave of arrests of Jewish forced labourers in February 1943. Ulli volunteered to join his wife. Partners from 'mixed marriages' and 'Geltungsjuden' were detained in a Jewish community building in Rosenstrasse. Elsa joined the women who were demonstrating for days in front of the building, and their protest eventually led to the release of their husbands and children. The four Chotzens were among those released. Afterwards, Bubi and Lisa moved back to Johannisberger Strasse, where they felt safer. The Scheurenbergs were deported to Theresienstadt, as were Ruth's mother and sisters.

Later Eppi wrote about his own situation: *'During this very tense time for us star bearers, I was very alert, especially because I was risking so much. I was determined to avoid deportation at all costs.'* He went into hiding, as he had once before in 1933, and lived illegally at the home of Božka's mother. He tried unsuccessfully to convince his brothers to do the same:

> *'I was disappointed and depressed! I promised to support them where I could when things got rough. But what I had to offer them through the help of others was by no mean enough for many. […] And, of course, I have grown to love the girls, so I have some understanding for the many unrealistic courses of action taken during these terrible times. They love their wives and see no other chance!'*

In April, Eppi registered again at the labour office for Jews at Fontanepromenade and was assigned to a job repairing areas damaged by bombs: The job provided urgently needed ration cards.

Bubi and Lisa were arrested again on 19 June 1943; the arrest of Ulli and Ruth followed shortly thereafter. This time Elsa was unable to prevent their deportation. The two couples were held for several days in the assembly camp at Große Hamburger Strasse. Their mother went there every day to bring them food and short messages and they were able to wave to each other. Several farewell letters were written during this time. In one of Ulli's letters, written in a childlike handwriting that was untypical for him, someone, probably Eppi, underlined certain letters in blue: The brothers had previously agreed on a secret code, but no one has ever been able to decipher it. **Fig. 12**

The day before his brothers were scheduled for deportation, Eppi received a summons from the Gestapo. He went to the meeting with great trepidation. During the interrogation, it became clear that he had been seen outdoors without the yellow star, but it turned out that the officer only had the personal details of his father, who had the same name, but was already deceased. The officer was infuriated by the mix-up, but as the situation began to escalate, another Gestapo employee entered the room and intervened. The second officer had been Elsa Chotzen's Gestapo contact, the man who had helped her protect her children in the past. Eppi was allowed to leave. He was the only one of the four sons who spent the entire war years in Berlin. He performed forced labour in a sandblasting workshop, which caused severe and permanent damage to his lungs.

On 29 June 1943, Bubi, Lisa, Ulli and Ruth Chotzen were deported on the 92nd 'elderly transport' to Theresienstadt, located nearly 300 kilometres from Berlin. One hundred people were on the passenger train, which departed from Anhalter Station at 6 o'clock in the morning. Their names were noted on the transport list with the additional obligatory middle names 'Israel' and 'Sara'. The reason for their

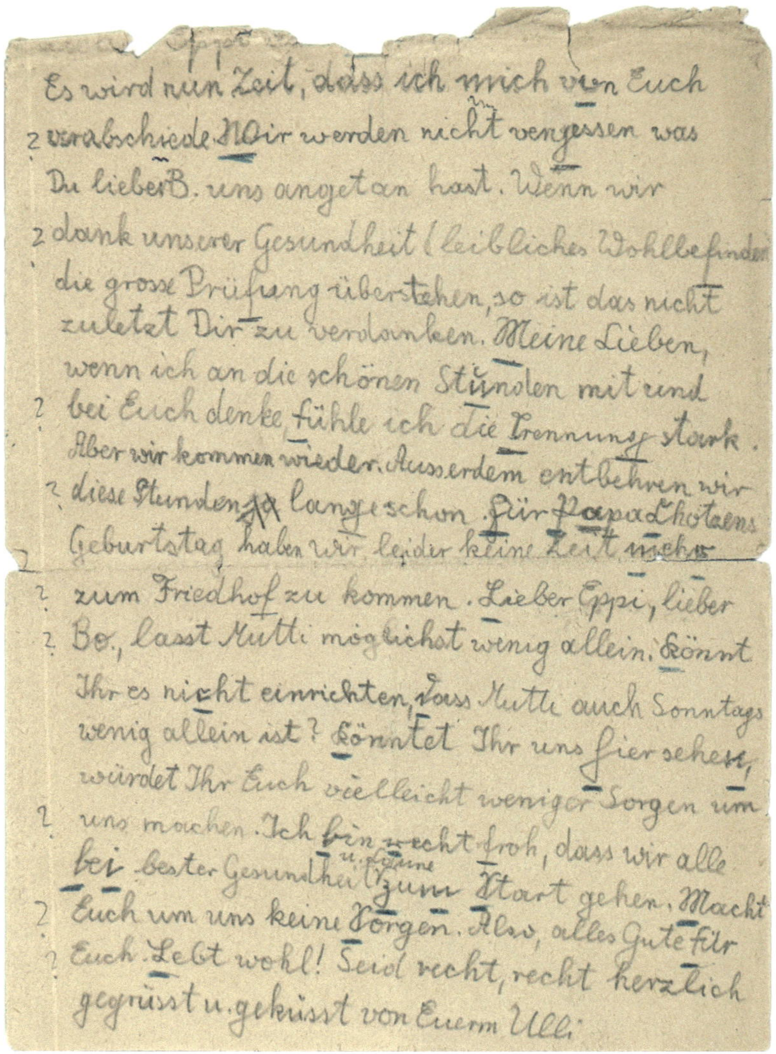

Es wird nun Zeit, dass ich mich von Euch
verabschiede. Wir werden nicht vergessen was
Du lieber B. uns angetan hast. Wenn wir
dank unserer Gesundheit (leibliches Wohlbefinden)
die grosse Prüfung überstehen, so ist das nicht
zuletzt Dir zu verdanken. Meine Lieben,
wenn ich an die schönen Stunden mit und
bei Euch denke, fühle ich die Trennung stark.
Aber wir kommen wieder. Ausserdem entbehren wir
diese Stunden ja lange schon. Für Papa Chotzens
Geburtstag haben wir leider keine Zeit mehr
zum Friedhof zu kommen. Lieber Eppi, lieber
Bo, lasst Mutti möglichst wenig allein. Könnt
Ihr es nicht einrichten, dass Mutti auch Sonntags
wenig allein ist? Könntet Ihr uns hier sehen,
würdet Ihr Euch vielleicht weniger Sorgen um
uns machen. Ich bin recht froh, dass wir alle
bei bester Gesundheit u. Laune zum Start gehen. Macht
Euch um uns keine Sorgen. Also, alles Gute für
Euch. Lebt wohl! Seid recht, recht herzlich
gegrüsst u. geküsst von Euerm Ulli.

Fig. 12 Ulli's farewell letter written in the assembly camp at Große Hamburger Strasse, undated (June 1943)

It is now time for me to say goodbye to you.
We will not forget what you dear B.[ozka]
have done for us. If we survive this great ordeal
thanks to our health (physical well-being),
it is not least of all thanks to you. My dear ones,
when I think of the beautiful hours with you,
I feel the separation strongly. But we will be back.
After all, we have had to do without these hours
for a long time. Unfortunately, we don't have
time to come to the cemetery for Papa Chotzen's
birthday. Dear Eppi, dear Bo, don't leave Mum
alone too much. Can you arrange for Mum to
not be alone much on Sundays, too? If you could
see us here, you might worry about us less.
I am quite happy that we are entering this in the
best of health and spirits. Don't worry about us.
All the best to you. Farewell! Very, very
warm greetings and kisses from your Ulli.

deportation was also recorded: They or their spouse had been classified as a 'Geltungsjuden'. **Fig. 13**

Theresienstadt is a difficult place to characterise. It is referred to interchangeably as a 'ghetto' and a (transit) 'camp'. The decision to set up Theresienstadt as an assembly and transit camp for Jews, most of whom came from the 'Protektorat' ('remaining Czechia'), Germany and Austria, was made in late September 1941. The SS were convinced that, because the 18th-century garrison town had been built as a fortress, it would be easy to seal off and control. They also noted that the existing barracks could accommodate large numbers of people and that the camp was conveniently located since the neighbouring town of Bohušovice was connected to the railway network. At the Wannsee Conference on 20 January 1942, the participants discussed establishing Theresienstadt as a 'ghetto for the elderly', to which people over 65 and German Jews who had been injured or awarded medals in World War I could be sent. They also considered allowing spouses of 'mixed marriages' and their children to be 'evacuated' to Theresienstadt. Being deported there was presented as a 'privilege'. The Nazis used the site in its propaganda efforts and took various measures to conceal its true purpose as a way station to Auschwitz. **Fig. 14**

The two couples wrote four postcards during their journey and threw them out the train window. Somebody found the postcards, took them to the post office in Dresden, and sent them to Johannisberger Strasse. Not wanting to cause Elsa any more worry than they already had, they kept their messages upbeat and optimistic. They were certain they would survive what awaited them, especially since they were sure that the war was nearing its end. The defeat at Stalingrad in late November 1942 had been a clear turning point. Bubi and Ulli wrote on their first postcard:

> *'We left Anhalter Station at 6:06 a.m. on the dot. 4 ladies your age, very nice, from our room, and all of us in one compartment, all with seats. I wear a white band as car attendant. The atmosphere is fabulous. Lisa is sleeping now; her head is on my lap. Until the next message, warm greetings and kisses from Bubi.'*

> *'Dear Mum! Hopefully you are still in bed at the moment and resting after all the excitement and strain. Eppi will surely be working and thinking of us, as you are. Don't worry about us. The food is good. But we have even better things from you. Everything went very smoothly. We are sitting comfortably; the weather is fine and we have a nice trip ahead of us. Now make sure that you have calm. Take care of yourself and look after your health. Give my best to Frida, Helga and especially*

Fig. 13 Excerpt from the deportation list of the 92nd elderly transport from Berlin to Theresienstadt from 29 June 1943, Signature 15510052a, page 11, Arolsen Archives
The four Chotzens are numbered 41 to 44.

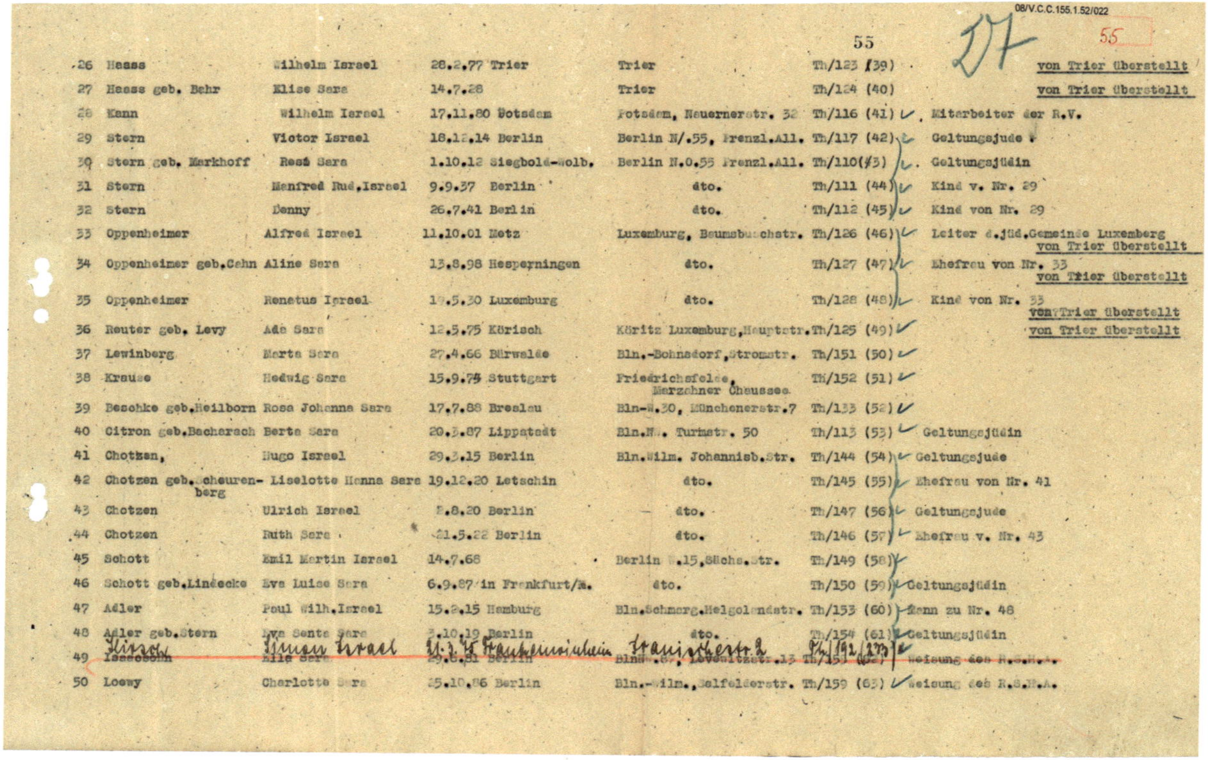

08/V.C.C.155.1.52/022

55

No.	Name	First names	Born	Place of birth	Address	Th no.	Remarks
26	Haass	Wilhelm Israel	28.2.77	Trier	Trier	Th/123 (39)	von Trier überstellt
27	Haass geb. Behr	Elise Sara	14.7.28		Trier	Th/124 (40)	von Trier überstellt
28	Kann	Wilhelm Israel	17.11.80	Potsdam	Potsdam, Neuernerstr. 32	Th/116 (41)	Mitarbeiter der R.V.
29	Stern	Victor Israel	18.12.14	Berlin	Berlin N/.55, Prenzl.All.	Th/117 (42)	Geltungsjude
30	Stern geb. Markhoff	Rosa Sara	1.10.12	Siegbold-Wolb.	Berlin N.O.55 Prenzl.All.	Th/110(43)	Geltungsjüdin
31	Stern	Manfred Rud.Israel	9.9.37	Berlin	dto.	Th/111 (44)	Kind v. Nr. 29
32	Stern	Denny	26.7.41	Berlin	dto.	Th/112 (45)	Kind von Nr. 29
33	Oppenheimer	Alfred Israel	11.10.01	Metz	Luxemburg, Baumsbuschstr.	Th/126 (46)	Leiter d.jüd.Gemeinde Luxemberg von Trier überstellt
34	Oppenheimer geb.Cahn	Aline Sara	13.8.98	Hesperningen	dto.	Th/127 (47)	Ehefrau von Nr. 33 von Trier überstellt
35	Oppenheimer	Renatus Israel	1?.5.30	Luxemburg	dto.	Th/128 (48)	Kind von Nr. 33 von Trier überstellt
36	Reuter geb. Levy	Ada Sara	12.5.75	Körisch	Köritz Luxemburg, Hauptstr.	Th/125 (49)	von Trier überstellt
37	Lewinberg	Marta Sara	27.4.66	Bärwalde	Bln.-Bohnsdorf, Stromstr.	Th/151 (50)	
38	Krause	Hedwig Sara	15.9.75	Stuttgart	Friedrichsfelde, Marzahner Chaussee	Th/152 (51)	
39	Beschke geb.Heilborn	Rosa Johanna Sara	17.7.88	Breslau	Bln-W.30, Münchenerstr.7	Th/133 (52)	
40	Citron geb.Bacharach	Berta Sara	20.3.87	Lippstadt	Bln.N.. Turmstr. 50	Th/113 (53)	Geltungsjüdin
41	Chotzen,	Hugo Israel	29.3.15	Berlin	Bln.Wilm. Johannisb.Str.	Th/144 (54)	Geltungsjude
42	Chotzen geb.Scheurenberg	Liselotte Hanna Sara	19.12.20	Letschin	dto.	Th/145 (55)	Ehefrau von Nr. 41
43	Chotzen	Ulrich Israel	2.8.20	Berlin	dto.	Th/147 (56)	Geltungsjude
44	Chotzen	Ruth Sara	21.5.22	Berlin	dto.	Th/146 (57)	Ehefrau v. Nr. 43
45	Schott	Emil Martin Israel	14.7.68		Berlin W.15, Sächs.Str.	Th/149 (58)	
46	Schott geb.Lindecke	Eva Luise Sara	6.9.87	in Frankfurt/M.	dto.	Th/150 (59)	Geltungsjüdin
47	Adler	Paul Wilh.Israel	15.2.15	Hamburg	Bln.Schmarg.Helgolandstr.	Th/153 (60)	Mann zu Nr. 48
48	Adler geb.Stern	Eva Senta Sara	3.10.19	Berlin	dto.	Th/154 (61)	Geltungsjüdin
49	~~Issacsohn~~ Hirsch	~~Ella Sara~~ Simon Israel	~~29.6.81~~ [illegible]	~~Berlin~~ [illegible]	~~Bln N.87, Levetzowstr.13~~ [illegible]	~~Th/155 (62)~~ Th/192 (273)	~~Weisung des R.S.H.A.~~
50	Loewy	Charlotte Sara	25.10.86	Berlin	Bln.-Wilm., Belfelderstr.	Th/159 (63)	Weisung des R.S.H.A.

to our friend Hanna. Thank you again, Bozka and Eppi and all the others. Greetings to everyone, Ulli.'

Although the postal service was highly unreliable in both directions, over the next 16 months, the Chotzens in Berlin and Theresienstadt engaged in a lively correspondence. With active assistance from Božka, who was able to procure both food and everyday products, including packaging material, through her employer, Elsa and Eppi sent care packages nearly every other day. In this way, they were able to support the two couples, as well as the wives' families who had been deported earlier and later reunited there with Bubi, Lisa, Ulli and Ruth. They were allowed to acknowledge receipt of the parcels on pre-printed forms and also send a handwritten postcard every 4 or 6 weeks. Between July 1943 and October 1944, 369 of these brief messages, a sign that they were still alive, reached Berlin. Elsa kept all of them. **Fig. 15** In their reply postcards, the prisoners frequently expressed not only gratitude, but also astonishment at the amount of food being sent. Elsa's household ledger shows that she had gone into debt for the first time in her life so that she could send the parcels. Moreover, goods were being rationed in the German Reich, which meant she was scrimping from her own portions to have food to send to her children. Eppi described the 'big parcel campaign':

> *'What efforts, difficulties, dangers had to be overcome in order to get the parcels ready and packed is impossible to imagine today. At least not by anyone who did not experience the situation that we Jews were in at that time, and certainly not by anyone who did not live through that time. When the most difficult and dangerous part was done, namely the things at home were ready to be packed, there were the additional problems of missing paper, cardboard boxes and, above all, usable string. Then off to the post office. In the beginning, when possible, I took it off my mother's hands. But one time she was there (we usually had several parcels) and witnessed their degrading treatment of me – I was wearing the star after all, and the Jewish names – Israel or Sarah every time – in the future she did that alone, too. All together demoralizing and too much for her!'*

Bubi and Ulli were deported to Auschwitz on 29 September 1944. They had no chance to inform their mother.

Since they were not allowed to write anything personal on the pre-printed parcel confirmation cards, Lisa's father, Paul Scheurenberg, resorted to a trick: to let Elsa and Eppi know that the two brothers were no longer in Theresienstadt, he signed his name as 'Bubiweg' (Bubi gone). By the time the card arrived in Berlin, the two daughters-in-law, Lisa and Ruth, had also left on a transport to Auschwitz.

The family members who had stayed in Berlin did not learn of the others' fate until after the war: Ruth appeared one day unexpectantly at their door, emaciated, exhausted and with a shaved head. She had been sent from Auschwitz to Merzdorf, a subcamp of Gross-Rosen, where she had performed forced labour in a spinning mill. After liberation, she set off on foot to Berlin, sustaining her hope for months that Ulli was still alive. But she was the only one to return: Lisa died under unclear circumstances in Auschwitz sometime in 1944; Ulli died in the Dachau subcamp in Landshut on 23 December 1944; Bubi died there too on 20 February 1945. Elsa did not receive official confirmation from Dachau of her sons' death until July 1946. She was later informed by the authorities that Erich and Ilse had died in Riga.

Ruth's mother and two sisters also survived, but Ruth stayed with Elsa until she learned of the death of the two sons, after which Ruth decided to emigrate to the United States. In 1946, Eppi became office manager of the denazification commission in Wilmersdorf. However in 1948 he was compelled to give up this job: his physical condition had rapidly deteriorated and he was no longer able to work. His mother-in-law died in 1952, followed by the unexpected death of his wife in 1959. He later was in a relationsship again and cared for his mother, Elsa, who was both physically and emotionally damaged, until her death. When Elsa died in 1982, she left Eppi all the documents she had collected from the time of their persecution.

After Eppi went through the photo albums, correspondences and documents, he began to write the family's story. He sent the manuscript to friends and fellow survivors and revised it several times after receiving their feedback. He also asked his friend Gerhard Schoenberner, who became the founding director of the House of the Wannsee Conference Memorial and Educational Site in 1992, for his opinion. The manuscript, however, was never published.

Eppi died the same year the memorial opened. In his will, he stipulated that part of the Family Archive, including the 369 postcards from Theresienstadt, should be given to the memorial. The Chotzen material was researched and catalogued by the historian Barbara Schieb. Everyone who has worked with this family history owe a great deal of gratitude to her for her seminal research. Her book 'Nachricht von Chotzen' was published in 2000. The following year, the first special exhibition about the Chotzen family was presented at the House of the Wannsee Conference. For the staff of an educational institution, this unprecedented collection is particularly valuable. By following the fate of a single family in Berlin, it demonstrates what the Nazi policies, and specifically the Wannsee Conference, meant: On 20 January 1942, fifteen men were invited by Reinhard Heydrich to a villa on Lake Wannsee to discuss the organisational details of murdering European Jews through a collaborative administrative process. The protocol of this meeting is a clear example of antisemitism and racism and evidence of a criminal and inhumane bureaucracy. Four of the 15 pages are concerned with the precise definition of the people targeted for deportation and murder. The definition was based on the Nuremberg Laws, which had been co-authored by Interior Minister Wilhelm Stuckart in 1935. Stuckart, who attended the conference, stressed the importance of adhering to these laws. Theresienstadt, the 'ghetto for the elderly' is the only transport destination mentioned by name in the protocol.

The violent end of the Chotzen family, which was discussed theoretically at a meeting of state secre-

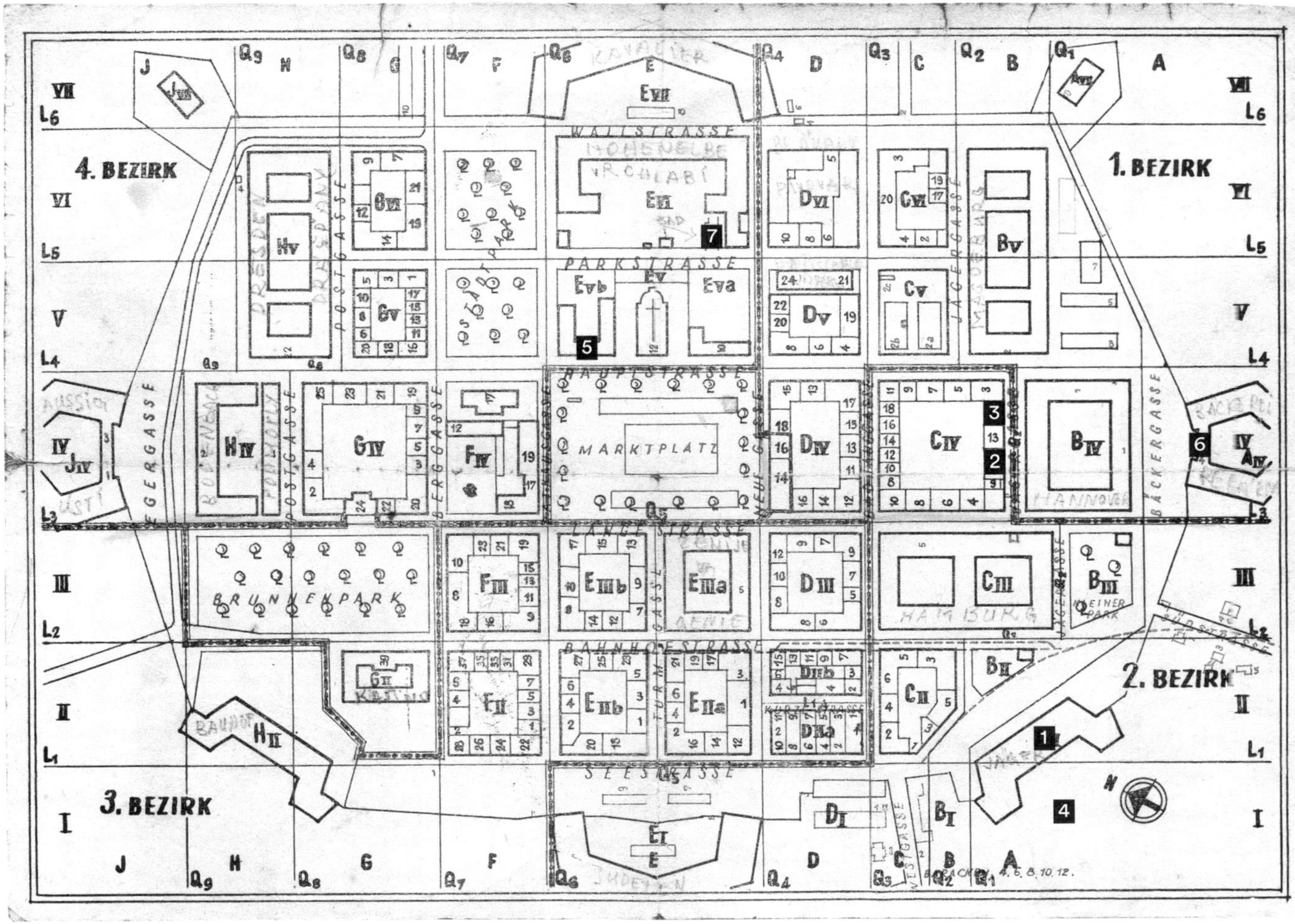

Fig. 14 City map of Theresienstadt (1941–1945), Terezín Memorial, APT Inventar-Nr. A 11808

1. Ulli and Bubi's address: Bäckergasse 2
2. Lisa's address: Jägergasse 11
3. Address of Ruth: Jägergasse 15
4. Soccer field: Südberg
5. Central post office: Hauptstraße 14
6. Bakery / grocery store: Bäckergasse, Block A IV
7. Central swimming pool: Parkstraße 10

taries, soon became a gruesome reality. Or perhaps the opposite is the case: an important part of the Wannsee Conference becomes personalised through the story of the Chotzen family.
Looking back half a century later, Eppi wrote:

> *'What was it? And how much of it*
> *prevails today?*
> *Was it stupidity? – Indifference? – Egoism?*
> *Were they just mean? – Lacking character? –*
> *Cowardly?*
> *And what made these "honourable" citizens*
> *ask: Why did she marry a Jew?! –*
> *They were referring to my mother.*
> *Is this still a civilised nation?'*

Fig. 15 Calendar with markings of the dates of writing in Theresienstadt

- Bubi
- Ulli
- Lisa
- Ruth
- Family Scheurenberg
- ■ Arrest / Deportation

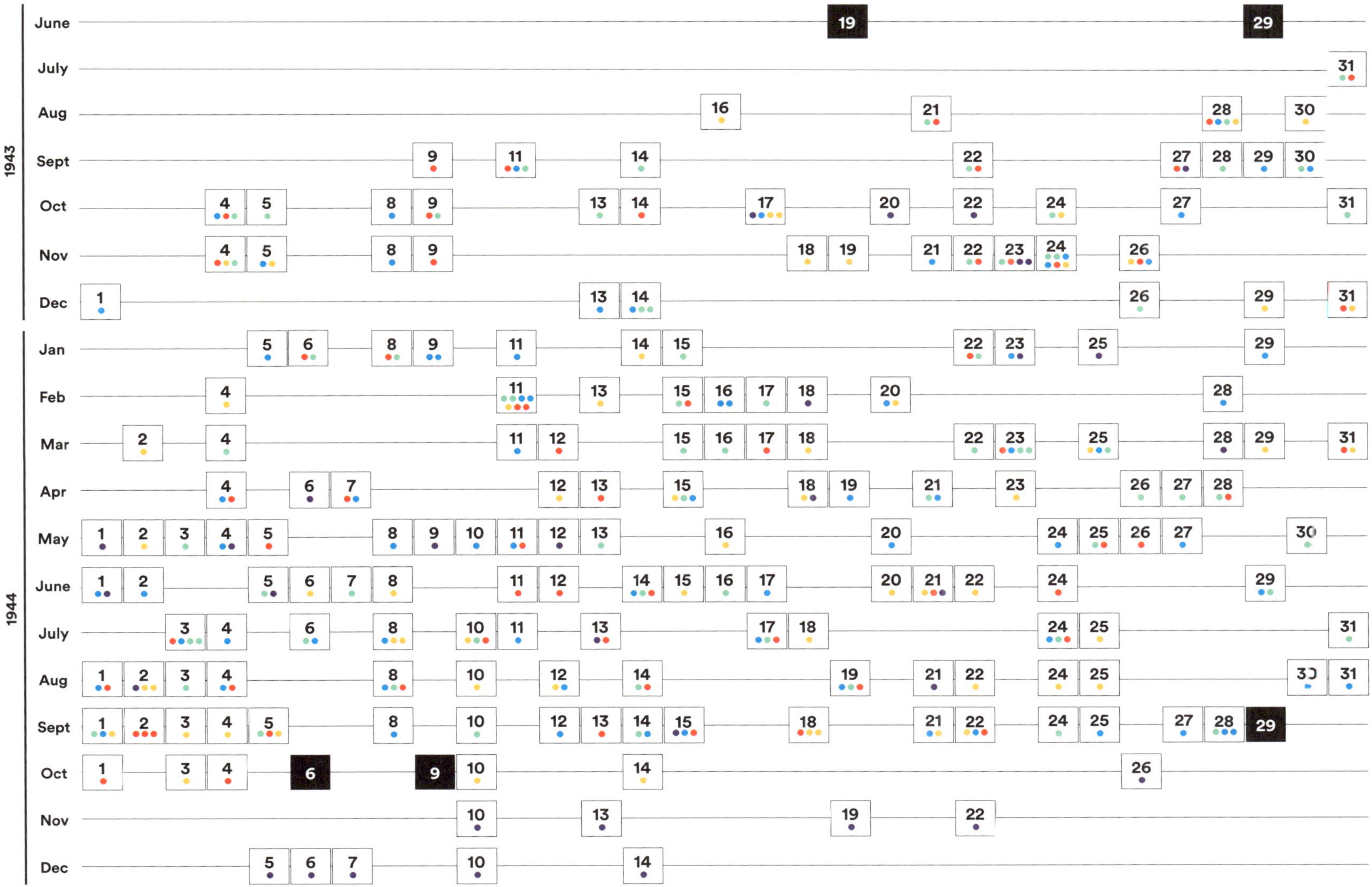
1943
June 19 29
July 31
Aug 16 21 28 30
Sept 9 11 14 22 27 28 29 30
Oct 4 5 8 9 13 14 17 20 22 24 27 31
Nov 4 5 8 9 18 19 21 22 23 24 26
Dec 1 13 14 26 29 31
1944
Jan 5 6 8 9 11 14 15 22 23 25 29
Feb 4 11 13 15 16 17 18 20 28
Mar 2 4 11 12 15 16 17 18 22 23 25 28 29 31
Apr 4 6 7 12 13 15 18 19 21 23 26 27 28
May 1 2 3 4 5 8 9 10 11 12 13 16 20 24 25 26 27 30
June 1 2 5 6 7 8 11 12 14 15 16 17 20 21 22 24 29
July 3 4 6 8 10 11 13 17 18 24 25 31
Aug 1 2 3 4 8 10 12 14 19 21 22 24 25 30 31
Sept 1 2 3 4 5 8 10 12 13 14 15 18 21 22 24 25 27 28 29
Oct 1 3 4 6 9 10 14 26
Nov 10 13 19 22
Dec 5 6 7 10 14

CREATING A MEMORY

Inbar Chotzen

Intense feelings overcame me when I first saw the postcards. The sensation was horrifying in its very tangibility. This was in 2016, when I went to see the Chotzen's postcards in the House of the Wannsee Conference archives. I was very aware that these postcards had been sent by my family members, shortly before they were murdered in the Holocaust. After years of not knowing my family's fate, here before me was proof, firsthand testimony, evidence of what had happened to them.

My starting point was the book "Nachricht von Chotzen" by Barbara Schieb. I read the book slowly, focusing on the photographs. I started my journey by creating many paintings in response to the photos. It was my way of "processing" the overwhelming information.

Old family photos have always been my main artistic focus. My paintings are created from a realistic perspective, with a combination of the imaginary. I use my own childhood photos as my references. In my work, I explore the connection between the present and the past, between the actual experience and the memory it leaves. My childhood photographs serve as raw material. Through the act of painting, I reexamine the childhood moments captured in the photographs. This act reveals the tension between private and collective memory. The figures – mother and daughter, girl and animal – are in an intermediate state between specific representation and archetype.

The Chotzens were photography enthusiasts, leaving behind hundreds of photos that are now part of the family's "Nachlass" (estate) in the House of the Wannsee Conference archives. Through the process of painting, I became familiar with the facial features and body postures of my family members, and I explored the photos for details and objects. I learned about their relationships and hobbies. Each detail was like a bridge to the past that brought them closer to me; a memory was created and they became part of me.

My family's postcards collection

Hebrew was the only language my grandparents spoke with us; it was yet another step towards breaking away from their past in Europe and starting a new life in the new land of Israel. When I first held the postcards, I could not read them, but I did notice that each postcard opened with the touching words "Liebe Mutti" and ended with words like "tausend Küsse," phrases that required no translation.

The sweet warm words sounded to me like a muffled cry for help.

The sense of warmth was heartbreaking. I couldn't stop thinking of their mother, Elsa Chotzen, collecting the postcards as signs of life; how a good day was a day a postcard was received at the family home at Johannisberger Straße 3 in Berlin-Wilmersdorf. And then of the days when the postcards had stopped coming.

My attention was also focused on the different handwriting in the postcards. Ruth's handwriting was so feminine, soft, round and meticulous. I recognized Bubi's decisive handwriting, which I had already seen in his photo albums. And Ulli's handwriting changed from one postcard to the next, from a child's handwriting to a man's.

In time, I was able to read the postcards in the book "Nachricht von Chotzen" by Barbara Schieb, although even then their meaning was not always clear. The situations they wrote about while imprisoned in Theresienstadt seemed surreal. Ruth wrote: "Received today tomatoes and leek from 31.8.44."

Evidence of receiving food parcels sent from home in Berlin to the camp exists in many of the postcards. Yet, as I read about tomatoes (!) and leeks (!) in the context of the Shoah, I initially found it hard to believe this was the case.

Ulli wrote about his birthday in a postcard from 3 August 1944: "Bubi and Lisa were there for coffee and cake, which Ruth had baked beautifully." I asked myself what was true and what was written under duress or censorship? Had this event really taken place?

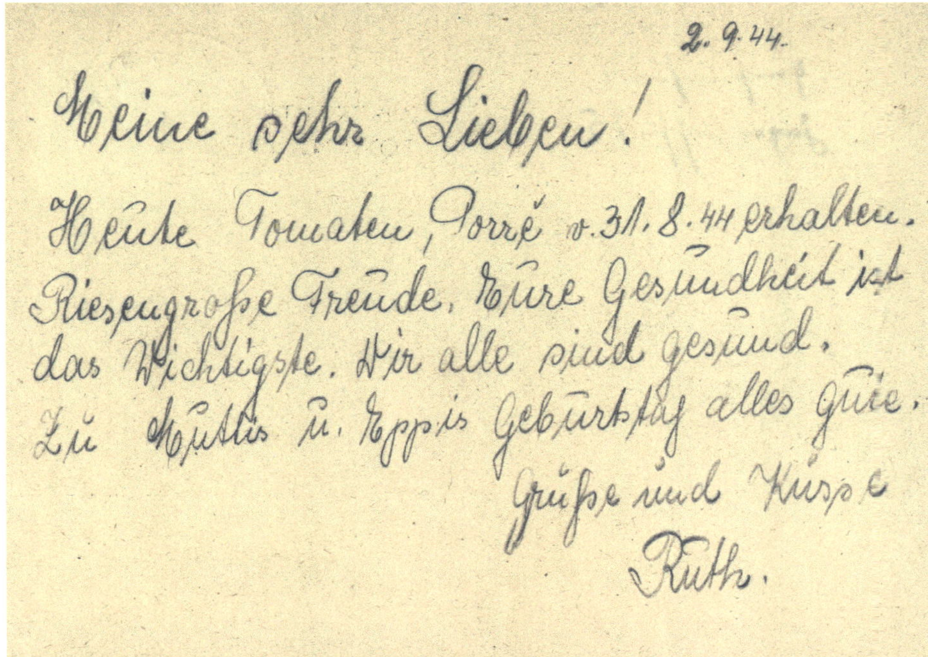
2.9.44.

Meine sehr Lieben!

Heute Tomaten, Porré v. 31.8.44 erhalten. Riesengroße Freude. Eure Gesundheit ist das Wichtigste. Wir alle sind gesund. Zu Muttis u. Eppis Geburtstag alles Gute.

Grüße und Küsse

Ruth.

Postcard from Ruth Chotzen, 2 September 1944

Ulli's words comforted me, as he probably hoped they had when his mother read them.

Artistic approach

My artistic approach here has been to portray my family as they were before being deported, i.e., young, athletic and free. I continued doing this while working with the postcards. My aim was to contrast their earlier lives as free people with their lives in the camp.

Inbar Chotzen:
Sketch for *Lisa cooking*, mixed media, 2016

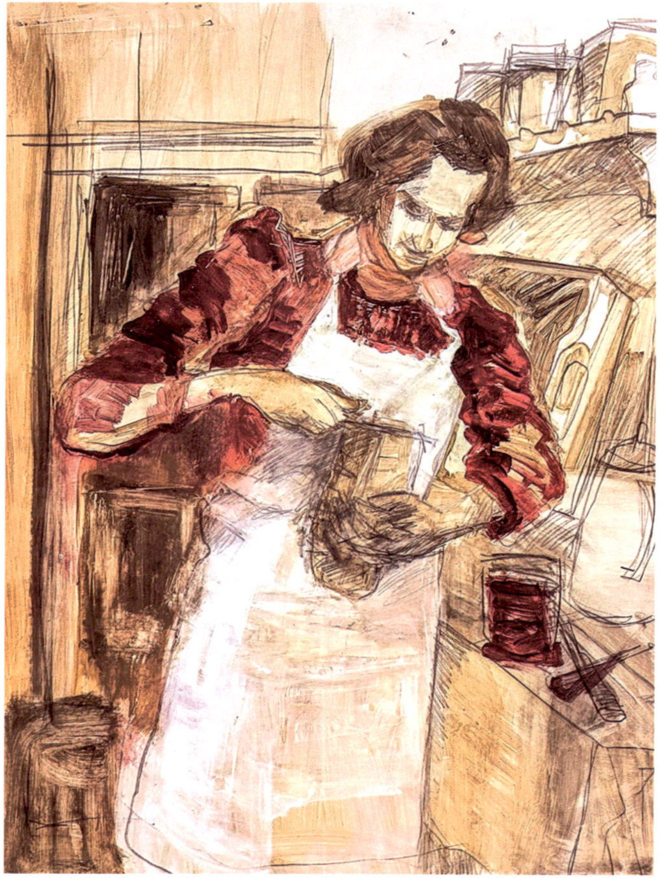

When painting my family, I avoid images from our collective memory of the Holocaust. In my work they are real people; I try to create complete portrayals of them as human beings, not "merely" as victims.

In the artworks presented here, I have tried to convey my feelings and thoughts. I have explored the contrast between the content of the postcards and the former lives of their authors in Berlin; I considered the situation in which the writers found themselves and their desire to protect and encourage their mother (and perhaps themselves). I explored the dissonance between their former lives in their warm home in Berlin, and the inhumane, life-threatening living conditions in the camp.

I was moved by the efforts of Bubi, Lisa, Ruth and Ulli, who wrote tender messages to their loved ones back home, even as they feared for their own lives. Their writing was a daring act and a way of overcoming their fears. Instead of desperately calling their mother for help, they wrote about how wonderfully they spend their free time and how they cared for each other.

When we read Bubi's words, "I work and sleep head to head with Ulli," an image comes to mind; prisoners lying crowded together on bunks in a concentration camp. But with his words, he wants to reassure his mother that he is taking very good care of his younger brother.

My work method was dictated by the technical restriction of using only scanned copies of the postcards. I developed the practice of separately drawing, painting or creating a print. I then combined the design and the postcard using digital editing.

Art holds a key to our hearts. Ever since the Old Masters first painted the sky, we have look at it through their eyes. Humbly, I hope you are able to see my family through my art and my eyes; I also hope you can speak of them, think of them and cherish their memory.

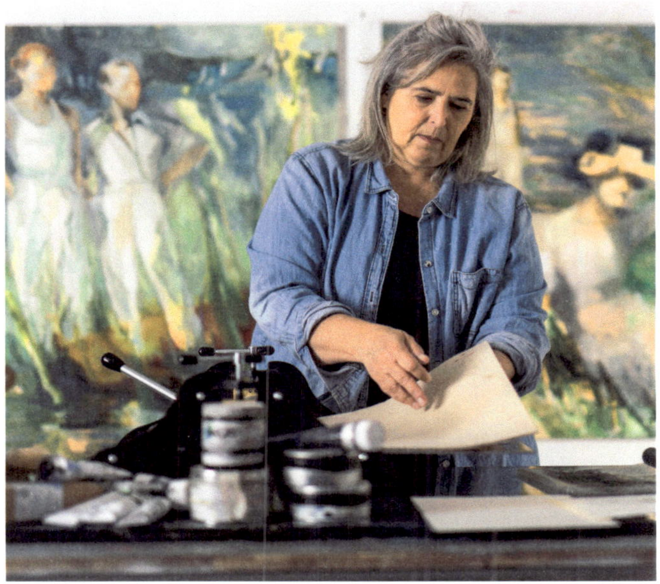

Inbar Chotzen in her studio 2025, Foto: Eran Akerman

THE POSTCARDS

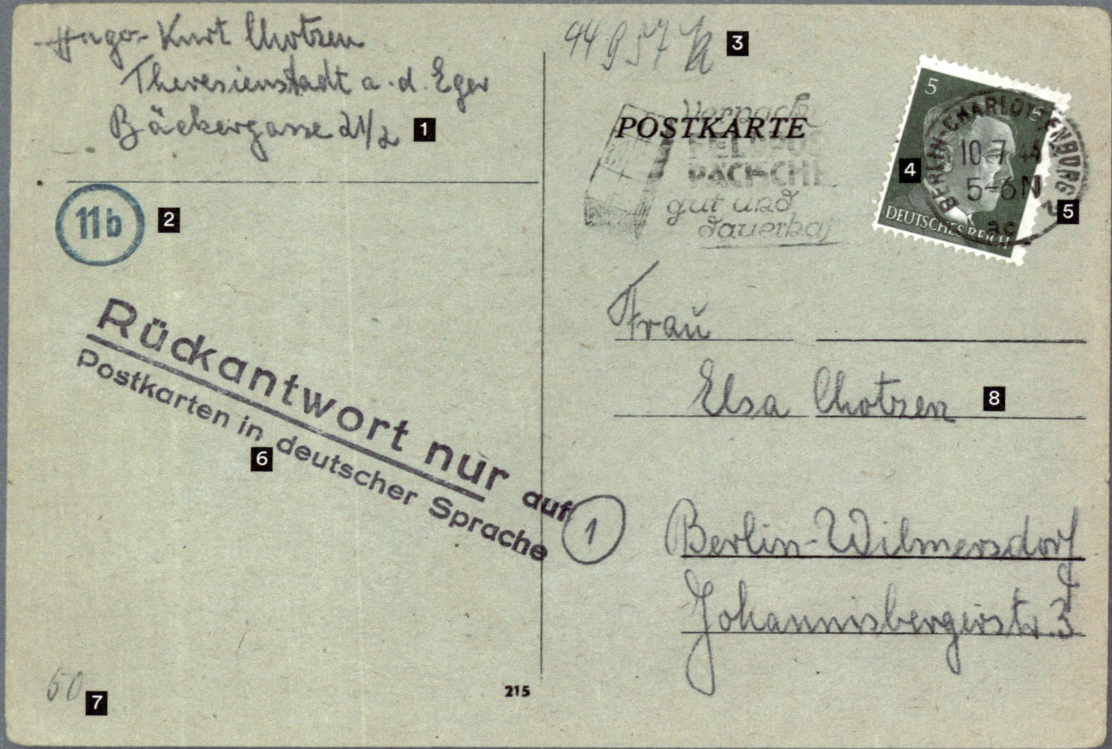
Hugo-Kurt Chotzen
Theresienstadt a. d. Eger
Bäckergasse 21/2 1

11b 2

44957 K 3

POSTKARTE

Verpacke Feldpost-Päckchen gut und dauerhaft

5 DEUTSCHES REICH 4

BERLIN-CHARLOTTENBURG 10.7.44 5-6N ac 5

Rückantwort nur auf Postkarten in deutscher Sprache 6

(1)

Frau
Elsa Chotzen 8
Berlin-Wilmersdorf
Johannisbergerstr. 3

50 7

215

Explanatory notes

1 **Return address:** From 1 August 1943 with street name and house number (here: 2), sometimes with a room number (here: 21), completed by the sender

2 **11b:** Postal code for the Protektorat. It was stamped or added to the card during the dispatch process.

3 **44957 (K):** The sender's personal number. It was no longer provided after July 1944. The four Chotzens had the numbers 44957 to 44960.

4 **Postal stamp:** This green 5-pfennig Adolf Hitler stamp, part of an ongoing series, was affixed to all postcards with personal text. The stamp was not added in Theresienstadt: It was applied by the Jewish communities in Prague, Vienna or Berlin, which sent the cards through the normal postal service. Parcel confirmation cards were franked with 60 pfennig.

5 **Postmark:** Text postcards are stamped in Berlin-Charlottenburg, parcel confirmation cards in Prague. Only then is the mail sent in the normal way.

6 **Stamp** 'Reply only to postcards in German language': Censorship was enforced by German employees of the Jewish self-administration. Some postcards contained a postmark stating: 'Reply only via the Reich Association of Jews in Germany.' On the first cards, the address is given as Kantstraße in Berlin. After the dissolution of the Reichsvereinigung in the summer of 1943, the address is then Iranische Straße: The Rest-Reichsvereinigung uses offices in the Jewish Hospital.

7 **Number** at lower left: Censor's number (here: 50)

8 **Addressee:** All postcards were addressed to Elsa Chotzen; some cards also contained the word 'Reich'. The cards were issued monthly together with the meal cards.

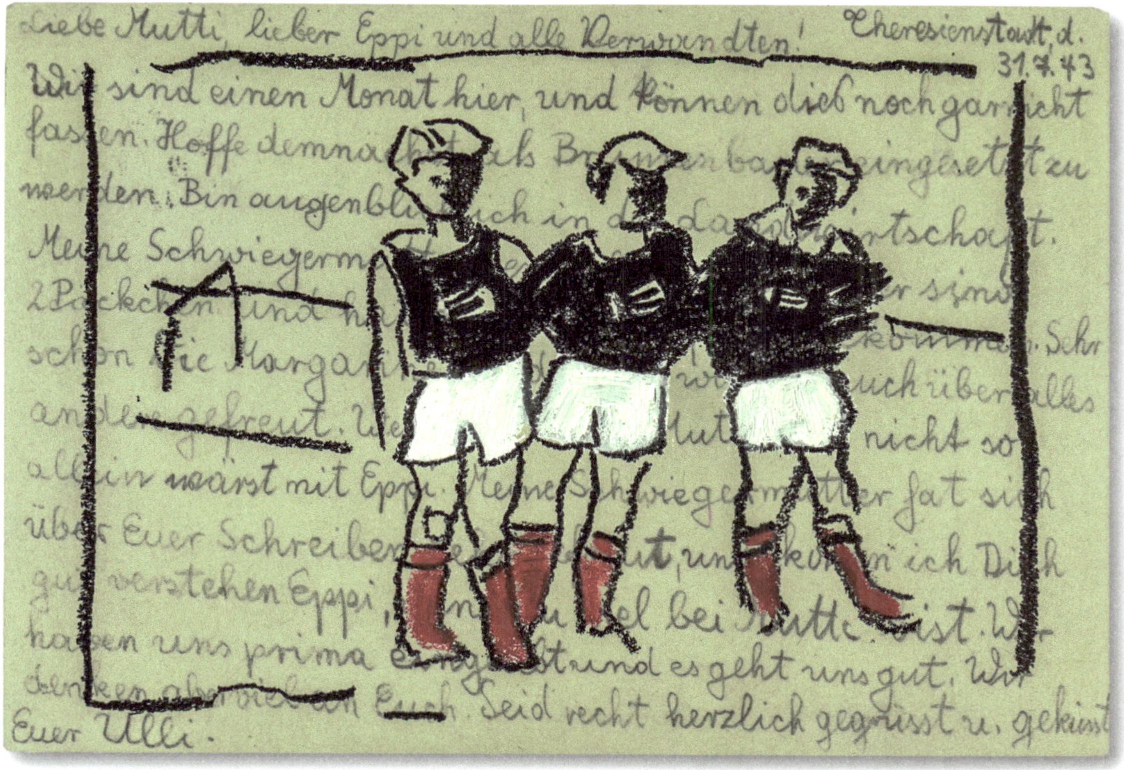

Storks, 2022

Painting and digital editing

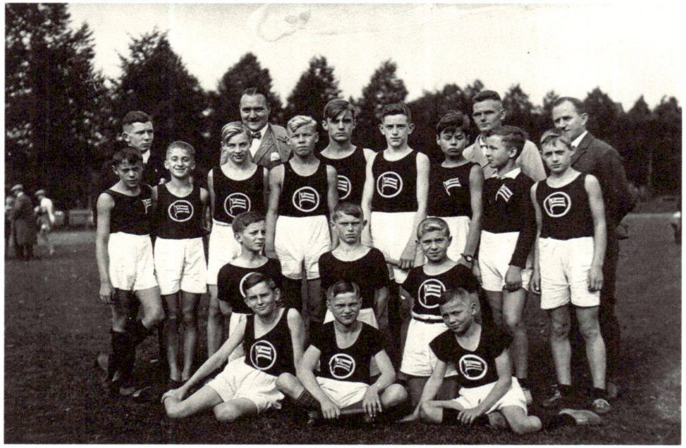

Bubi sits front row centre with Erich next to him on the right. Erich wrote beneath this photo: 'The old guard. BSV Youth' from Erich's photo album (1917–1937)

INBAR CHOTZEN

For the postcard 'Storks' I was inspired by photos of the boys in their junior hockey team's jerseys. Ulli's attempt to sound relaxed and calm is heartbreaking; between his written lines, I sense how much he missed home and his mother. This handsome boy was struggling to be brave for his mother's sake.

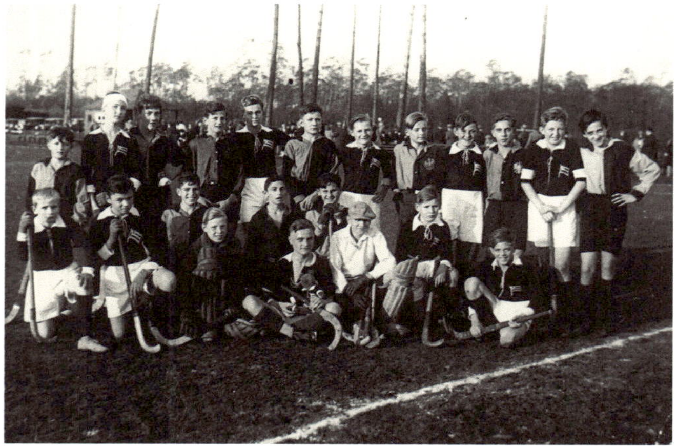

The 1st boys' hockey team B.S.V.-B.S.C., Bubi sits cross-legged in the middle, from Bubi's photo album (1923/24–1936)

EPPI CHOTZEN

The nearby Berlin sports club [founded in] 1892 became a second home to me after the First World War, but even more so for my three brothers. As soon as it was possible, at around the age of six, they were the most eager members of the 'Störche'. That's what the members were called and may well still be today, because of the red socks, the black and white jerseys and the white pants the first teams wore and still wear.

Memories [The final solution has caught up with us], unpublished

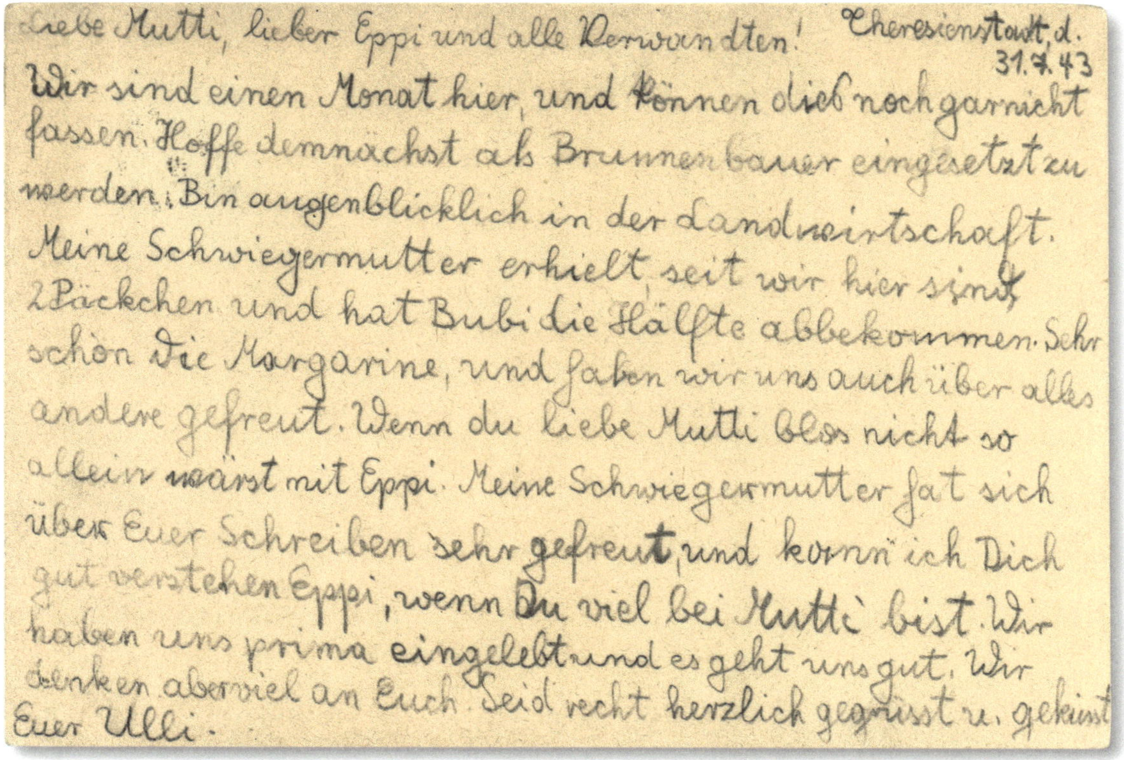
Liebe Mutti, lieber Eppi und alle Verwandten! Theresienstadt, d. 31.7.43

Wir sind einen Monat hier, und können dies noch garnicht fassen. Hoffe demnächst als Brunnenbauer eingesetzt zu werden. Bin augenblicklich in der Landwirtschaft. Meine Schwiegermutter erhielt, seit wir hier sind, 2 Päckchen und hat Bubi die Hälfte abbekommen. Sehr schön die Margarine, und haben wir uns auch über alles andere gefreut. Wenn du liebe Mutti bloss nicht so allein wärst mit Eppi. Meine Schwiegermutter hat sich über Euer Schreiben sehr gefreut, und kann ich Dich gut verstehen Eppi, wenn Du viel bei Mutti bist. Wir haben uns prima eingelebt und es geht uns gut. Wir denken aber viel an Euch. Seid recht herzlich gegrüsst u. geküsst

Euer Ulli.

First postcard from Ulli, 31 July 1943

postmark: 10 September 1943, Berlin-Charlottenburg 2

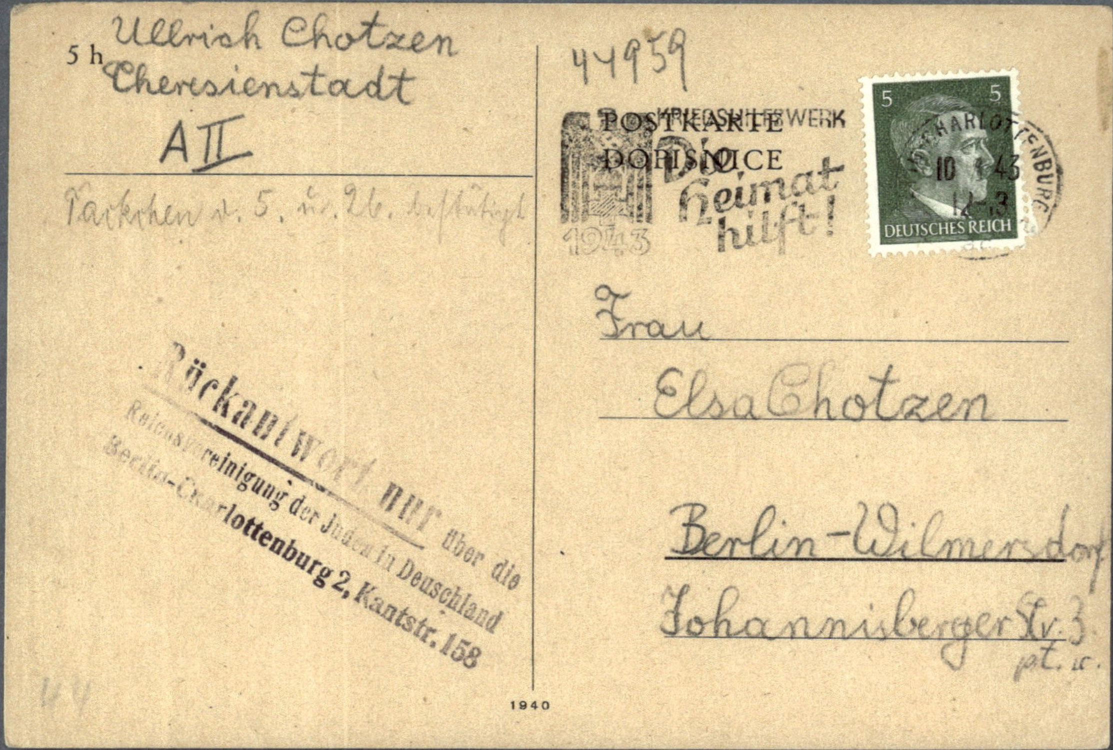
Ullrich Chotzen
5 h Theresienstadt
A II

Päckchen v. 5. u. 26. bestätigt

Rückantwort nur über die
Reichsvereinigung der Juden in Deutschland
Berlin-Charlottenburg 2, Kantstr. 158

1940

44959

POSTKARTE
DOPISNICE

KRIEGSHILFSWERK
Die Heimat hilft!
1943

5 5
DEUTSCHES REICH
CHARLOTTENBURG
10 1 43

Frau
Elsa Chotzen
Berlin-Wilmersdorf
Johannisberger Str. 3
pt. r.

About postal traffic

This postcard documents Ulli's initial communication with mother and brother following the deportation on 28 June 1943. Ulli's wife Ruth also sent a postcard to Berlin that day. Her card was postmarked ten days later in Berlin-Charlottenburg and was probably delivered soon thereafter. Ulli's card – the first sign that he was still alive – took a month longer to arrive.
The handwriting on the card is similar to that on his farewell letter: Ulli wrote in Latin script with some letters in cursive. The card may contain a hidden message, but, if it did, it has yet to be deciphered.

Situation in Theresienstadt

The return address is marked as Theresienstadt AII. This refers to the *Jägerkaserne*, a small barrack built into the entrenchments. Like all new arrivals, the four Chotzens were held in a 'sluice' for at least one or two days and registered in the detention system. During the process they had to hand over their valuables, but were allowed to keep their clothes and a few personal items. Then they were assigned to housing, separated by gender. The brothers stayed together.

Dear Mum, dear Eppi and all my relatives!

Theresienstadt,
31.7.43

We've been here a month already and still can't get our heads around it. I hope to soon be employed as a **well builder**. I'm currently working in **agriculture**.
My **mother-in-law** has received 2 parcels since we arrived and Bubi was given half. The margarine was very nice and we were also happy about everything else. If only you, dear mum, weren't so alone with Eppi. My mother-in-law was very happy about your letter and I can understand you well, Eppi, when you're with Mum a lot.
We have settled in really well and are doing fine. But we think of you a lot. Best wishes and kisses.
Yours, Ulli

Until 1938, Ulli had attended the building trade school in Kurfürstenstraße and studied civil engineering and **well construction**. Like his brothers Eppi and Bubi, he was made to perform forced labour in this field.

agriculture: In Theresienstadt, all 'able-bodied' prisoners between the ages of 16 and 60 were assigned to forced labour soon after they arrived. Prisoners aged 14 or younger and older prisoners up to the age of 65 were also assigned to unskilled labour, depending on their health. A regular work day lasted 11.5 hours for men and an hour less for women. The 'labour centre' of the Jewish self-administration oversaw the assignment of work. People were rarely assigned work in their actual professions, but sometimes they could change to a different job.

Ulli's **mother-in-law**, Klara Cohn, and his two sisters-in-law, Ursula and Lieselotte Cohn, were deported on the first transport from Berlin to Theresienstadt on 6 June 1942. It took six months for Ruth to learn where her relatives were. When Ruth was deported to Theresienstadt she was reunited with her mothers and sisters. She moved in with her mother and older sister, Ursula, at Jägergasse 15. Liselotte Cohn lived in the youth centre at Hauptstraße 14.

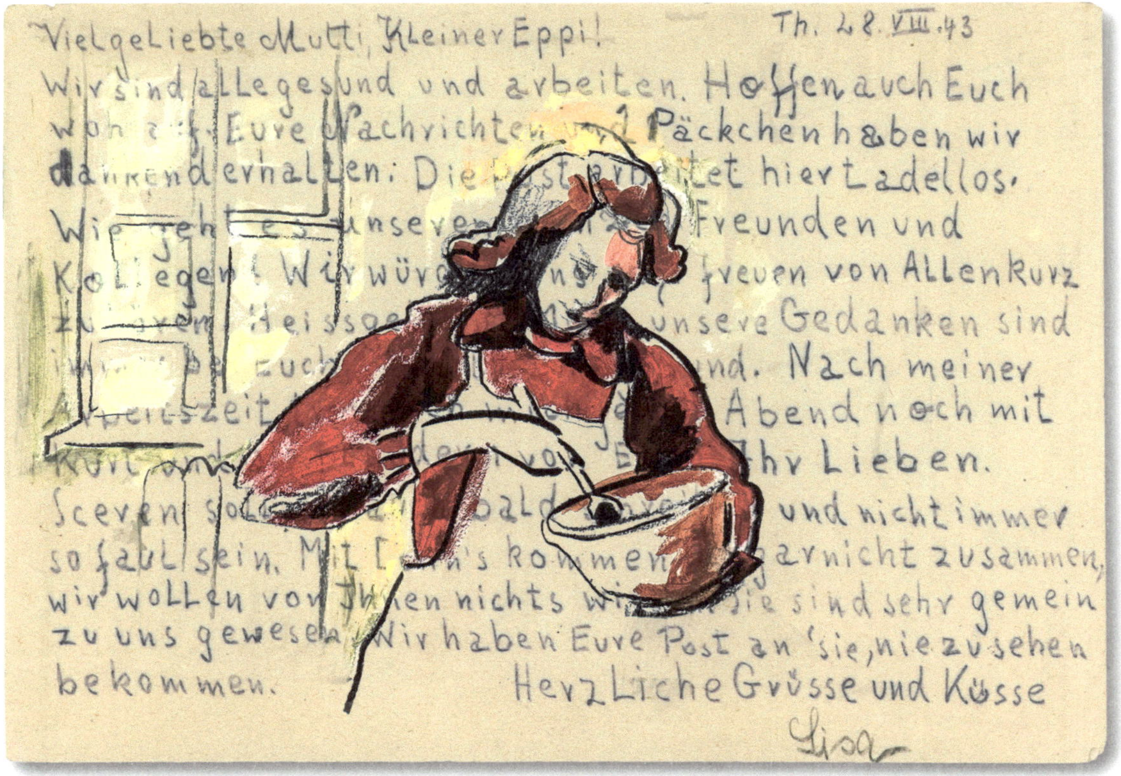

Lisa cooking, 2019

Painting and digital editing

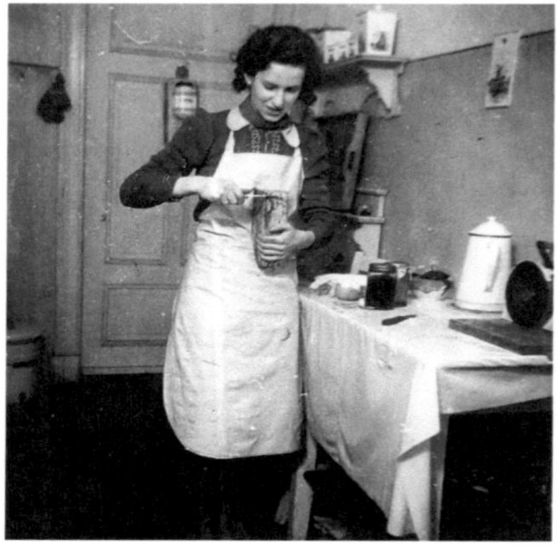

In one version of his memoirs, Eppi included photos of family members, including this one of Lisa in the kitchen.

INBAR CHOTZEN

In sketches for the postcard 'Lisa Cooking', I looked at a photo taken in 1941 in their apartment in Elsässer Strasse 54. Only once have I seen someone holding and slicing bread this way; it was in an old photo of my grandmother as a pioneer in the Kibbutz. It was thus clear to me that, next to Lisa, a jar of jam was on the table, waiting to be spread onto the bread. I imagined it was a jar of homemade red jam. From then on, for me Lisa's colour was red; it represented a young, vibrant woman who had just found the love of her life.

After their wedding on 18 November 1941, Bubi and Lisa subletted a room on the ground floor of Elsässer Strasse 54, where they shared a kitchen and bathroom with an elderly woman. This building, in which Lisa's family also lived after they were forced to leave Reinickendorf, belonged to the Jewish community. This was where people were housed after the antisemitic housing policy dictated they leave their homes. Bubi and Lisa's landlady took her own life in her bedroom after receiving her deportation order in early 1942. According to the memoir written by Klaus Scheurenberg, Lisa's brother, the landlady left behind a farewell letter *'[w]ith well wishes for Lisa and Kurt. And the message that she was glad to have lived her life. She had experienced so many wonderful things, seen so much, read so much. [...] She wrote in her slightly old-fashioned way that she didn't know why her life should end in misery and agony after all that beauty.'*[1] Throughout the year, other residents in the building were also deported. At the end of 1942, Bubi and Lisa moved back to the Chotzens' family home in Johannisberger Straße where they hoped they would be safer.

1 Klaus Scheurenberg: Ich will leben – Ein autobiografischer Bericht. Berlin 1982, p. 70.

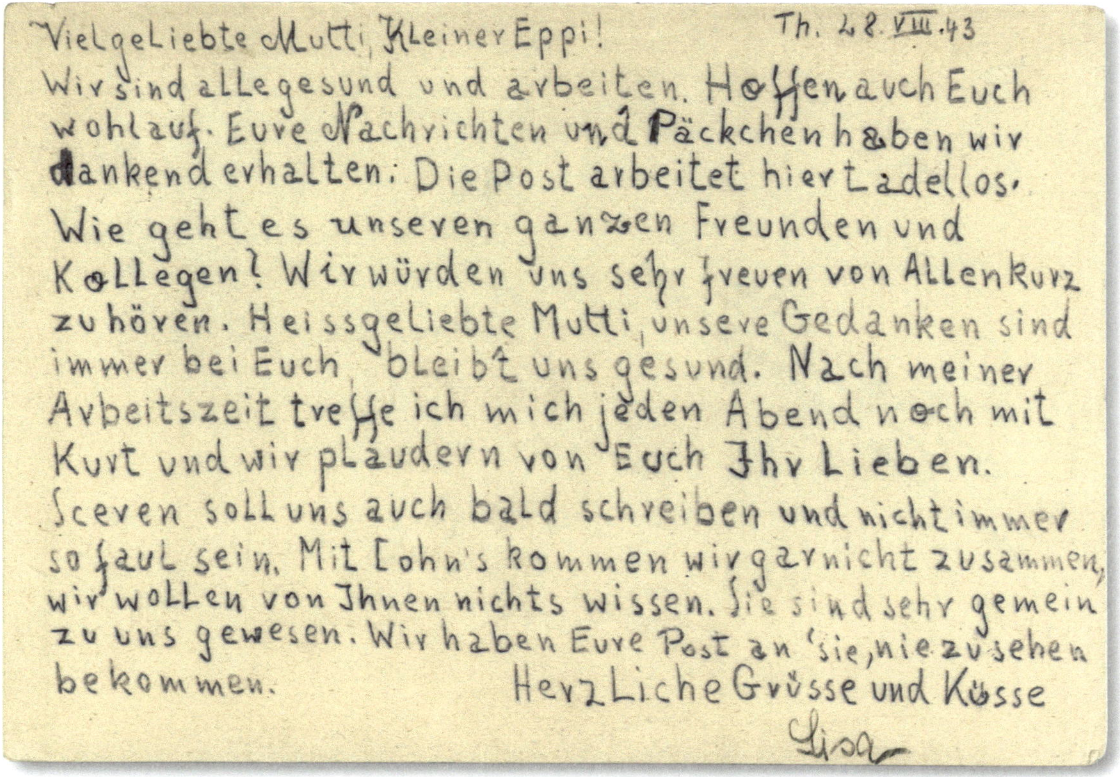

Vielgeliebte Mutti, Kleiner Eppi! Th. 28. VIII. 43
Wir sind alle gesund und arbeiten. Hoffen auch Euch
wohlauf. Eure Nachrichten und Päckchen haben wir
dankend erhalten; Die Post arbeitet hier tadellos.
Wie geht es unseren ganzen Freunden und
Kollegen? Wir würden uns sehr freuen von Allen kurz
zu hören. Heissgeliebte Mutti, unsere Gedanken sind
immer bei Euch, bleibt uns gesund. Nach meiner
Arbeitszeit treffe ich mich jeden Abend noch mit
Kurt und wir plaudern von Euch Ihr Lieben.
Sceven soll uns auch bald schreiben und nicht immer
so faul sein. Mit Cohn's kommen wir garnicht zusammen,
wir wollen von Ihnen nichts wissen. Sie sind sehr gemein
zu uns gewesen. Wir haben Eure Post an sie, nie zu sehen
bekommen. Herzliche Grüsse und Küsse
Lisa

Third postcard from Lisa, 28 August 1943
postmark: 8 November 1943, Berlin-Charlottenburg 2

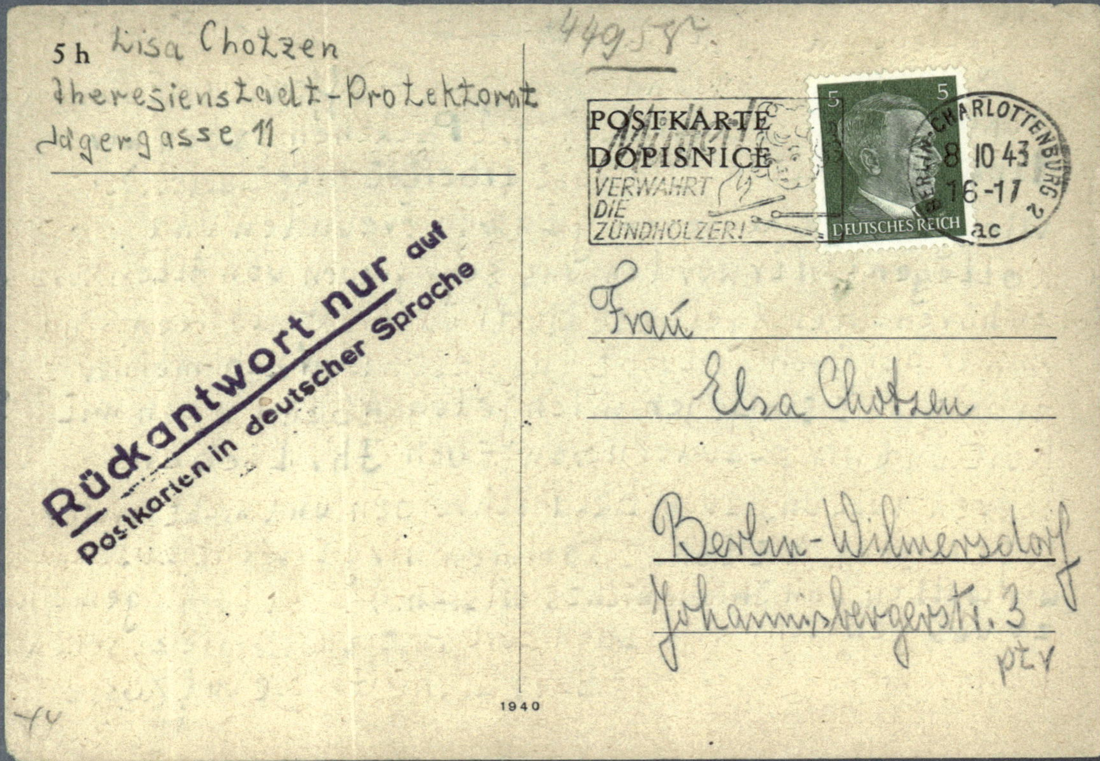

5 h Lisa Chotzen
Theresienstadt-Protektorat
Jägergasse 11

44958

POSTKARTE
DOPISNICE
VERWAHRT
DIE
ZÜNDHÖLZER!

5 DEUTSCHES REICH 5

BERLIN-CHARLOTTENBURG 2
8.10.43 16-17
ac

Rückantwort nur auf
Postkarten in deutscher Sprache

Frau
Elsa Chotzen
Berlin-Wilmersdorf
Johannisbergerstr. 3
ptr

1940

About postal traffic

This postcard was written by Bubi; only the signature and the recipient's address were written by Lisa. Bubi pretended to be his wife to avoid detection by the censor. This was the first time he and Lisa were allowed to send home a postcard with personal text. Although the two cards were sent on the same day, they arrived in Berlin a month apart. On the same day Ulli and Ruth both completed a confirmation card for a parcel that was packed in Berlin on 17 August. Since their deportation, the four Chotzens had been allowed to send five messages – signs that they were alive – to Berlin. By the end of August, however, only one of these cards had arrived, written by Ruth on 31 July 1943.

The handwriting here, like the card Bubi signed with his own name that same day, is unusual. On later postcards Bubi always wrote in cursive.

The return address, Jägergasse 11, was where Lisa was housed. This street ran parallel to Bäckergasse, where Ulli and Bubi lived. Lisa's brother, Klaus, wrote in his memoir that Lisa's first accommodation was in a hot attic without running water or sanitary facilities, and that she had lost her will to live there. Her family, who had been in Theresienstadt for a few weeks by then, were able to get her moved into her mother's room in Jägergasse.

Situation in Theresienstadt

The forced resettlement of the town, which was designed for approximately 7,000 residents, began in November 1941. Within six months, occupancy had reached its peak during which 58,500 people were squeezed into the closed-off area. This overcrowding disrupted the food supply, which led to increased malnutrition. Although the number of residents in Theresienstadt sank after several transports left for Auschwitz, the living conditions remained difficult; in summer 1943, new arrivals were still being forced to sleep on the bare floors of unfurnished attics.

Dearly loved Mum, little Eppi! Th., 28.VIII 43
We are all healthy and working. Hope you are well, too. We gratefully received your messages and parcels.The postal system works perfectly here. How are all our friends and colleagues? We would enjoy hearing from everyone. Dear Mum, our thoughts are always with you, stay healthy. Every evening **after my work shift** I meet up with Kurt and we chat about you all, our dear ones. **Sceren** should write us soon and not always be so lazy. We don't see the **Cohns** at all. We don't want anything to do with them. They have been very unkind to us. We never received the mail you sent them.

Warm greetings and kisses
Lisa

After my work shift: Over time, the pretence of a 'normal' life with work and free time was perfected in Theresienstadt. In May 1943, a monetary economy was introduced and the prisoners were paid for their forced labour in ghetto 'crowns', which could only be used in Theresienstadt. The wages varied depending on the difficulty of the labour. The same was true for how many calories one was entitled to per day.

Sceren, also spelled Szeren, was a cousin of Bubi's on the father's side of the family who lived in Budapest. Bubi had last visited her and her family there in 1936. His brother Erich had travelled to Hungary in 1938. Bubi also mentioned her in the postcard he wrote that same day. The significance of this is unclear.

The Cohns is a reference to Ruth's mother, Klara Cohn, and her sisters. Bubi's message conveys how desperately Elsa's children needed food and contact from home: The Cohns had apparently received mail from Berlin that they hadn't shown Bubi. The surviving correspondence also includes a postcard from Lieselotte Cohn to Elsa Chotzen dated 9 August 1943: 'Our mum received your parcel with great joy. The pudding, the sugar and the other items were very nice. [...] This time we didn't share the parcel with Bubi, as we had two.'

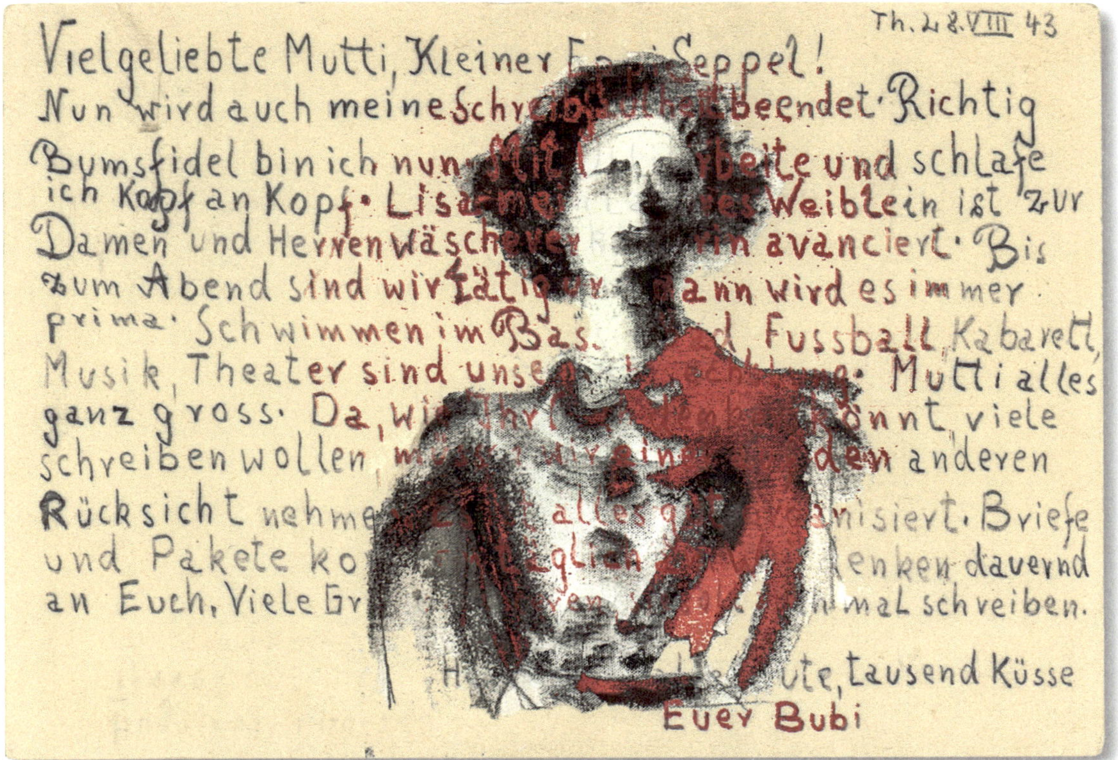

Lisa in red dress, 2024
Ink drawing and digital editing

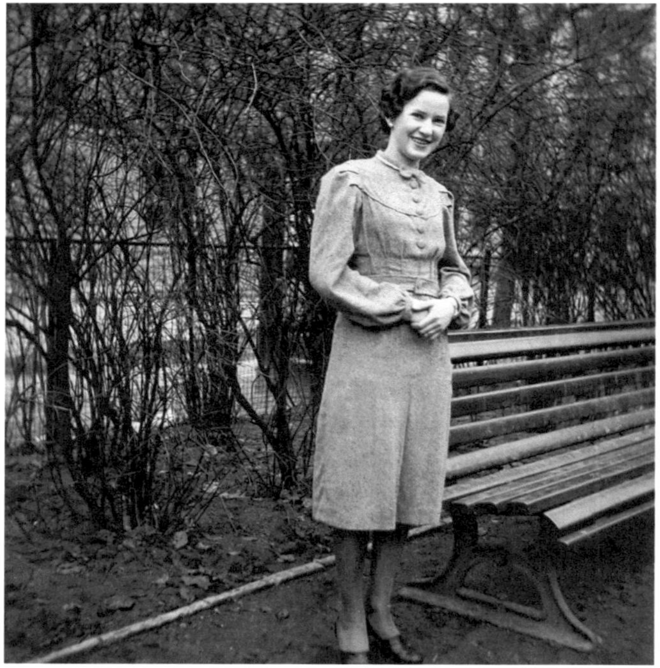

Lisa Scheurenberg, probably 1940, from Bubi's photo album (1936–1941)

Lisa is wearing the same dress in many photos. This is a reflection both of the wartime economy and the Nazi's antisemitic policies: A few weeks after food rationing was introduced, restrictions were also placed on the purchase of textiles during the war. One could only buy new clothes with an allocated 'Reich clothing card'. From 6 February 1940, Jews were no longer entitled to clothing cards.

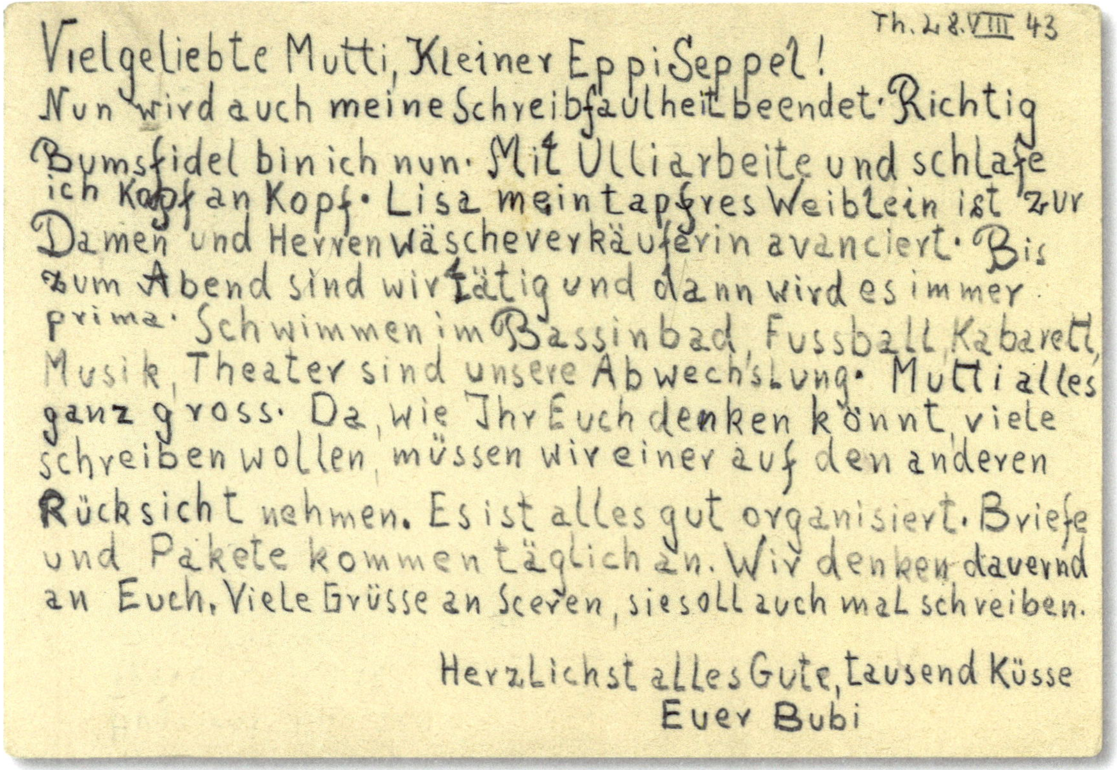
Th. 28.VIII 43

Vielgeliebte Mutti, Kleiner EppiSeppel!
Nun wird auch meine Schreibfaulheit beendet. Richtig Bumsfidel bin ich nun. Mit Ulli arbeite und schlafe ich Kopf an Kopf. Lisa mein tapfres Weiblein ist zur Damen und Herrenwäscheverkäuferin avanciert. Bis zum Abend sind wir tätig und dann wird es immer prima. Schwimmen im Bassinbad, Fussball, Kabarett, Musik, Theater sind unsere Abwechslung. Mutti alles ganz gross. Da, wie Ihr Euch denken könnt, viele schreiben wollen, müssen wir einer auf den anderen Rücksicht nehmen. Es ist alles gut organisiert. Briefe und Pakete kommen täglich an. Wir denken dauernd an Euch. Viele Grüsse an Sceren, sie soll auch mal schreiben.

Herzlichst alles Gute, tausend Küsse
Euer Bubi

First postcard from Bubi, 28 August 1943
postmark: 8 November 1943, Berlin-Charlottenburg 2

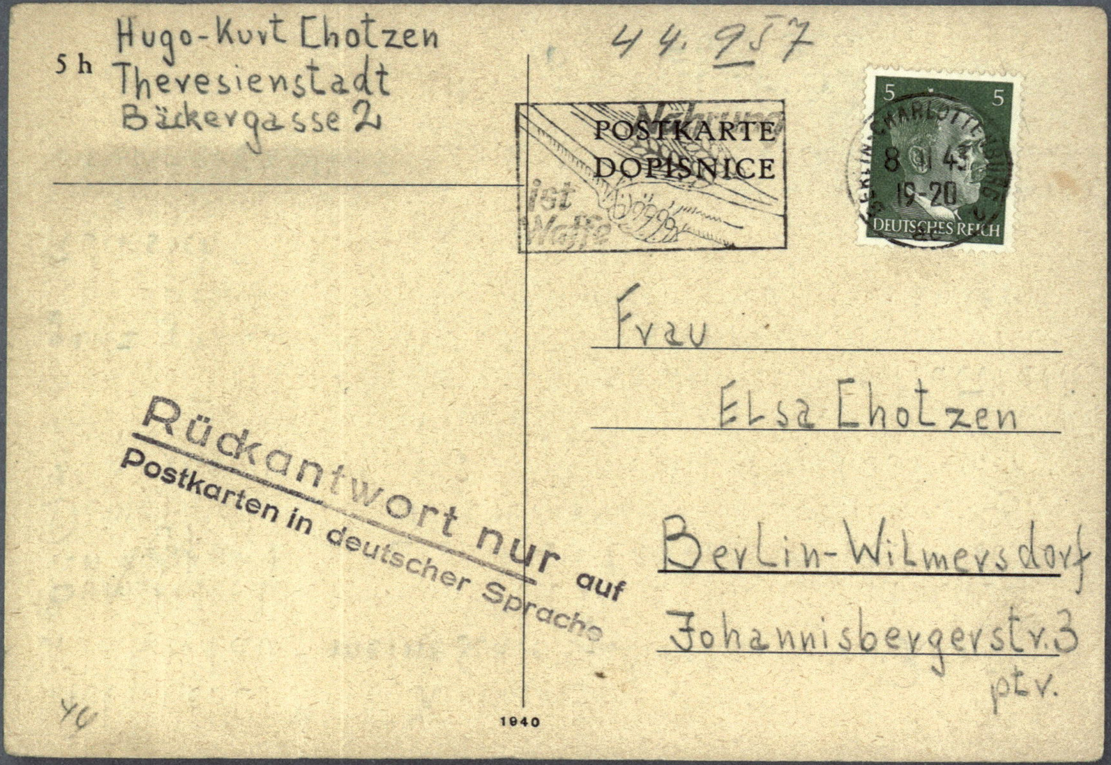
Hugo-Kurt Chotzen
5 h Theresienstadt
Bäckergasse 2

44.957

POSTKARTE
DOPISNICE

5 5
DEUTSCHES REICH

Frau
Elsa Chotzen
Berlin-Wilmersdorf
Johannisbergerstr. 3
ptr.

Rückantwort nur auf
Postkarten in deutscher Sprache

40

1940

About postal traffic

This card was written almost a month after Ulli sent his first postcard. It is Bubi's first known correspondence with Elsa and Eppi.
The handwriting on the card stands out. He wrote future messages in cursive – perhaps in response to the censorship authorities' demand that all postcards be legible. There may, however, also be a secret code hidden here.
The return address is Bäckergasse 2. Street names, which replaced the building names that had previously been used for addresses, were not introduced in Theresienstadt until 1 August 1943. Bubi and Ulli continued to live in the Jägerkaserne, before designated as A II. Bäckergasse was located at the town's southern outer wall and ran parallel to Jägergasse, where their wives, Ruth and Lisa, lived.
On 28 August 1943, the Jewish self-administration published 'Daily Order No. 354', which announced new blackout times and the timetable for submitting postcards. The schedule was based on transport numbers. The four Chotzens' number was I/97. 'I' stands for Berlin; '97' refers to the number of transports from the Reich capital.

Situation in Theresienstadt

The town was formally run by a Jewish self-administration, which received its instructions from the SS: The arrival and departure of transports, the expected productivity results of forced labour, the allocation of food to the population – this was all decided by the SS. However, the prisoner's 'council of elders', which was headed by sociologist Paul Eppstein during the time the Chotzens were there, was responsible for deciding who would be deported, how work positions were distributed and who received the allocated food. Notices, which were initially published as numbered 'daily orders', also informed the ghetto residents of when they could do laundry, post mail, go shopping or visit the sick. The transport number of the train that brought people to Theresienstadt was used as an organisational tool.

Th., 28.VIII 43

Beloved Mum, little **EppiSeppel**!

Enough of my laziness in writing. I am now quite chipper. **I work and sleep head-to-head with Ulli.** Lisa, my brave girl, has advanced to the position of **ladies' and men's undergarments seller**. We work until evening and then things are fine. **Swimming in the pool**, football, cabaret, music, theatre are our diversions. Mum, everything is grand. As you can imagine, many want to write, so we must show consideration. Everything is well organised. Letters and parcels arrive daily. We think of you always. Many greetings to Sceren, tell her to write, too.

All the best, a thousand kisses

Your Bubi

EppiSeppel: Seppel had been Joseph's nickname, until he changed it to 'Eppi' as a small child.

Laziness in writing: Bubi wrote another postcard under Lisa's name that day. Elsa and Eppi will have recognised his handwriting.

I work and sleep head-to-head with Ulli: Bubi and his brother performed agriculture labour together. The work was hard, but it had advantages. Klaus Scheurenberg wrote: *'My brother-in-law Bubi was part of a work detail that did gardening and agricultural work outside the camp every morning. From time to time, he was able to "smuggle" a green leaf of lettuce or something like that. He was a strong young man of 25 who was always hungry.'*[1] Harvesting vegetables or fruit for personal consumption was strictly forbidden of course, and the labour crews were checked at the camp gate. Anyone caught with smuggled food faced severe punishment.

Ladies' and men's undergarments seller: Like so much else in Theresienstadt, the term 'ladies' and men's undergarments seller' was a euphemism. The 'shops' did not offer new goods. Instead, clothes that were taken from new arrivals in the 'sluice' or removed from the dead were redistributed through ration cards, for which one had to apply. This was Lisa's job for at least nine months.

Swimming in the pool: The so-called 'central pool' was located in the Hohenelb barracks at Parkstraße 10. Children, women and men were permitted to go there separately at designated times to wash themselves. Because the pool was very small, most people only used the shower. Jiří Brady, a survivor who was deported to Theresienstadt when he was 14, described the baths as follows: *'When I received a red or white note with the letter M or J on it, I took a towel, soap and washcloth and went to the Hohenelbe central bath. I stood there with a group of men and boys waiting for the door to open. ... The central bath had two shower rooms and a pool that was rarely used. A boy operated the tap in the room: he turned it on twice in seven-minute intervals. In between, you soaped yourself up.'*[2]

1 Klaus Scheurenberg: Ich will leben, bid., p. 140.

2 see https://www.ghetto-theresienstadt.de/lexikon/vedem, accessed on 31.3.2025

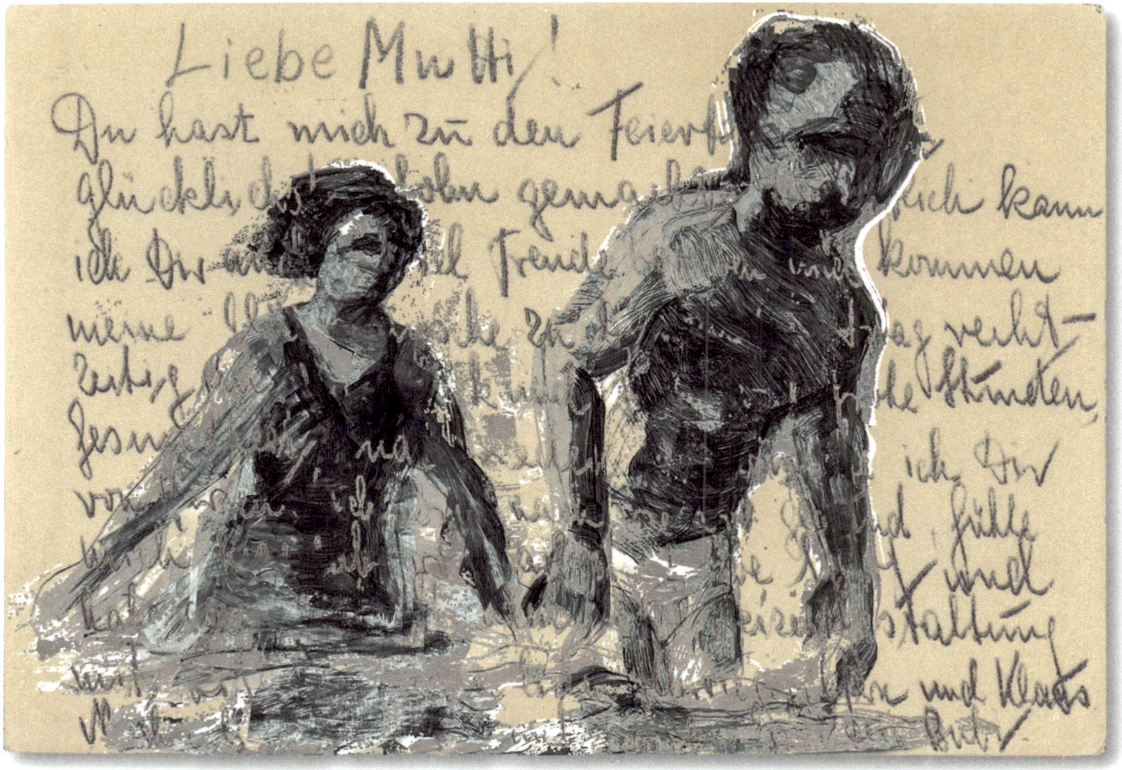

The Expulsion, 2024

Ink drawing and digital editing

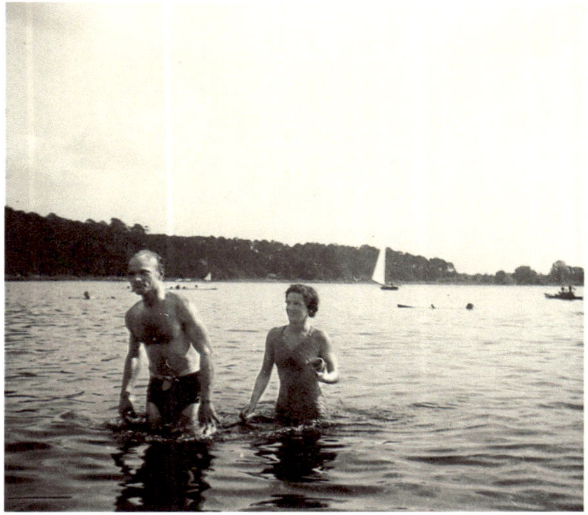

Bubi and Lisa bathing in the Havel, 1940/41, from Bubi's photo album (1936–1941)

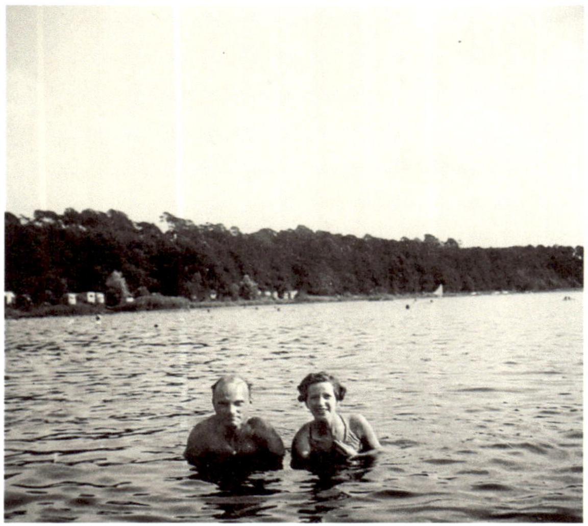

INBAR CHOTZEN

The illustration in the postcard 'The Expulsion' is based on my eponymous painting from 2021. This painting was inspired by the painting 'Escape of Eden' by Abel Pann. In both the painting and the postcard I expressed my outrage and sorrow. It is also based on a photo of Lisa and Bubi swimming in the Havel; they look carefree, but the truth behind the photo is that in 1940, Jews were banned from swimming in public pools.

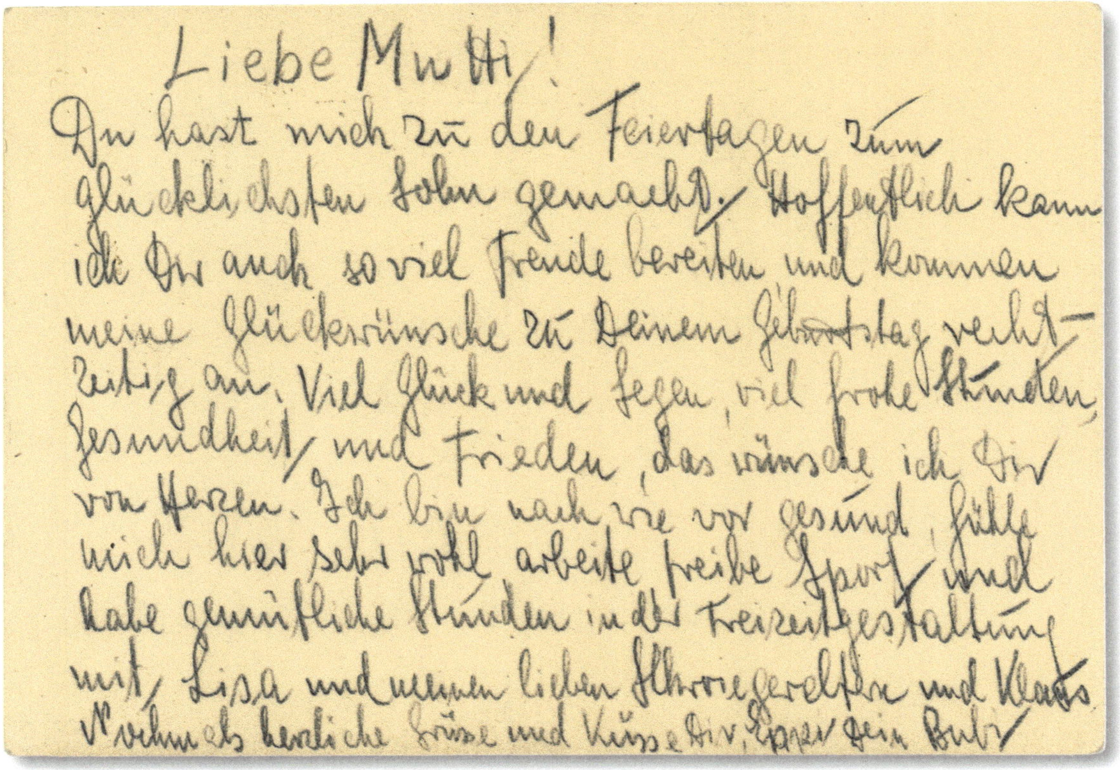

Liebe Mutti!
Du hast mich zu den Feiertagen zum
glücklichsten Sohn gemacht. Hoffentlich kann
ich Dir auch so viel Freude bereiten und kommen
meine Glückwünsche zu Deinem Geburtstag recht-
zeitig an. Viel Glück und Segen, viel frohe Stunden,
Gesundheit, und Frieden, das wünsche ich Dir
von Herzen. Ich bin nach wie vor gesund, fühle
mich hier sehr wohl, arbeite, treibe Sport und
habe gemütliche Stunden in der Freizeitgestaltung
mit Lisa und meinen lieben Schwiegereltern und Klaus.
Nochmals herzliche Grüsse und Küsse Dir, Immer Dein Bubi

Second postcard from Bubi, undated
postmark: 17 November 1943, Berlin-Charlottenburg

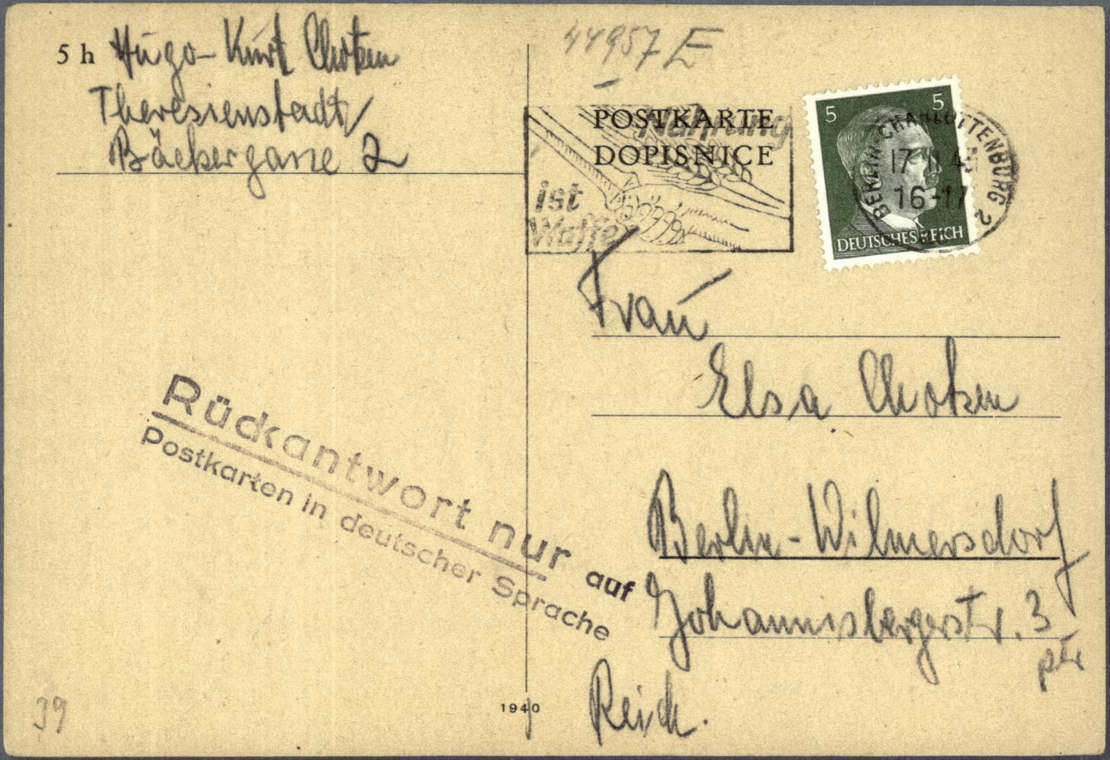

5 h Hugo-Kurt Chotzen
Theresienstadt/
Bäckergasse 2

44957 E

POSTKARTE
DOPISNICE

ist Waffe

5 DEUTSCHES REICH 5

BERLIN-CHARLOTTENBURG 2

Frau
Elsa Chotzen
Berlin-Wilmersdorf
Johannisbergerstr. 13

Reich

Rückantwort nur auf
Postkarten in deutscher Sprache

39

1940

About postal traffic

This is the second postcard Bubi was allowed to send with a personal text. According to 'Daily Order No. 363' published by the Jewish self-administration on 24 September 1943, those with the transport number I/97 were allowed to send mail again on 28 September 1943, exactly one month after Bubi's first postcard. Between these two dates, he was also permitted to send one parcel confirmation, which, based on the postmark, left the camp relatively swiftly.

Situation in Theresienstadt

The decision was made to send to Theresienstadt not only Jews from the 'Protektorat', but also Jews from Germany and Austria. The town was declared a 'ghetto for the elderly' and 'privileged'. At the same time, deportations began leaving Theresienstadt for the East. Most of the people on these transports were sent directly to their death: from spring 1942, roughly 87,000 people were deported in 63 transports. Only about 3,800 of them survived the war.

Most of the prisoners who were sent to Theresienstadt between 1941 and 1945 came from five cities: Prague, Vienna, Berlin, Brno and Frankfurt am Main. From 1943, Jews arrived from other German-occupied countries, in particular the Netherlands and Denmark.

The transport lists of the Jewish self-administration and the files in the SS office were destroyed as evidence before the war ended. Consequently, there is no complete list of all transports to and from Theresienstadt.

Dear Mum!

You made me the happiest son **on the holidays**. I hope I can bring you just as much joy and that my **birthday** greetings arrive in good time. Good luck and blessings, many happy hours,health and peace, that's what I wish you from the bottom of my heart. I am still healthy, feel quite well here, work, **play sports and spend pleasant hours in my free time** with Lisa, my dear in-laws, and **Klaus**.

Warm greetings and kisses to you again, Eppi, Your Bubi

On the holidays: Bubi had evidently received a parcel containing good wishes for the holidays of Rosh ha-Shanah (the Jewish New Year) and Yom Kippur (the Jewish Day of Atonement). In 1943, these fell on 29/30 September and 9/10 October respectively.

Elsa's **birthday** was on 31 October. The postcard reached her on 17 November 1943 at the earliest.

Play sports and spend pleasant hours in my free time: Given that they had to perform at least 54 hours of hard labour per week, the Chotzens probably preferred to spend the little free time they had together or playing sports. Klaus Scheurenberg, Lisa's brother, recalls in his autobiography:
I saw her [Lisa] one evening after work in the late autumn of 1943. She had crawled into a corner of the yard with Bubi. She had touchingly set a miniature table on a stool I had built. She had stuck a bit of greenery into a little old tube in place of flowers. Two tin plates and two spoons completed the picture of the festive table. They ate and looked at each other. Two young people, she 23, he 25, cheated out of their lives. They had no idea that they had only 14 more months to live.[1]
Physical exercise had been important to the boys since their early childhood, and Bubi and Ulli were certain that they could endure the strenuous forced labour because their bodies were 'well-trained' and 'strong'. This was something they mentioned regularly in the postcards they sent home. They probably tried to stay fit in Theresienstadt. The author and survivor of Theresienstadt, H. G. Adler wrote that football was the most popular sport there, especially among the younger children. They played on the 'Süd-berg', a hill close to where Bubi and Ulli were housed. The young prisoners even organised a league and played tournaments.[2]

Klaus refers to Klaus Scheurenberg, Lisa's brother and Bubi's brother-in-law, who was 18 years old at the time.

Bubi probably sent **warm greetings and kisses to Eppi** again because his older brother's birthday had been the day before, on 27 September.

1 Klaus Scheurenberg: Ich will leben, ibid., p. 166f.

2 H. G. Adler: Theresienstadt 1941–1945. Das Antlitz einer Zwangsgemeinschaft. Göttingen 2005, p. 604

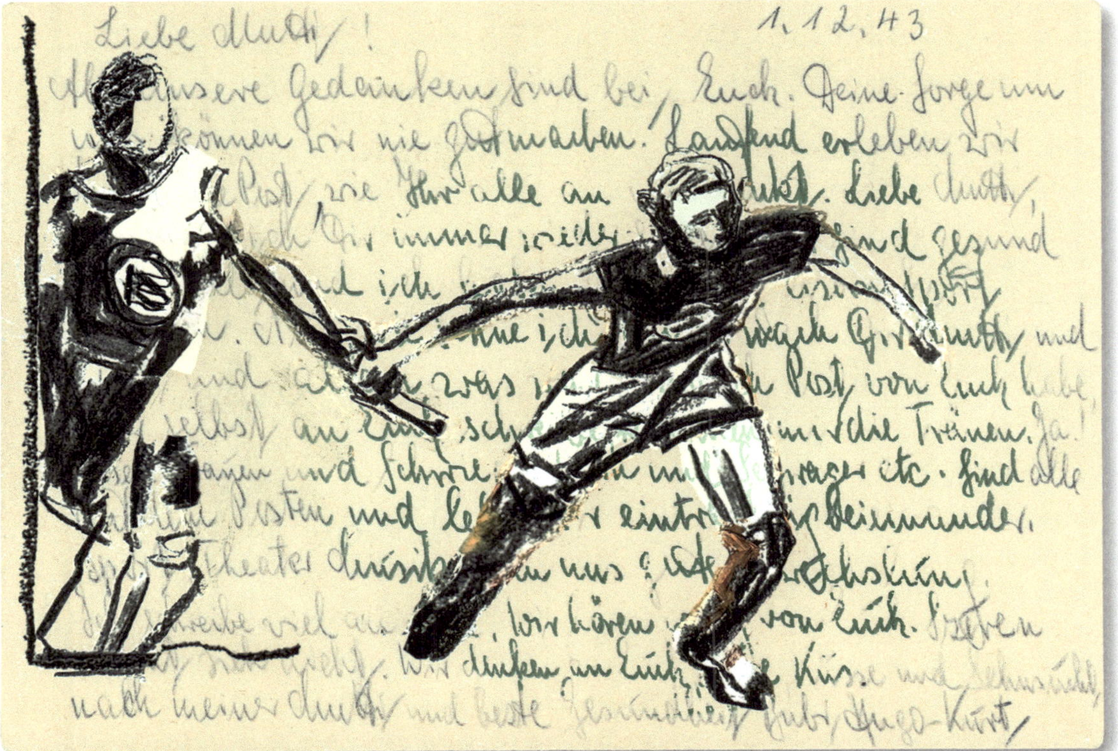

Running, 2019

Charcoal and digital editing

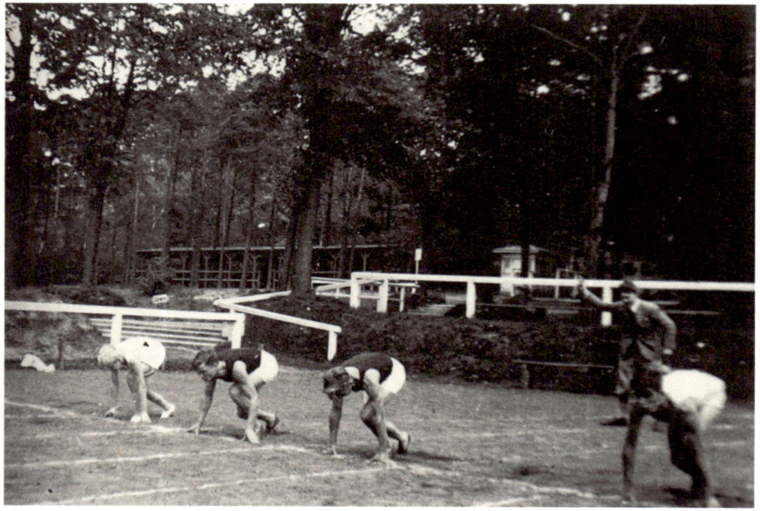

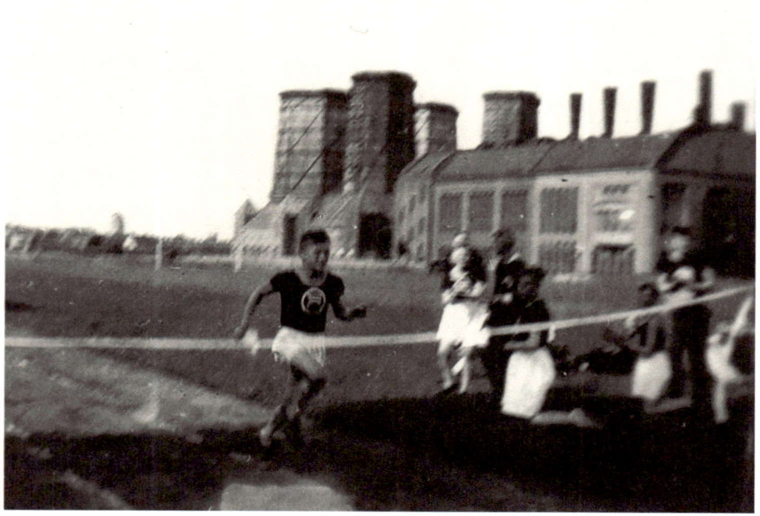

Bubi in a relay race. Beneath the photo series he wrote: 'training', 'contest', 'finished...winner!' From Bubi's photo album (1923/24–1936)

EPPI CHOTZEN

Before the Nazi era, I have no memory of any particular interactions with our neighbours that was marked by the slightest hint of hostility or dislike.
This does not mean, of course, that there were no Nazis or hateful people in our neighbourhood prior to this.
The whole atmosphere clearly demonstrated what had long been brewing. When they first deliberately began to fly the flags around 1933, very few areas remained without swastika flags in Johannisbergerstrasse.
Up to that point, it was normal for us to play with the others, arguing, roughhousing, and breaking the occasional window. We mostly played sports along with everyone else.

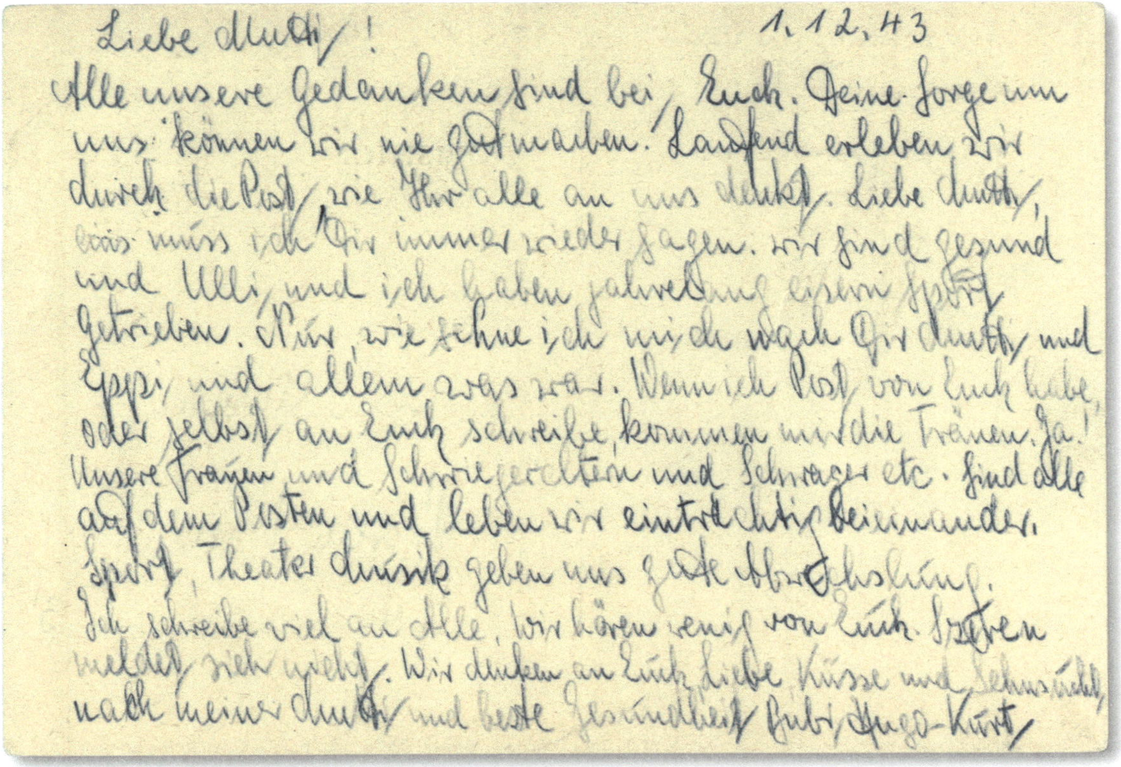
Liebe Mutti! 1.12.43

Alle unsere Gedanken sind bei Euch. Deine Sorge um uns können wir nie gutmachen. Laufend erleben wir durch die Post, wie Ihr alle an uns denkt. Liebe Mutti, was muss ich Dir immer wieder sagen. Wir sind gesund und Ulli und ich haben jahrelang einen Sport getrieben. Wir, wie sehne ich mich nach Dir Mutti und Eppi und allem was war. Wenn ich Post von Euch habe oder selbst an Euch schreibe, kommen mir die Tränen. Ja! Unsere Frauen und Schwiegereltern und Schwager etc. sind alle auf dem Posten und leben wir einträchtig beieinander. Sport, Theater Musik geben uns gute Abwechslung. Ich schreibe viel an Alle, wir hören wenig von Euch. Sieben meldet sich nicht. Wir denken an Euch. Liebe Küsse und Sehnsucht nach meiner Mutti und beste Gesundheit Bubi, Hugo-Kurt.

Sixteenth postcard from Bubi, 1 December 1943
postmark: 25 February 1944, Berlin-Charlottenburg 2

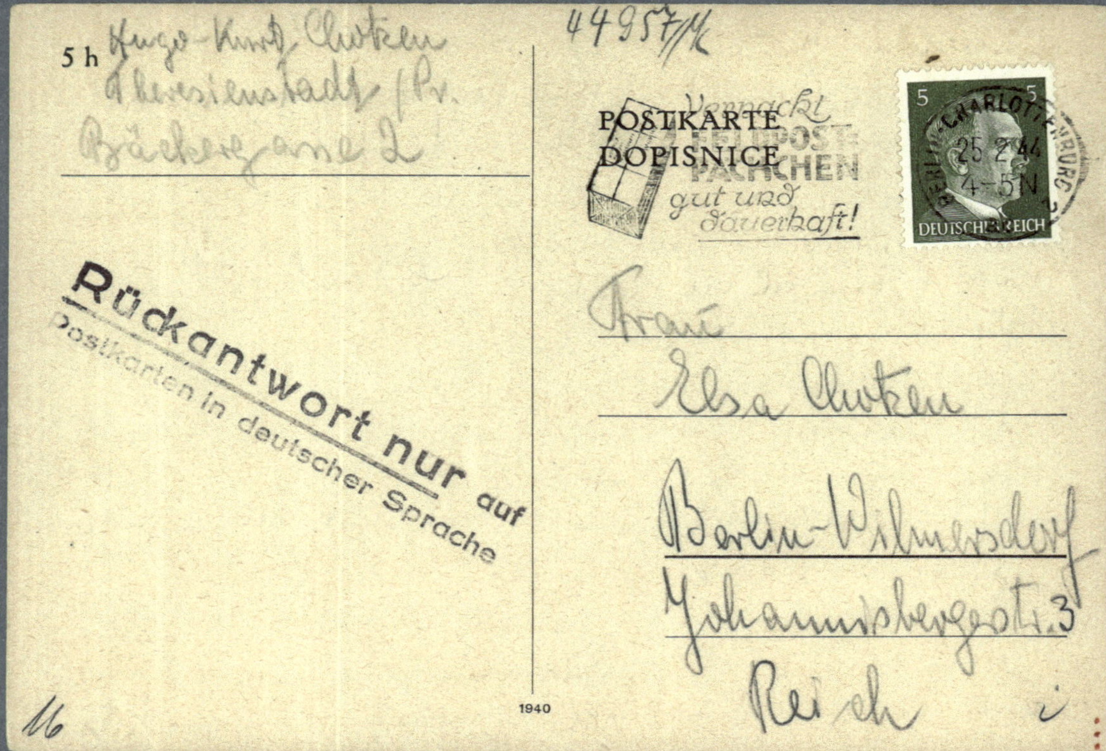

5 h Hugo-Kurt Chotzen
Theresienstadt / Pr.
Bäckergasse 2

44957/K

POSTKARTE
DOPISNICE

Verpackt
Feldpost-
Päckchen
gut und
dauerhaft!

5 5
DEUTSCHES REICH

BERLIN-CHARLOTTENBURG 2
25.2.44
4-5N

Frau
Elsa Chotzen
Berlin-Wilmersdorf
Johannisbergerstr. 3
Reich

Rückantwort nur auf
Postkarten in deutscher Sprache

16

1940

About postal traffic

This is the third preserved postcard with a personal text from Bubi. It took nearly three months to be delivered to Berlin from Theresienstadt. By the time it arrived, he had already sent another 13 more – signs that he was still alive.
Based on the 'daily orders' from the Jewish self-administration, Bubi would have been allowed to write also on 16 October and 23 November 1943. The Family Archive, however, only contains ten parcel confirmations from Bubi during these two months.

Situation in Theresienstadt

A two-man delegation from the German Red Cross, accompanied by Eberhard von Thadden, the Foreign Office's 'Jewish advisor', visited Theresienstadt in the summer of 1943. The two men were appalled by the conditions there and confidentially reported their concerns to an official from the International Red Cross. The aid organisation subsequently demanded another visit. To refute rumours circulating about the humanitarian conditions in the concentration camps, the SS pursued an extensive 'beautification campaign' in Theresienstadt that began in late 1943: Now referred to officially as a 'Jewish settlement area', Theresienstadt was used in Nazi propaganda to appease foreign countries.

Dear Mum! 1.12.43
All our thoughts are with you. We can never make up for all your worries about us. We see from the continuous post how much you are thinking of us. Dear Mum, I have to tell you one thing over and over again: we are healthy and Ulli and I have been doing sport for years. But how I long for you, Mum, and Eppi, and everything that used to be. When I receive mail from you or write you myself, I cry. Yes! Our wives and parents-in-law and brothers-in-law, etc. are all fit and we are living together harmoniously. **Sports, theatre, music provide us with a good diversion**. I write a lot to everyone. We hear little from you. **Szeren** doesn't write. We are thinking of you, love, kisses and longing for my Mum, and best health, Bubi, Hugo-Kurt.

Sports, theatre, music provide us with a good diversion: Over time, an astonishingly wide range of cultural activities took place in Theresienstadt. This was partly due to the many artists imprisoned there, but also because Theresienstadt played an important function in Nazi propaganda. The first theatre performances in 1941/early 1942 were held in secret, but after the 'beautification campaign' began in late 1943, they were tolerated and even encouraged. The SS allowed readings, cabaret, concerts and sporting events to take place, to give the impression that the town's forced residents were enjoying themselves.
Lisa, Ulli and Ruth never wrote about attending any cultural or sporting events in their 'free time'. In Bubi's later messages, he also ceased to mention any cultural events.

Szeren was the brothers' cousin who lived with family in Hungary. Bubi asked about her in several postcards. On 4 August 1944, he wrote to his mother saying they have received the first postcard from Budapest. The family in Hungary did not survive the Holocaust.

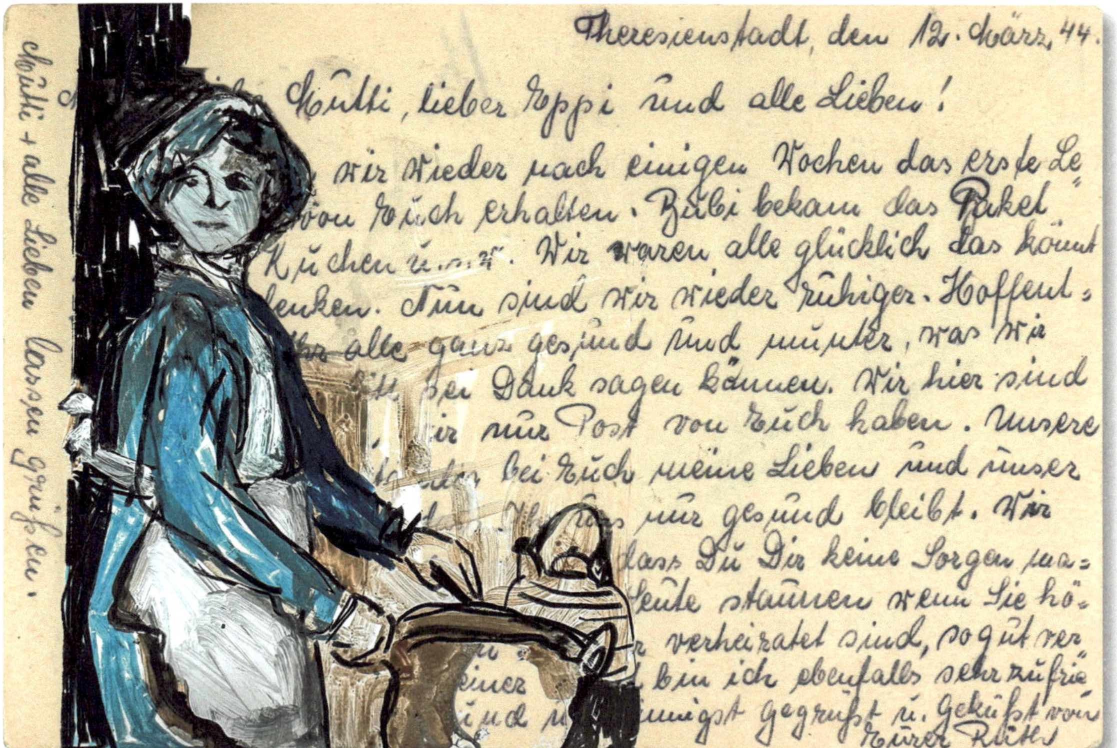

Mutti in her Kitchen, 2020

Painting and digital editing

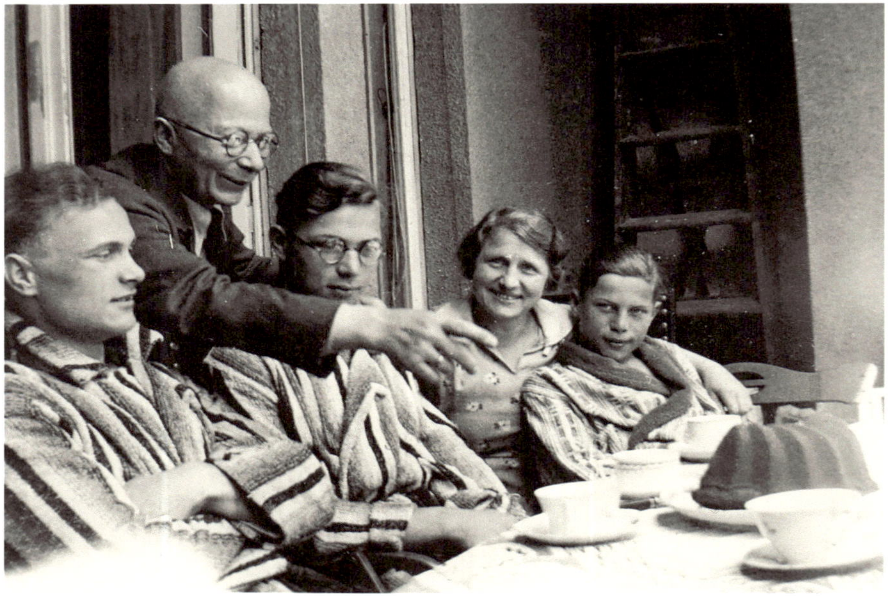

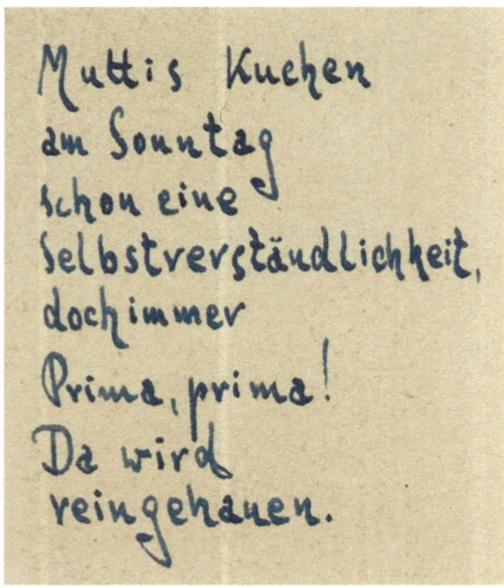
Muttis Kuchen
am Sonntag
schon eine
Selbstverständlichkeit,
doch immer
Prima, prima!
Da wird
reingehauen.

Bubi, Josef, Erich, Elsa and Ulli on their balcony, 10 June 1934. Bubi's caption: 'We could always count on Mum's cake every Sunday and it was always great, great! We relished it.' From Bubi's photo album (1936–1941)

INBAR CHOTZEN

All the postcards were addressed to Mutti, i.e., Elsa Chotzen, the children's mother. Elsa was a great inspiration to me; her heroic struggle to save her family from the clutches of the Gestapo is a story of the heroism of a mother lioness. Her image appears in several of the paintings and postcards I created. I use the color royal blue for her, influenced by Vermeer's "Woman reading a letter."

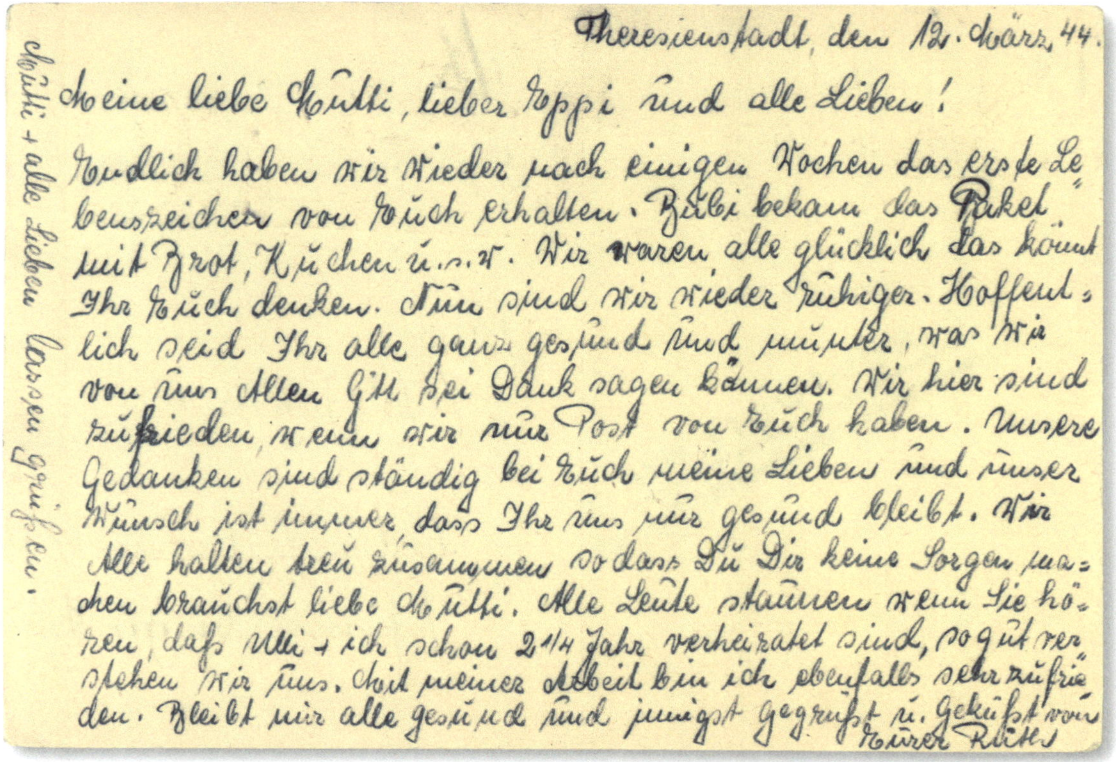
Theresienstadt, den 12. März. 44.

Meine liebe Mutti, lieber Peppi und alle Lieben!

Endlich haben wir wieder nach einigen Wochen das erste Lebenszeichen von Euch erhalten. Bubi bekam das Paket mit Brot, Kuchen u.s.w. Wir waren alle glücklich das könnt Ihr Euch denken. Nun sind wir wieder ruhiger. Hoffentlich seid Ihr alle ganz gesund und munter, was wir von uns Allen Gtt sei Dank sagen können. Wir hier sind zufrieden, wenn wir nur Post von Euch haben. Unsere Gedanken sind ständig bei Euch meine Lieben und unser Wunsch ist immer dass Ihr uns nur gesund bleibt. Wir Alle halten treu zusammen so dass Du Dir keine Sorgen machen brauchst liebe Mutti. Alle Leute staunen wenn Sie hören, daß Uli + ich schon 2 1/4 Jahr verheiratet sind, so gut verstehen wir uns. Mit meiner Arbeit bin ich ebenfalls sehr zufrieden. Bleibt mir alle gesund und innigst gegrüßt u. geküßt von Eurer Ruth

Mutti + alle Lieben lassen grüßen.

Twenty-fourth postcard from Ruth, 12 March 1944
postmark: 6 April 1944, Berlin-Charlottenburg 2

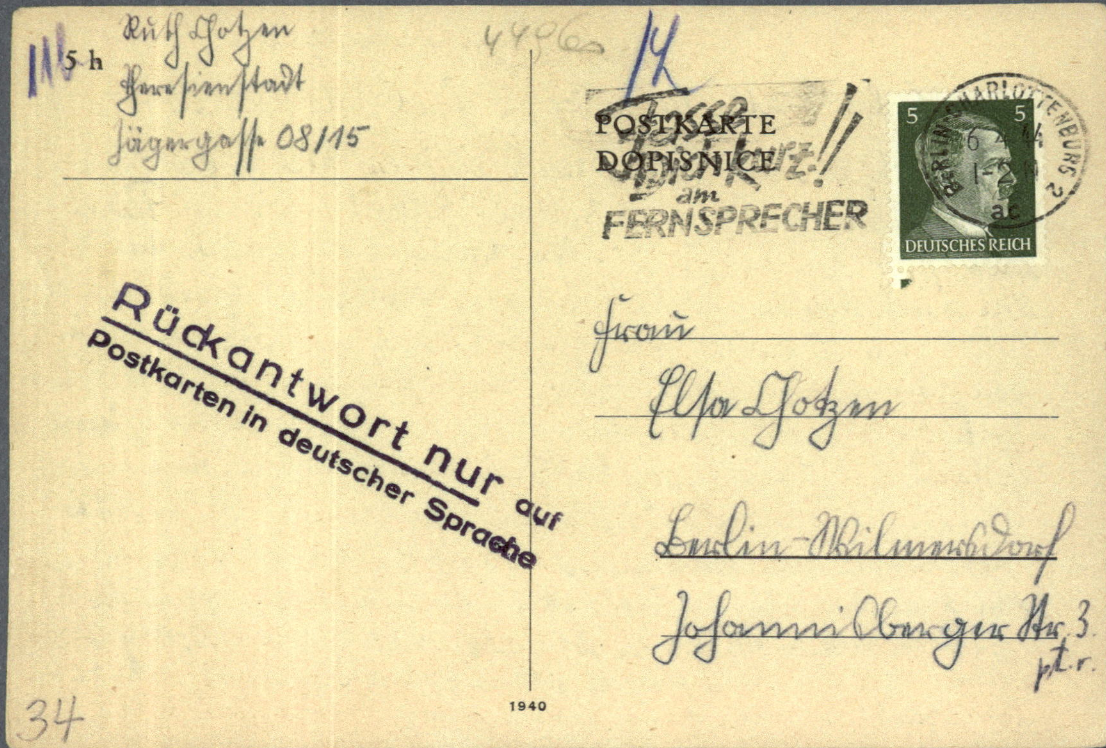
Ruth Gotzen
Theresienstadt
Jägergasse 08/15

5 h

POSTKARTE
DOPISNICE

Fasse Dich kurz! am FERNSPRECHER

DEUTSCHES REICH

Rückantwort nur auf Postkarten in deutscher Sprache

Frau
Elsa Gotzen
Berlin-Wilmersdorf
Johannisberger Str. 3
p.t.r.

1940

About postal traffic

By the time this card arrived, 16 postcards with personal text – five of them from Ruth, had already been delivered to Berlin. Nine months had passed since the two couples were deported. Ruth signed the cards with her own name, but also used one of the writing allowances of each of her sisters, Ursula and Lieselotte, and her mother Klara. The handwriting is clearly identifiable as Ruth's. Her husband Ulli wrote the return and recipient addresses on the front of the postcard. This was a way for him to send a sign home, too.

Situation in Theresienstadt

The 'beautification campaign', carried out in anticipation of a visit to Theresienstadt by the International Red Cross, was in full swing at this time. SS-Obersturmführer Karl Rahm had been camp commandant of Theresienstadt since 8 February 1944. In his standard work on Theresienstadt, the author H. G. Adler wrote:

He was the right man for the dictated farce as he knew how to give the 'beautification' verve, tempo and ideas, just as he skilfully knew how to play himself off as a supposedly better Nazi and helper of the Jews […]. During deportations and otherwise, Rahm behaved just as inhumanly as the other SS officers.[1]

1 H. G. Adler: Theresienstadt 1941–1945, ibid., p. 165

Theresienstadt, 12 March, '44

My dear Mum, dear Eppi and all my loved ones!

Finally, **after some weeks**, we have received **the first sign of life** from you again. Bubi received the parcel with bread, cake, etc. We were all happy, as you can imagine. Now we are at peace again. Hopefully you are all safe and sound, for which we can all **thank G'd.** We are happy just to get mail from you. Our thoughts are always with you, my dears, and it is our wish that you stay healthy. We all stick together faithfully so you don't have to worry, dear Mum! Everyone is amazed when they hear that Ulli + I have been married for 2 ¼ years, that's how well we get on. **I'm also very happy with my work.** Stay healthy, with warmest greetings and kisses from

your Ruth.

Mum + all loved ones send their regards.

After some weeks, the first sign of life: Based on the content of the postcard, we can deduce that the correspondence between Berlin and Theresienstadt had stalled for a time. However, this contradicts the frequent assurances from other family members that the mail system always works – a claim that was probably made to appease the censorship. Not only did the deportees not receive any mail from home – throughout March the Berliners only received pre-printed parcel confirmations that did not permit any personal comments.

Thank G'd: This spelling with the omitted vowel reflects Ruth's Jewish identity. She avoided mentioning the name of God, as is customary in Judaism.

I am also very happy with my work. In her first postcard to Elsa, dated 31 July 1943, Ruth wrote: 'I work in an office'. She explained in an interview decades later that after arriving in Theresienstadt, her first job was cleaning toilets. Her mother, who was the 'house eldest', managed to get her a different job at the labour office.

Mum + all loved ones: Ruth sends greetings from her mother, Klara Cohn, and her sisters, who were also receiving care packages from Elsa.

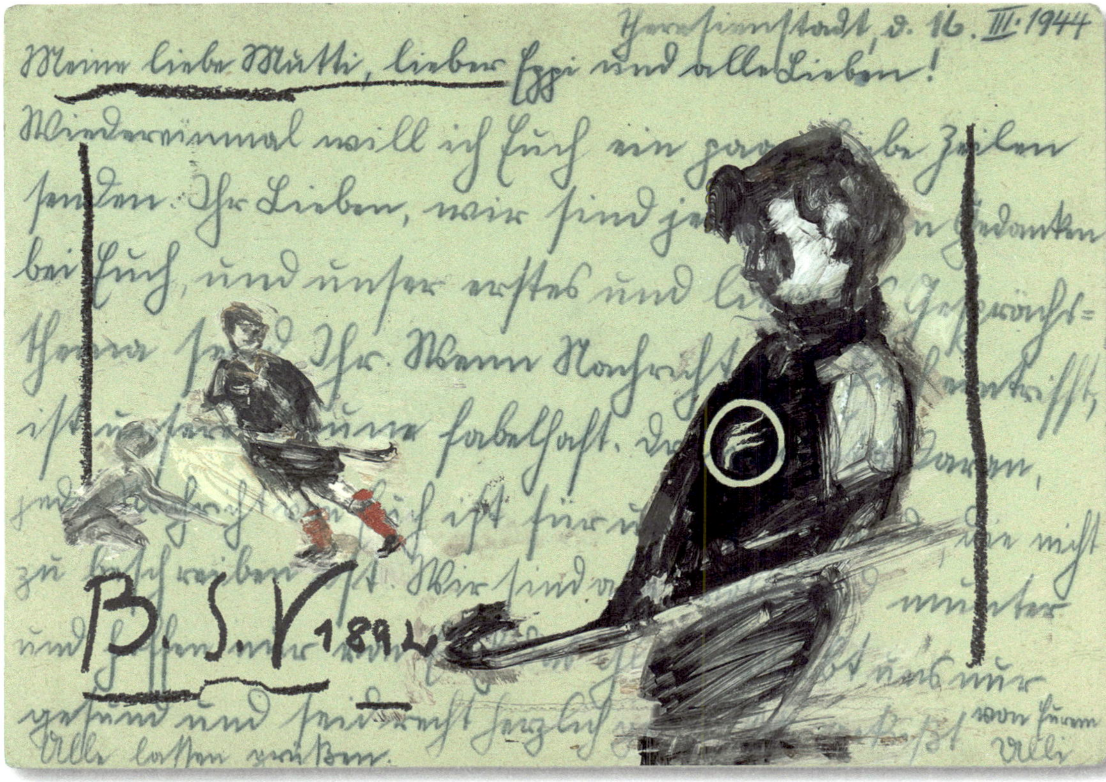

Hockey, 2020

Painting and digital editing

EPPI CHOTZEN

My brother Ulli was even assigned as a basketball judge at the 1936 Olympics. I have his Olympic badge and Olympic pin in my desk. After the Olympics, it all ended very quickly for Jews in general sports.
We were still able to play in Jewish sports clubs until 1938. Everything was banned after that.

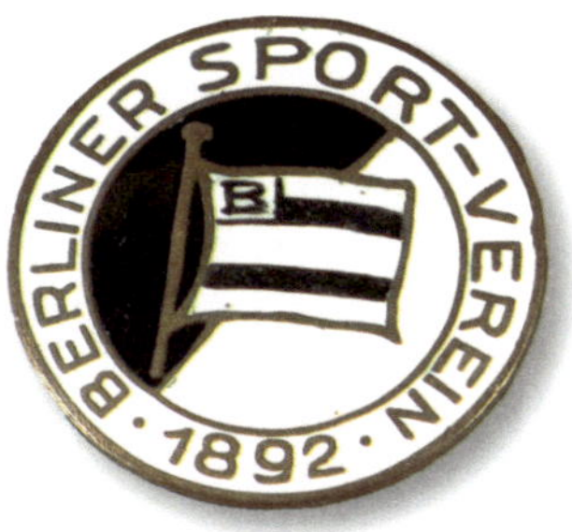

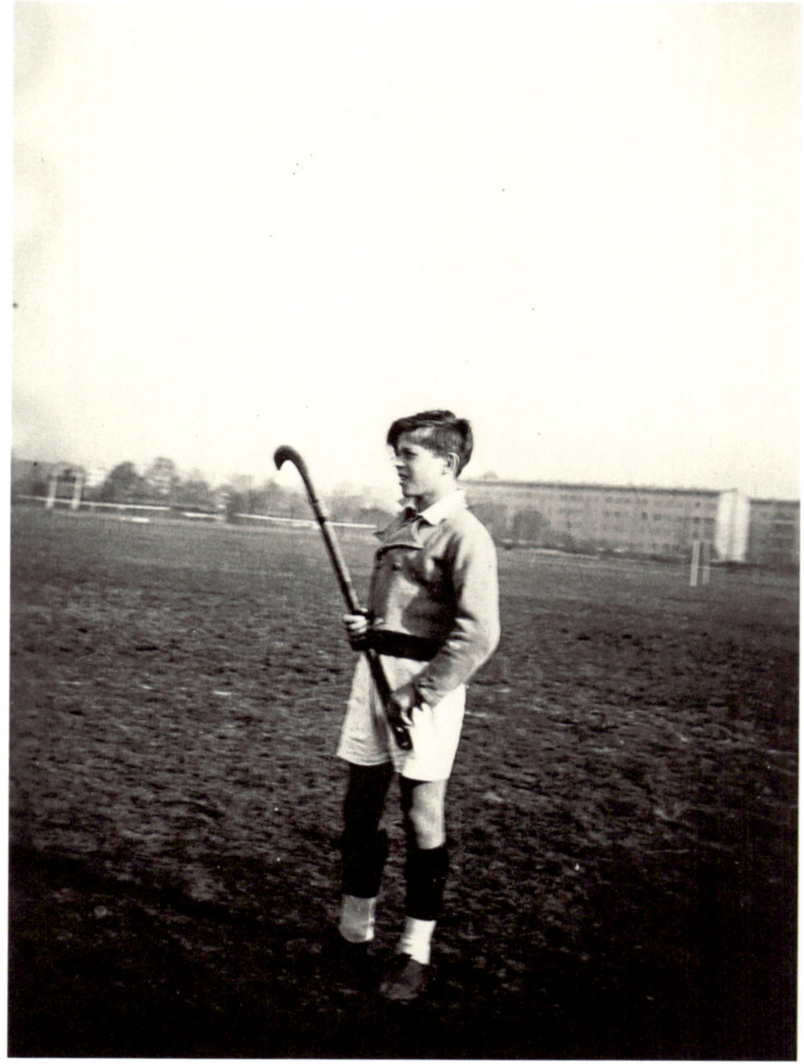

Ulli on the hocky field. Early 1930s, from Bubi's photo album (1923/24–1936)

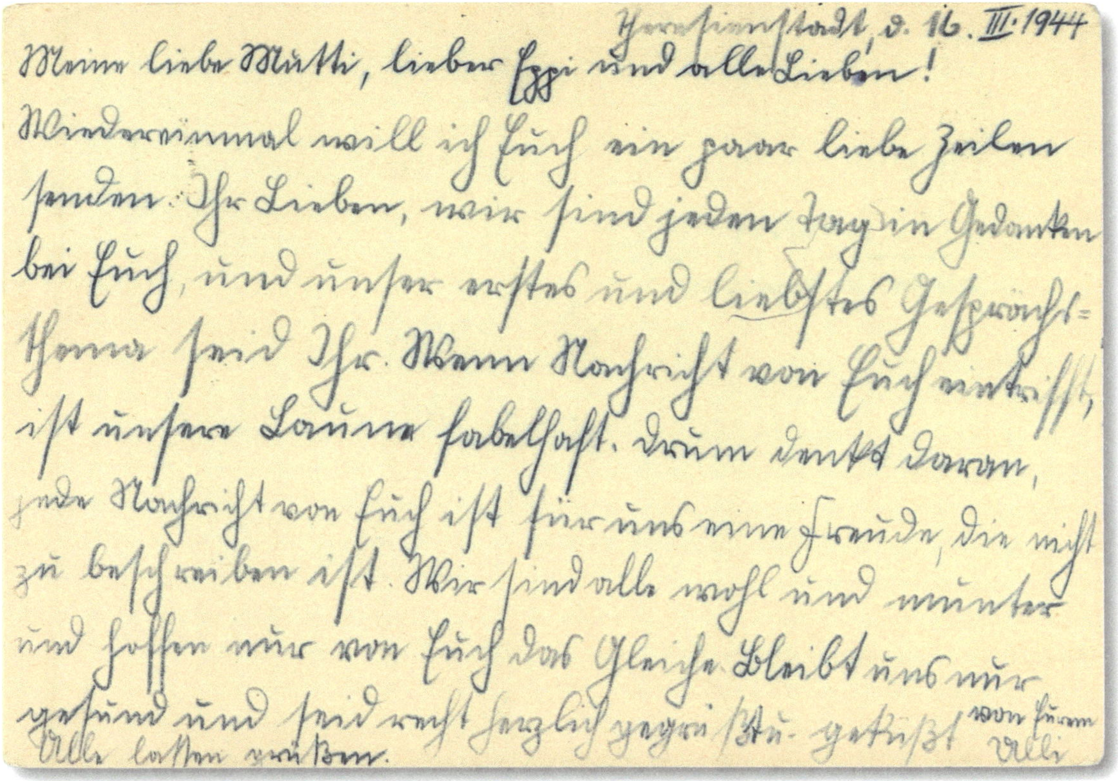

Theresienstadt, d. 16. III. 1944

Meine liebe Mutti, lieber Eggi und alle Lieben!

Wiedereinmal will ich Euch ein paar liebe Zeilen senden. Ihr Lieben, wir sind jeden Tag in Gedanken bei Euch, und unser erstes und liebstes Gesprächs=thema seid Ihr. Wenn Nachricht von Euch eintrifft, ist unsere Laune fabelhaft. Darum denkt daran, jede Nachricht von Euch ist für uns eine Freude, die nicht zu beschreiben ist. Wir sind alle wohl und munter und hoffen nun von Euch das Gleiche. Bleibt uns nur gesund und seid recht herzlich gegrüsst und geküsst von Eurem Ulli

Alle lassen grüßen.

Thirty-third postcard from Ulli, 16 March 1944

postmark: 3 May 1944, Berlin-Charlottenburg 2

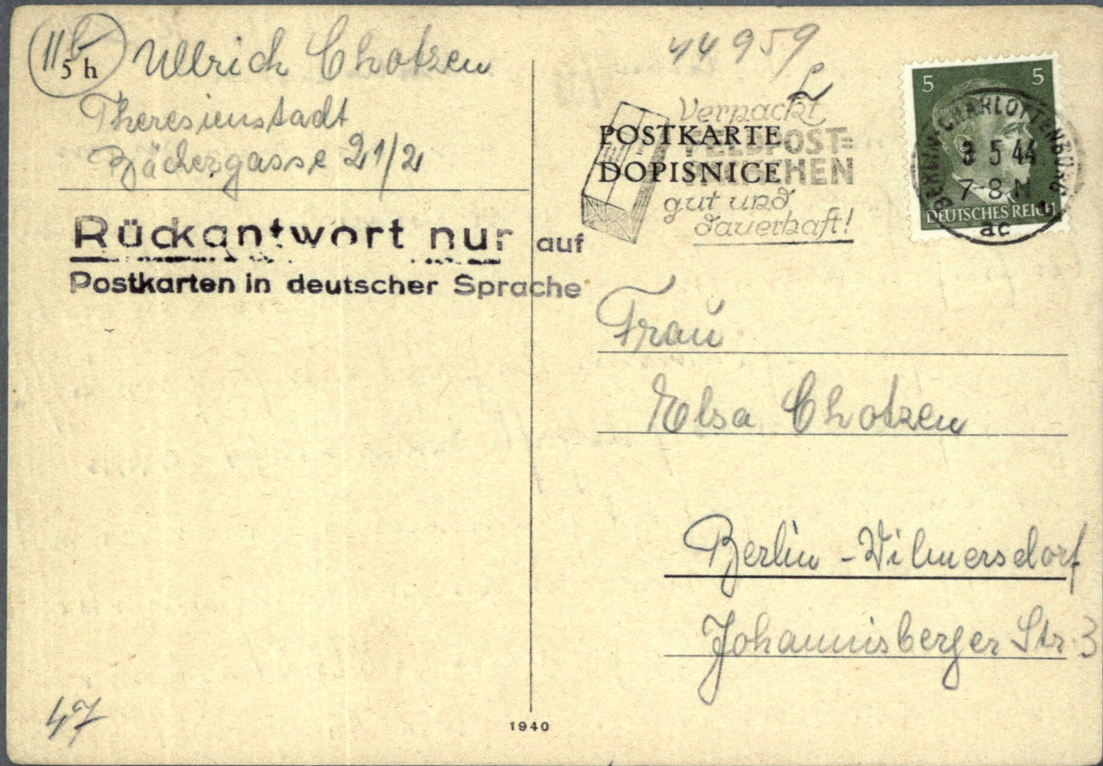

11 5 h Ulrich Chotzen
Theresienstadt
Bäckergasse 21/2

44959
L

Rückantwort nur auf Postkarten in deutscher Sprache

POSTKARTE
DOPISNICE

Verpackt ... FELDPOST- ... HEN gut und dauerhaft!

5 DEUTSCHES REICH 5

BERLIN-CHARLOTTENBURG 3.5.44 7-8 N ac

Frau
Elsa Chotzen

Berlin-Wilmersdorf
Johannisberger Str. 3

47

1940

About postal traffic

This card was in transit for seven weeks. It was the sixth personal postcard Ulli sent home, including one in which he used the name of his sister-in-law Ursula Kohn. Eighteen postcards with personal text had arrived in Berlin by 3 May 1944. On three occasions, several cards arrived on the same day, although they had been written several weeks apart. Ulli and his wife, Ruth, wrote this card together; again Ruth wrote the addresses on the front.

Situation in Theresienstadt

In 'Daily Order No. 423' of 16 March 1944, the ghetto court announced that anyone caught using someone else's meal card, accepting parcels intended for another person or stealing blankets would be punished with up to 10 days' detention. In his book, H. G. Adler wrote that the ghetto court was a total farce and that the larger, more consequential theft of community was never prosecuted: The SS men were able to divert food on a much larger scale and sell it for their own profit. And employees of the 'Jewish self-administration' diluted food in the kitchens.
In the spring of 1944, all the streets in the town were improved as part of the 'beautification campaign'. The town square, which had previously been off-limits to prisoners, was now made accessible. Lawns were created and 1,200 rose bushes were planted. A bandstand was constructed, benches were installed and a playground was built.

Theresienstadt, 16. III. 44

My dear Mum, dear Eppi and all our dear ones!

I wish to send you a few nice lines again. Dearest ones, we think of you every day and you are our first and dearest topic of conversation. When a message from you arrives, our mood is terrific. Every message we receive from you is an indescribable joy. We are **all well and chipper** and hope the same for you. Please stay healthy, I send warm greetings and kisses, Your Ulli.

Everyone sends their regards.

I wish to send you a few nice lines again. Ulli's opening sentence suggests he can decide when he writes his family. This could be understood as a sign of self-assertion.

All well and chipper: H. G. Adler wrote that, in addition to the fear of finding one's name on the next 'transport list', the prisoners' most important concern was food. Officially, the residents of Theresienstadt were supposed to receive the same amount of food as everyone in the 'Protektorat', where food was also rationed during wartime. In truth, however, the conditions in the sealed garrison town were much worse: fraud and embezzlement were rampant on many levels and the prices of fresh, black-market goods were very high. Hunger was a part of everyday life and the food that was available was low in quality and often inedible. Those suffering malnutrition were much more susceptible to disease.

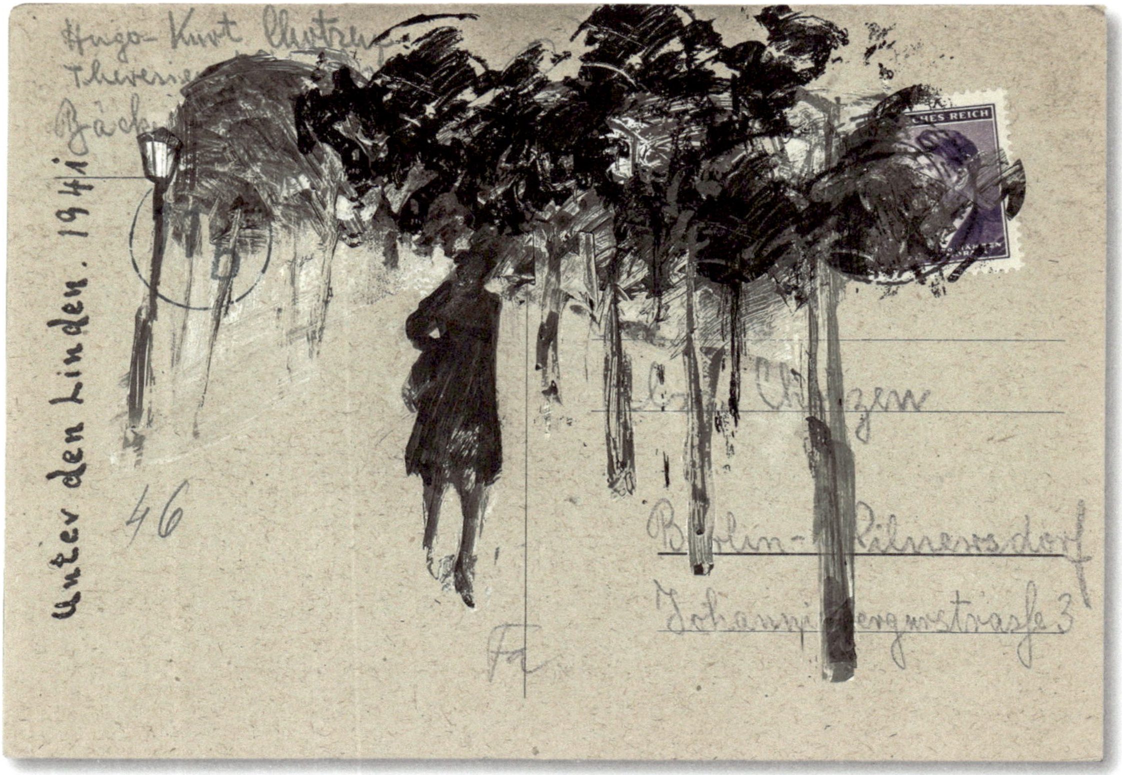

Berlin Life 1941, 2019/24

Ink drawing and digital editing

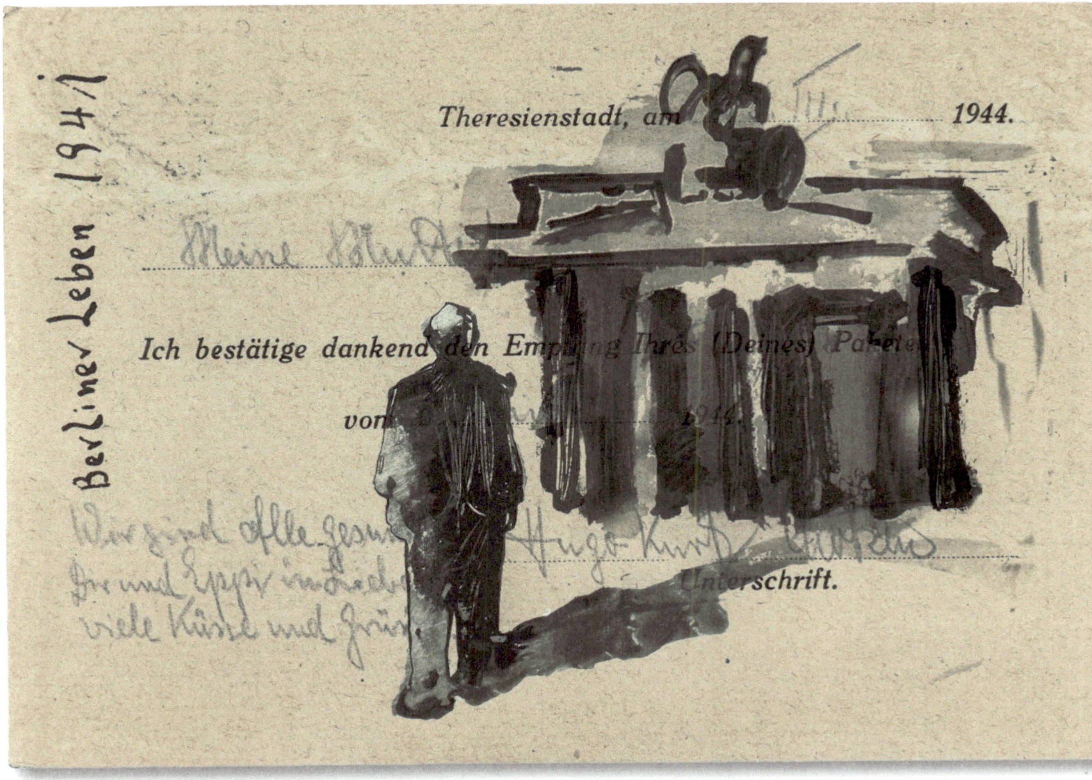
Berliner Leben 1941
Theresienstadt, am 1944.
Ich bestätige dankend den Empfang Ihres (Deines) Paketes
vom 1944.
Unterschrift.

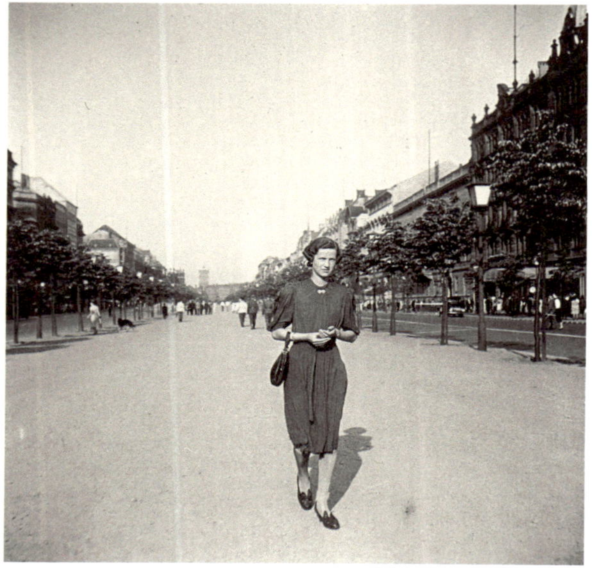

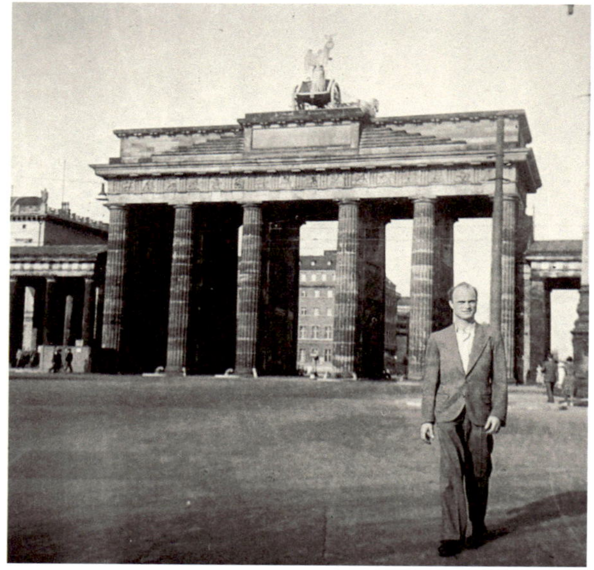

Illegal trip to the city centre on 22 June 1941, from Bubi's photo album (1923/24–1936)

On 22 Juni 1941, the day Germany invaded the Soviet Union, Bubi and his girlfriend Lisa photograph each other on Unter den Linden and at the Brandenburg Gate. Jews had been banned from entering the city centre since late 1938. Their deliberate violation of anti-Jewish laws is an act of resistance. The "Yellow Star" was introduced three months after these photographs were taken. Beginning in late 1941, Jews were no longer allowed to own cameras.

INBAR CHOTZEN

In my interpretation of the photos, the trees along Unter den Linden turn into black clouds hovering over them as omens of the terrible fate awaiting them. The writing on the postcard in Bubi's handwriting "Berliner Leben 1941" and "Unter den Linden 1941" is taken from his photo album.

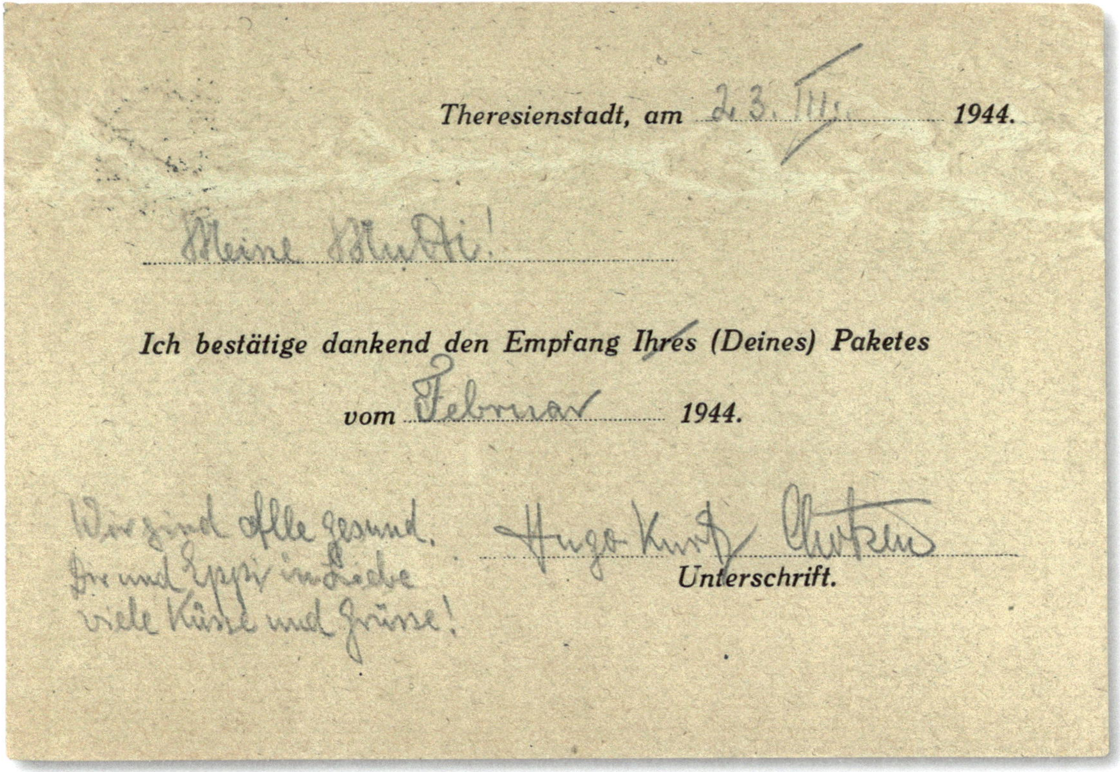

Theresienstadt, am 23. III. 1944.

Meine Mutti!

Ich bestätige dankend den Empfang Ihres (Deines) Paketes

vom Februar 1944.

Wir sind alle gesund.
viele Küsse und Grüsse!

Unterschrift.

Thirty-second postcard from Bubi, 23 March 1944
postmark: 20 April 1944, Prague

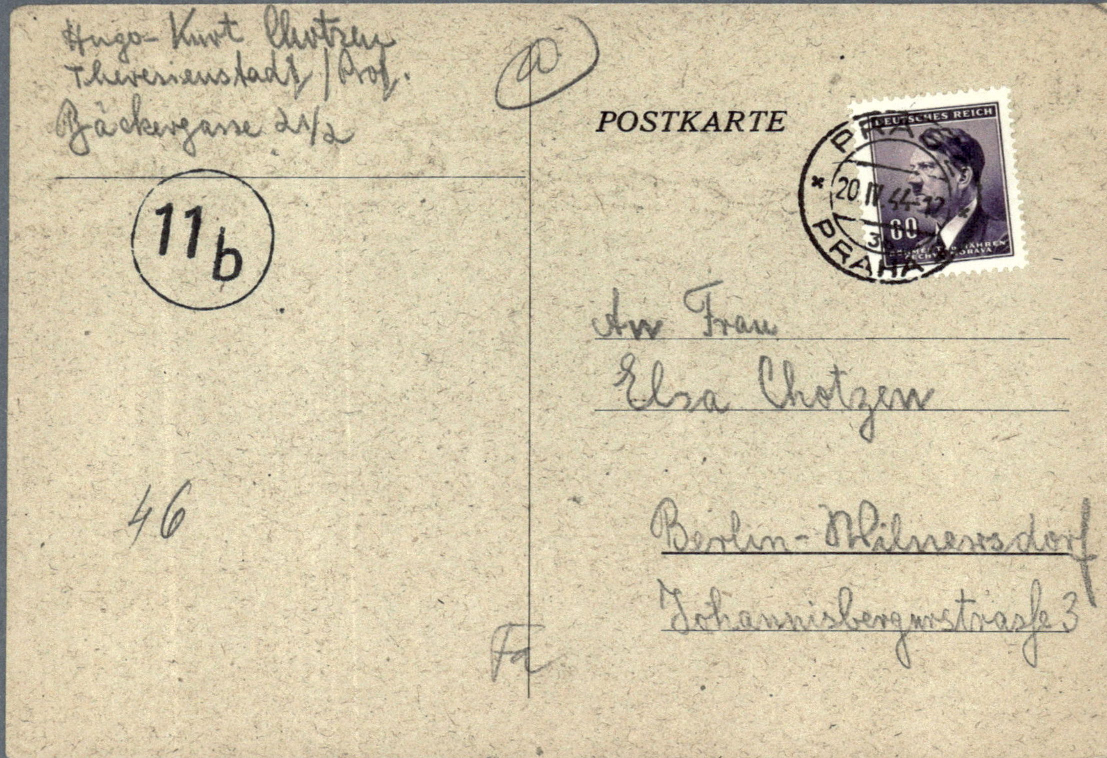
Hugo-Kurt Chotzen
Theresienstadt / Prot.
Bäckergasse 21/2

POSTKARTE

11b

46

An Frau
Elsa Chotzen
Berlin-Wilmersdorf
Johannisbergerstrasse 3

About postal traffic

This is the first parcel confirmation card that also included a personal note. In the following months, all four Chotzens sent several forms with a short personal text, although this was not allowed. Word may have spread that the censor was letting these postcards go through – or that certain censors were turning a blind eye. Every piece of mail that reached Berlin was a sign of life and the personal messages made them even more special.
The prisoners were handed the pre-printed cards when they picked up their parcel. Beginning in autumn 1943, they had to pay up to 50 ghetto 'crowns' to receive their care packages.
This card is also an indication of how long it often took for a postcard to be delivered. On 23 March, Bubi confirmed receiving a parcel that had been sent in February. Elsa and Eppi received this confirmation on 20 April. They often had to wait many months before learning whether their lovingly packed parcels were ever received. Sometimes they heard nothing.

EPPI CHOTZEN

In any case, the three of us – my mother, Božka and I – were determined to do everything in our power to make things easier for our deported loved-ones for as long as possible. We were frequently saddened by the fact that we couldn't do more, but we were often rewarded when the confirmation cards arrived. Everyone who was allowed to write – my brothers, their wives, their parents, i.e., the Scheurenbergs and Cohns – always expressed their gratitude and joy!

Theresienstadt, on 23. III. *1944*

Mum!

I gratefully acknowledge receipt of your parcel

from February *1944.*

We are all healthy.
Many loving kisses and
greetings to Eppi and you!

Hugo-Kurt Chotzen
Signature

We are all healthy: As with all areas of life, food allocation was centrally controlled by the Jewish self-administration. Bread and watery soups or stews were the only items served every day, and they were measured down to the exact gram. Other foods, such as milk, margarine, meat, fresh fruit and vegetables, could be obtained once a week at most and were not always available. Spices and baking powder had to be purchased in the 'grocery stores'. H. G. Adler wrote: *'The store was a farce, but its goods nevertheless helped to spice up the bland dishes somewhat.'*[1] Thus, during imprisonment, malnutrition continued to worsen, making people more susceptible to diseases. Bubi wrote home on 20 May 1944: 'Lisa is gaining weight, which I'm very happy about.' Lisa was already noticeably thin before the deportation.

1 H. G. Adler: Theresienstadt 1941–1945, ibid., p. 356.

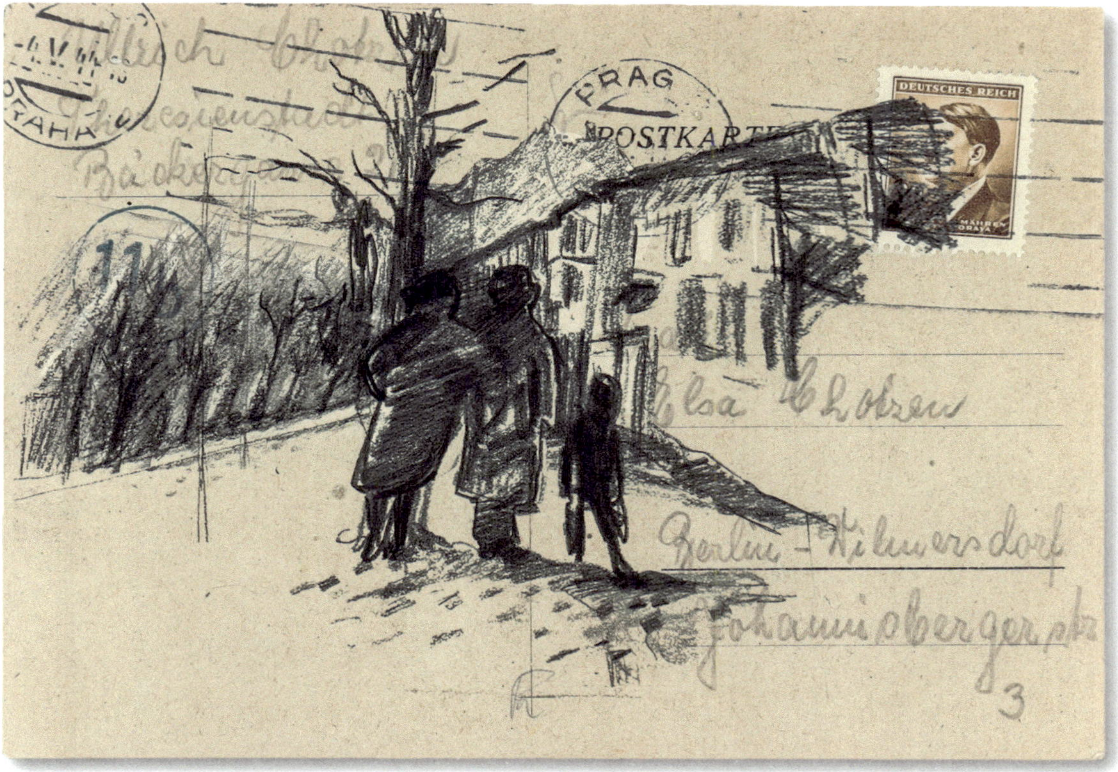

'Shpatzirn', 2019

Charcoal and digital editing

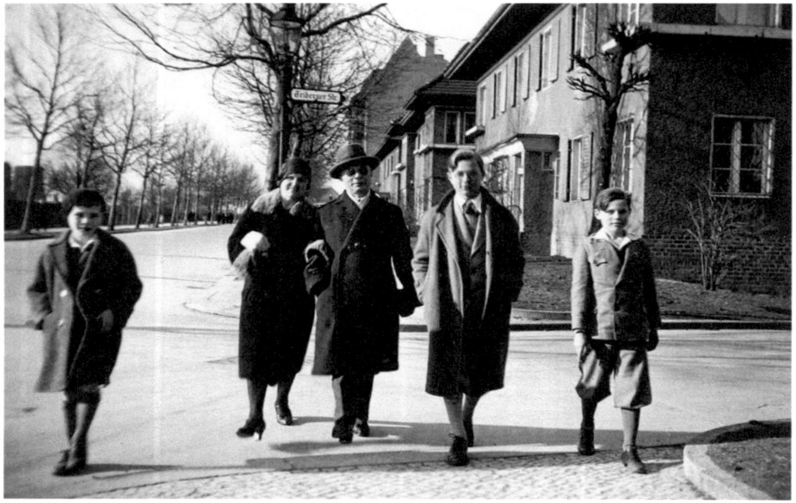

Family stroll in the late 1920s: Elsa, Josef, Erich, Ulli and an unidentified person on the left, from the children's photo album (1929–1937)

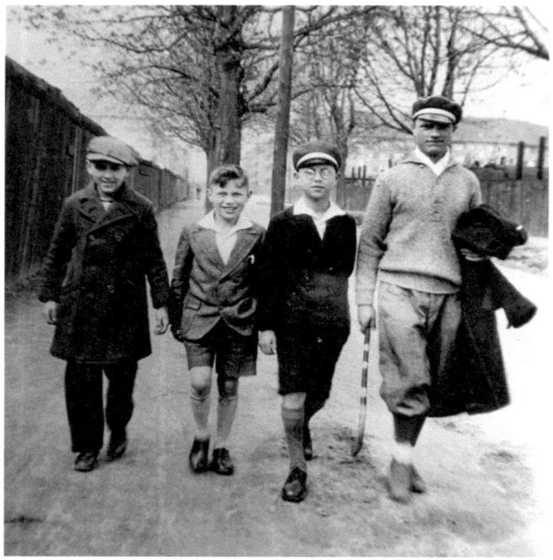

From right to left: Bubi, Erich, Ulli and a friend on the way to the field hockey game, from Bubi's album (1923/24–1936)

EPPI CHOTZEN

We brothers had all grown up in Johannisbergerstrasse and were popular with our friends and sport buddies. It never occurred to us to hide our Judaism. [...] We had certainly become a well-known family here in the area and had contact with many people over the many years.

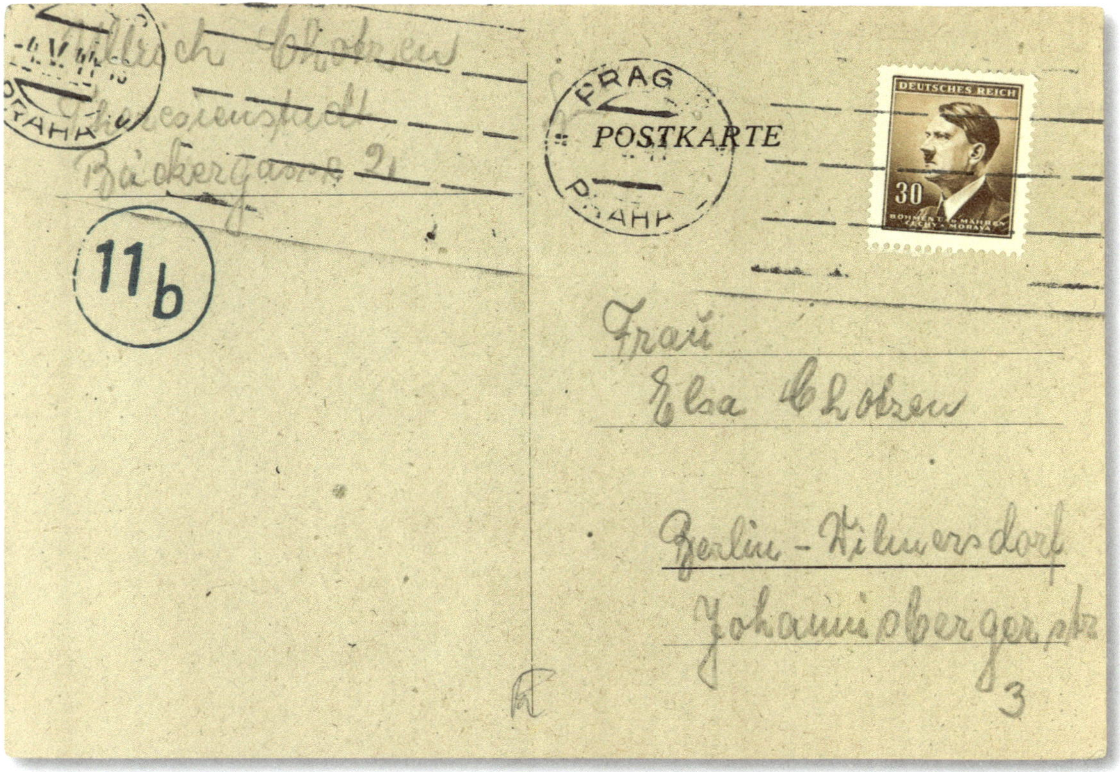

Thirty-eighth postcard from Ulli, 15 April 1944
postmark: 4 May 1944, Prague 2

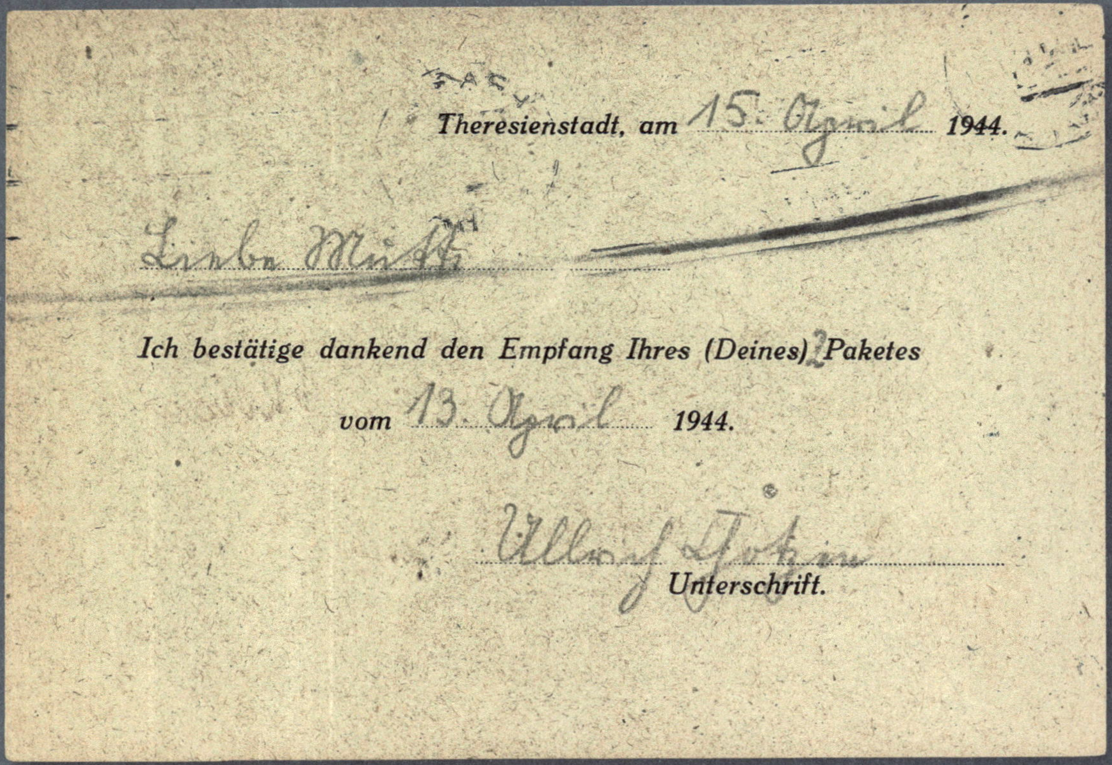

Theresienstadt, am 15. April 1944.

Liebe Mutti

Ich bestätige dankend den Empfang Ihres (Deines) 2 Paketes

vom 13. April 1944.

[illegible]

Unterschrift.

About postal traffic

In the nearly 10 months since his deportation, Ulli was able to send 38 cards demonstrating he was still alive. Yet only six of these contained a personal message. It is highly likely that Elsa and Eppi received a parcel confirmation from Ulli the day before this card arrived. Messages from Bubi, Ruth, Lisa and Ursula Cohn (written in Ruth's handwriting) were also stamped in Prague on 4 May 1944. The two different handwritings indicate that Ulli and Ruth wrote this card together, too.

Situation in Theresienstadt

As part of the 'beautification' process, the daily orders were renamed 'Notices from the Jewish Self-Administration'. The first of these newly designed notices, which now also included drawings, were published on this day. In addition to providing information about the second 'rat control campaign', it instructed the residents on how to treat the newly landscaped areas. Point 3 stated:

Protect the blossoms!

The green spaces are an innovation that is very important for the health of the inhabitants of Theresienstadt. They reduce dust and improve the air. Therefore, you must treat them with care and protect them from damage. The tree blossoms require special protection. Damaging plants, in particular by tearing off flower branches, will be punished.

Theresienstadt, on 15 April *1944*

Dear Mum!

I gratefully confirm receipt of your **2 parcels**

from 13 April *1944.*

Ullrich Chotzen

Signature

2 parcels: Not only do postcards arrive in large numbers in Berlin on some days, but parcels are also handed out at unpredictable intervals in Theresienstadt. In this postcard, Ulli expresses his thanks for two packages. It seems unlikely that Elsa and Eppi would have sent two packages to the same person on the same day. However, the frequency with which care packages were sent from Berlin is a clear sign of how obvious the need for this food support was.

That mail could be sent in and out of the fortress walls as of autumn 1942 was something that distinguished Theresienstadt from other camps. The Nazis worried that unrest might spread within the German population if nothing was heard from the 'privileged' people after their deportation. Although mail and packages were subject to complex regulations, from 1943 onward, it was generally possible for cards to be sent every four to six weeks. Theresienstadt prisoners were allowed to write on one side of the postcard in legible German. The 30-word limit was later lifted. Prisoners could write that receiving packages was permitted, but not specify what they needed. All messages were censored by the 'self-administration' and then sent to the Jewish communities in Prague, Vienna or Berlin. Most parcels were delivered, but they were usually inspected in the mailroom and often arrived with items missing. Because of the inadequate food situation, these care packages from outside were essential for survival. During their entire time in Theresienstadt, the Chotzens received mostly food parcels from Elsa, Eppi and Božka. Those who did not have relatives on the outside were dependent on parcels from the Red Cross or the Jewish communities, which also supported Theresienstadt.

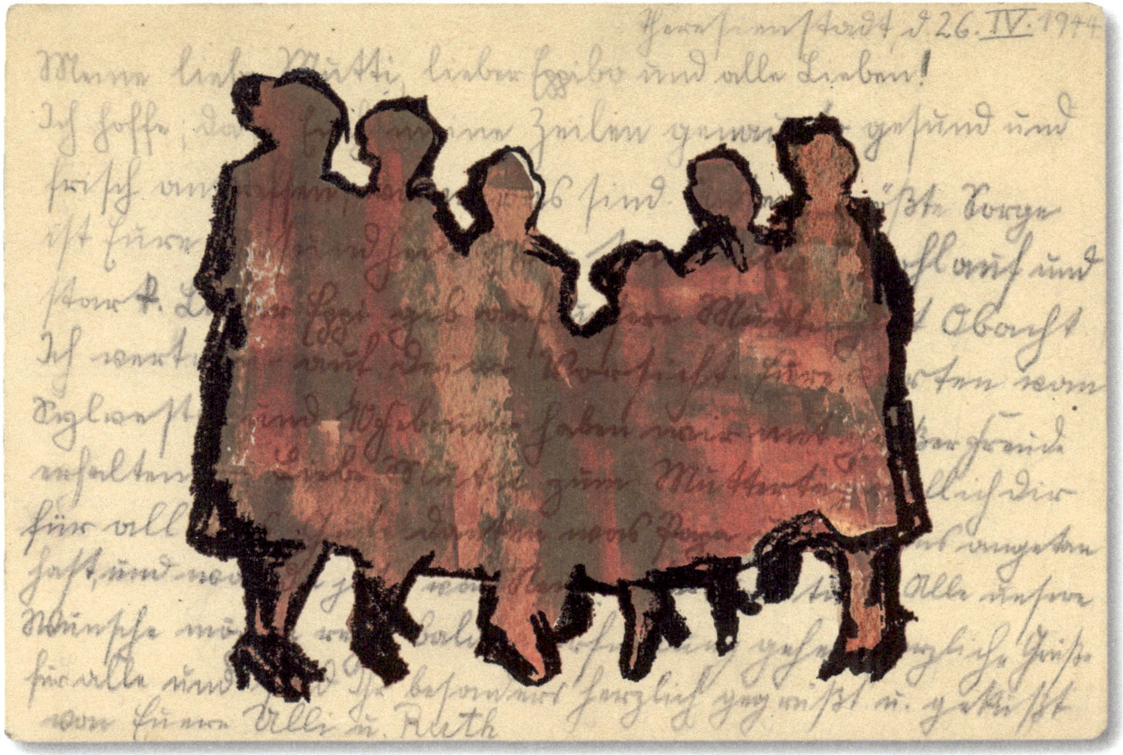

Family, 2021

Silk print and digital editing

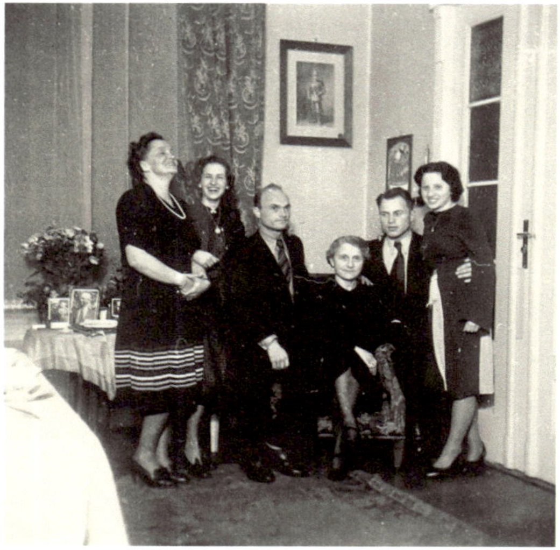

Elsa turned 55 on 31 Oktober 1942. Her three remaining sons and her daughters-in-law gathered at the Johannisberger Straße flat for the occasion. This is when Eppi and Bubi took the last group photo of the family. From left: Božka, Ilse, Bubi, Elsa, Ulli and Ruth.

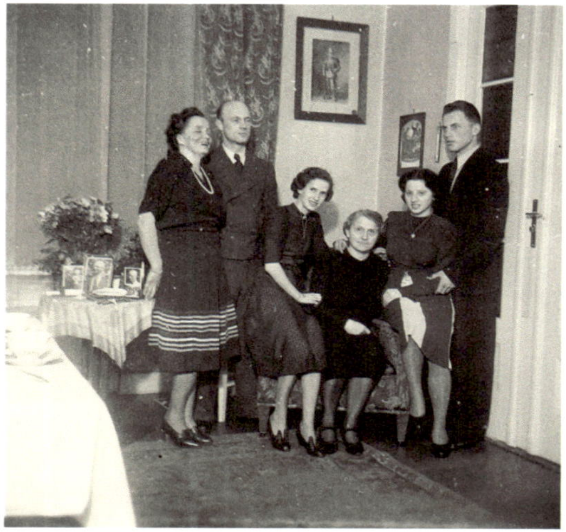

From left: Božka, Eppi, Ilse, Elsa, Ruth and Ulli. On the wall behind them hangs a picture of father Josef as a soldier in the First World War. From Eppi's pocket album

EPPI CHOTZEN

Later, at the end of 1941, we – my parents, my three brothers and their wives, whom they had married one after the other in November and December, and I – were all registered together for a very short time in the much-too-small Johannisbergerstrasse flat. [...] there were nine of us, all full-grown adults with a yellow star on their chest, that is, except for my mother. And there was also one outside on the apartment door.

At Elsa's birthday celebration, three people were already missing: The father had died in the Jewish Hospital at the start year. Erich, who was deported to Riga with his wife, Ilse, was also dead.

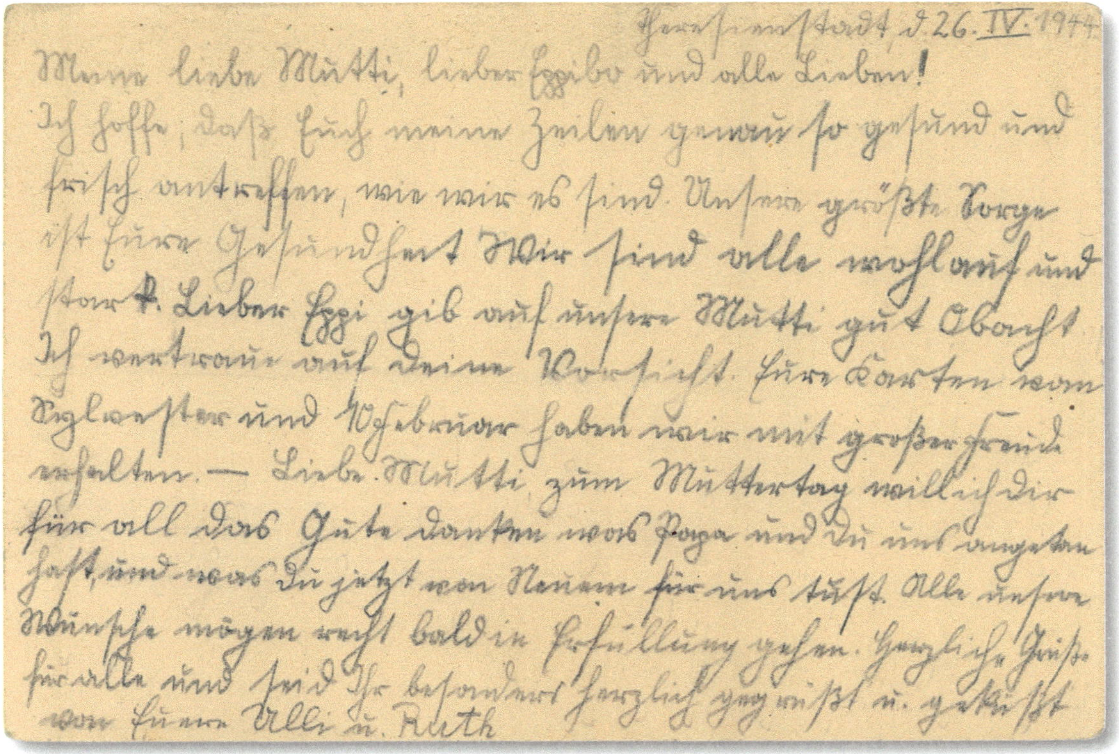

Theresienstadt, d. 26. IV. 1944
Meine liebe Mutti, lieber Eggi und alle Lieben!
Ich hoffe, daß Euch meine Zeilen genau so gesund und frisch antreffen, wie wir es sind. Unsere größte Sorge ist Eure Gesundheit. Wir sind alle wohlauf und stark. Lieber Eggi gib auf unsere Mutti gut Obacht. Ich vertraue auf deine Vorsicht. Eure Karten von [illegible] und [illegible] haben wir mit großer Freude erhalten. — Liebe Mutti zum Muttertag will ich dir für all das Gute danken was [illegible] und Du uns angetan hast, und was Du jetzt von Neuem für uns tust. Alle unsere Wünsche mögen recht bald in Erfüllung gehen. Herzliche Grüße für alle und seid Ihr besonders herzlich gegrüßt u. geküßt von Eurer Ulli u. Ruth

Fortieth postcard from Ulli, 26 April 1944
postmark: 5 June 1944, Berlin-Charlottenburg

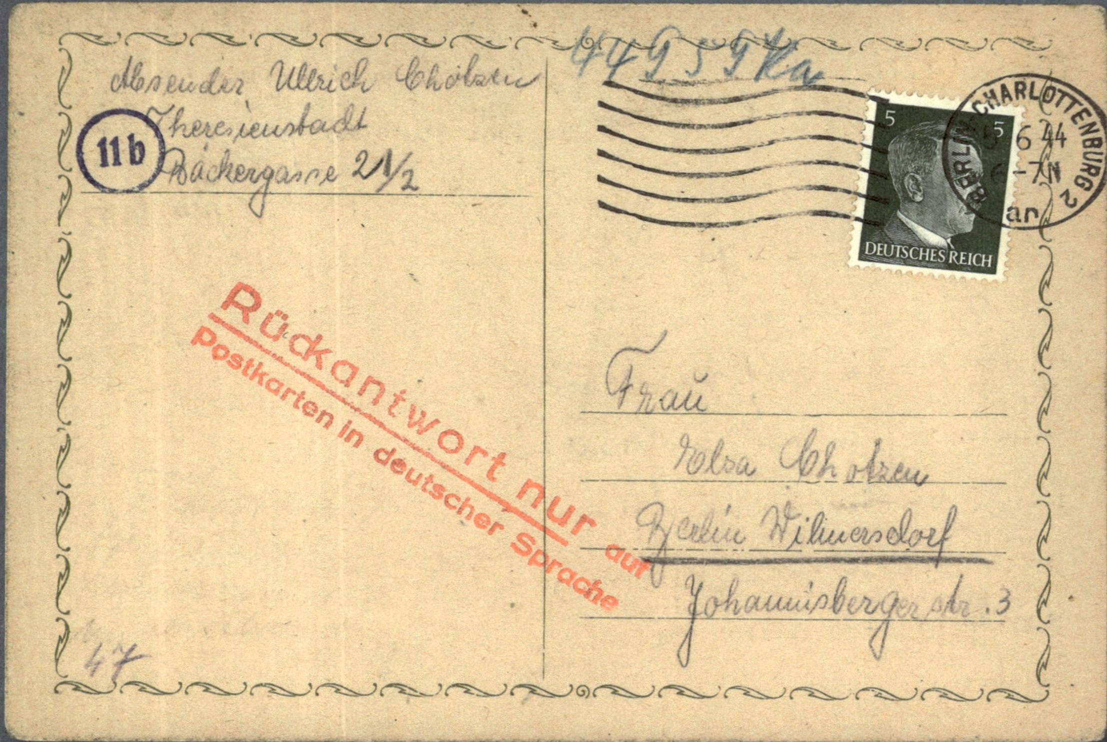
Absender Ullrich Cholzen
Theresienstadt
Bäckergasse 21/2

11b

44959 Ka

5
DEUTSCHES REICH

BERLIN-CHARLOTTENBURG 2
6.44

Rückantwort nur auf
Postkarten in deutscher Sprache

Frau
Elsa Cholzen
Berlin Wilmersdorf
Johannisbergerstr. 3

47

About postal traffic

Ulli's seventh postcard with a personal text was in transit for many weeks before it reached his mother in Berlin. Mail delivery from Berlin to Theresienstadt was heavily delayed during this time: Ulli expressed his thanks for cards from New Year's and 10 February 1944. After this postcard arrived, Elsa and Eppi had to wait more than a month before receiving any news from Theresienstadt. The next card was written by Bubi.
Ulli wrote the text, but the handwriting on the front was clearly that of his wife, Ruth.

Theresienstadt, 26. IV. 1944

My dear Mum, dear **Eppibo** and all our dear ones!
I hope that my lines find you as healthy and fit as we are. **Our greatest concern is for your health.** We are all in good health and strong. Dear Eppi, look after our mum. I trust your prudence. We received your cards from New Year's and 10 February with great joy. – Dear Mum, for **Mother's Day** I wish to thank you for all the good that you and **Papa** did for us and for all you are doing now. May all our wishes come true very soon. Warm greetings to you all and greetings and kisses especially to you both from your Ulli and Ruth

Eppibo: Ulli combined the nicknames of his brother Eppi and Eppi's girlfriend, Božka. He may have wanted to avoid writing her name to protect her. Because Božka was not Jewish, it was illegal for her to be in a relationship with Eppi. Božka's role in sending the parcels was crucial. She worked for the Danish Consulate and was often able to obtain food and other items that were not available to Jews.

Our greatest concern is for your health: In Elsa's compensation claim from 4 February 1959, a doctor completed a form with a description of Elsa's health history: In 1936 she began to suffer from stomach pain; her condition dramatically deteriorated after the death of her husband and the deportation of her son Erich and her daughter-in-law Ilse. 'June/July 1942 first shots of pain in the heart area, shortness of breath and strong palpitation of the heart. These attacks have been recurring since then. Necrosis of the hands and feet, pain in right arm. Since 1942 poor sleep, prone to depression and crying.'

Mother's Day fell on 14 May in 1944. The postcard arrived more than three weeks later.

Papa: Josef Chotzen died in the Jewish Hospital on 27 January 1942.

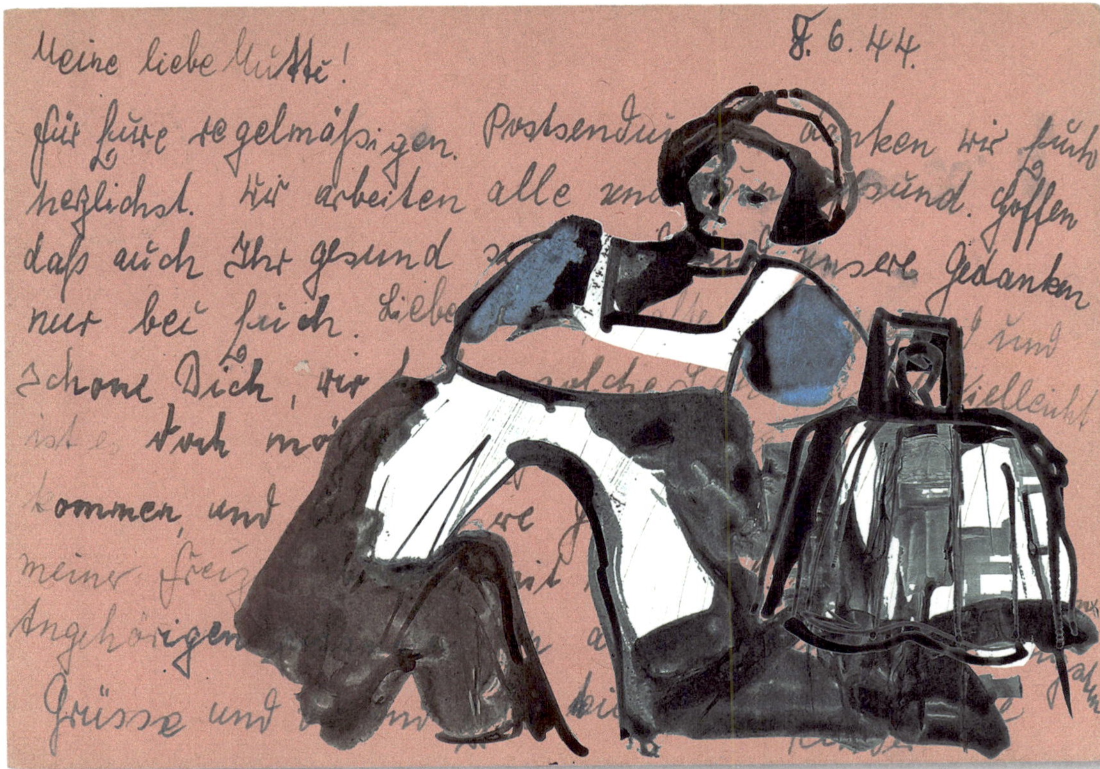

Mutti in a White Apron, 2024

Ink drawing and digital editing

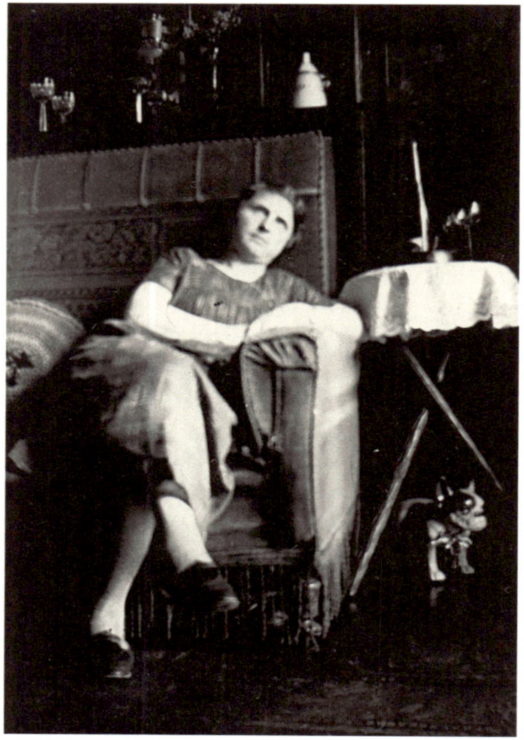

Elsa at home in her living room, 1930s, from Bubi's photo album (1923/24–1936)

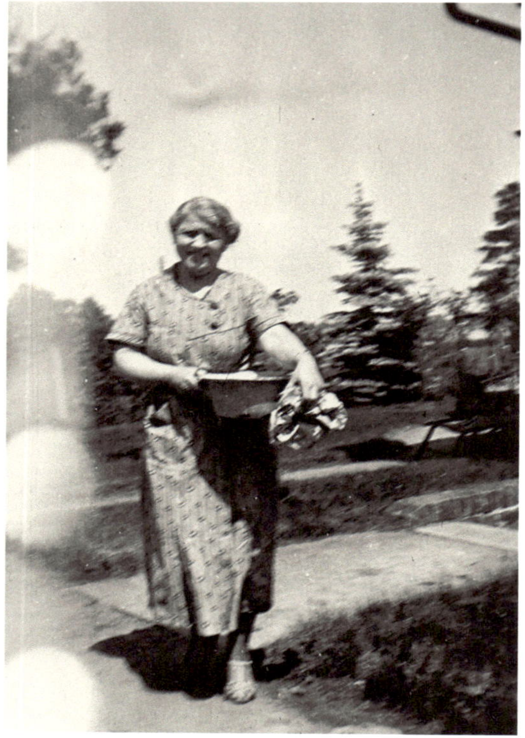

Elsa on holiday in Teupitz, 1940, from Bubi's photo album (1923/24–1936)

INBAR CHOTZEN

The painting "Mutti in a White Apron" is based on a photo of Elsa. Looking at it, I had the impression that this shot was taken through the loving eyes of one of her sons and that the young photographer took the picture from a very low angle. Elsa seems to be taking a break from the hectic life of a mother of four boys. The white apron symbolizes her role in the household, although we know this was simply part of her admirable character.

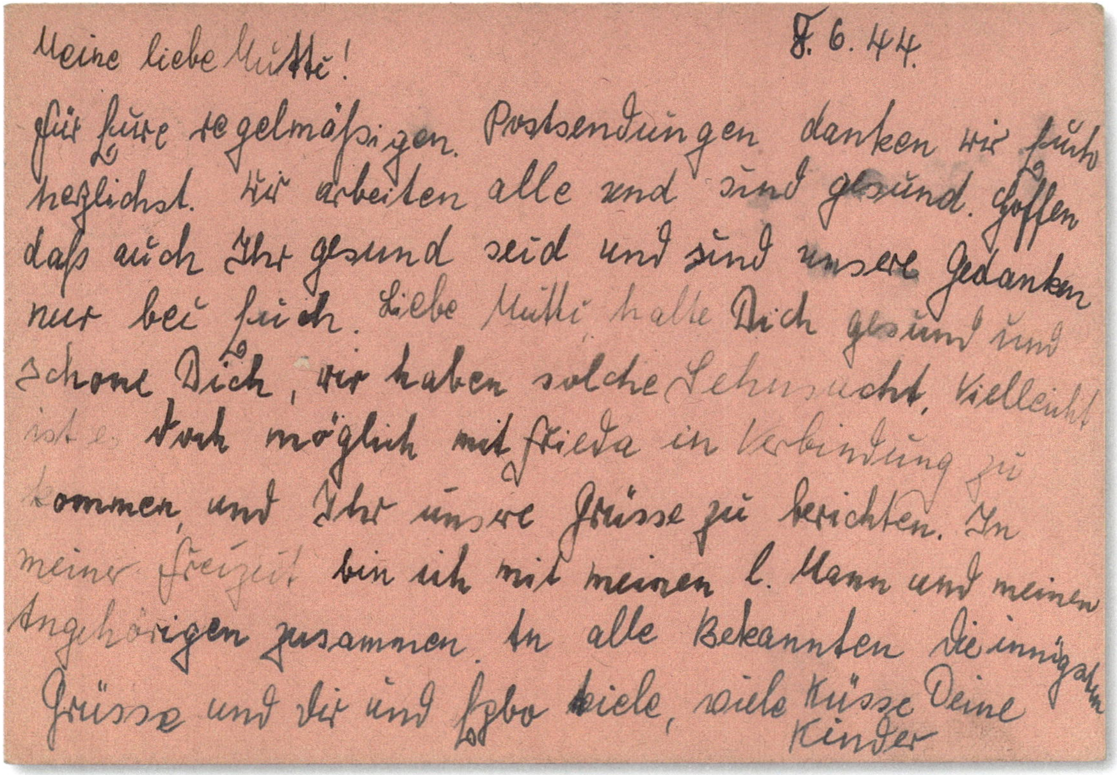

Meine liebe Mutti! 8. 6. 44.

Für Eure regelmäßigen Postsendungen danken wir Euch herzlichst. Wir arbeiten alle und sind gesund. Hoffen daß auch Ihr gesund seid und sind unsere Gedanken nur bei Euch. Liebe Mutti halte Dich gesund und schone Dich, wir haben solche Sehnsucht. Vielleicht ist es doch möglich mit Frieda in Verbindung zu kommen, und Ihr unsere Grüsse zu berichten. In meiner Freizeit bin ich mit meinem l. Mann und meinen Angehörigen zusammen. An alle Bekannten die innigsten Grüsse und dir und Ebo viele, viele Küsse Deine Kinder

Thirty-fifth postcard from Lisa, 8 June 1944
postmark: 10 July 1944, Berlin-Charlottenburg

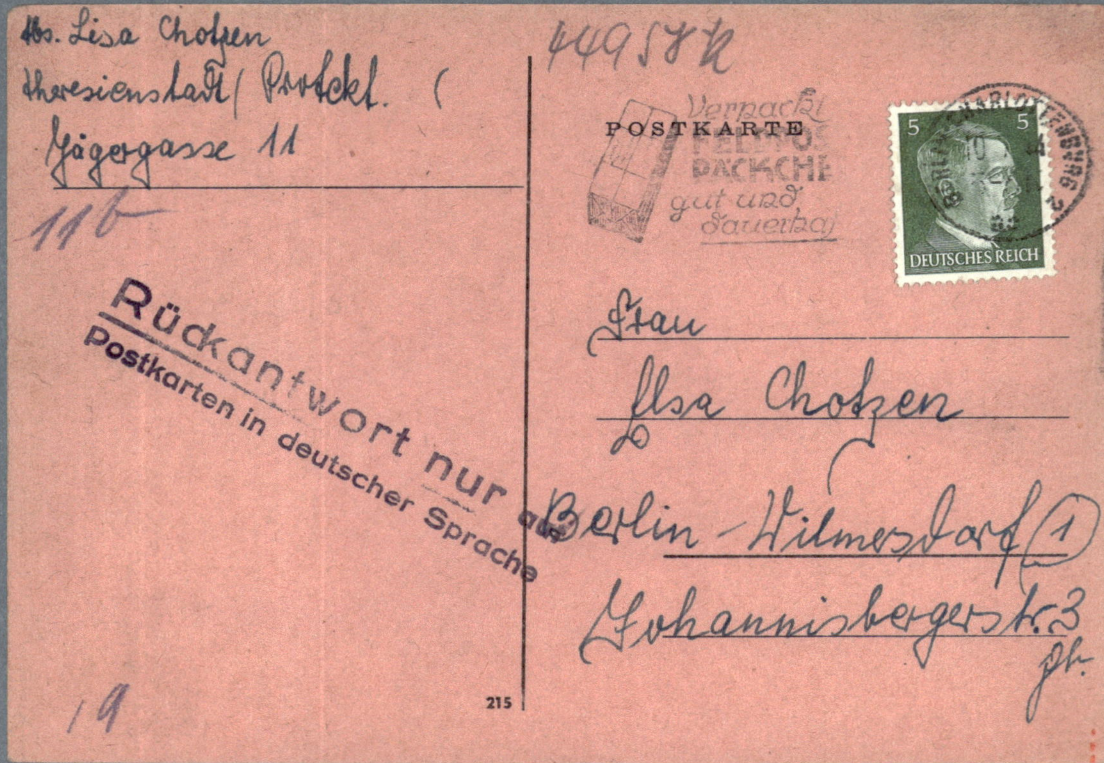
Theresienstadt
Jägergasse 11
POSTKARTE
DEUTSCHES REICH
Rückantwort nur
Postkarten in deutscher Sprache
215
Frau
Ilsa Chotzen
Berlin-Wilmersdorf (1)
Johannisbergerstr. 3

About postal traffic

This was Lisa's fifth postcard with a personal message. She also managed to send two other cards to Elsa under different names: one as Vera Samuel and the other as Eva Cahn. These women were probably neighbours from Jägergasse 11, where Lisa lived with her mother.

On 10 July 1944, when this card was stamped in Berlin-Charlottenburg, cards from Ulli, Ruth and Bubi also arrived. Ulli's card was written on 7 June; Ruth's on 11 June and Bubi's on 17 June. They took about a month to arrive, which was relatively fast.

Situation in Theresienstadt

In 'Notices from the Jewish Self-Administration No. 18' of 8 June 1944, the residents of Theresienstadt were asked to protect themselves from typhus and enteritis (intestinal inflammation) by paying particular attention to hygiene: They should wash their hands regularly, wash vegetables before eating them and not use the local waste water. The last demand was an indication of the poor hygienic conditions in Theresienstadt, which suffered from a massive water shortage. Residents would only have used waste water if no fresh water was available.

My dear Mum! 8.6.44

We thank you dearly for sending mail regularly. We are all working and are healthy. Hope that you are healthy, too. Our thoughts are always with you. Dear Mum, stay healthy and take care of yourself. We are filled with longing. If it is possible to connect with **Frieda** please send her our greetings. **I spend my free time with my husband and relatives.** Warm greetings to all my acquaintances and to you and **Epbo**. Many, many kisses, Your

Children

Frieda was the Scheurenberg's domestic worker. She also sent care packages to Theresienstadt.

Free time: Lisa's brother, Klaus Scheurenberg, described these meetings in his autobiography: *In the evenings we met in the yard in the barracks where he [Bubi] also slept, or in the small square behind the house where my mother and Lisa vegetated. We tried to maintain our family life even if only for an hour. We succeeded at first, but not later.*[1]

Epbo: Like her brother-in-law Ulli, who addressed a card to 'Eppibo', Lisa also combined the nickname of the oldest brother, Eppi, and the name of his girlfriend, Božka, whom she wished to thank for helping to send parcels.

1 Klaus Scheurenberg: Ich will leben, ibid., p. 140.

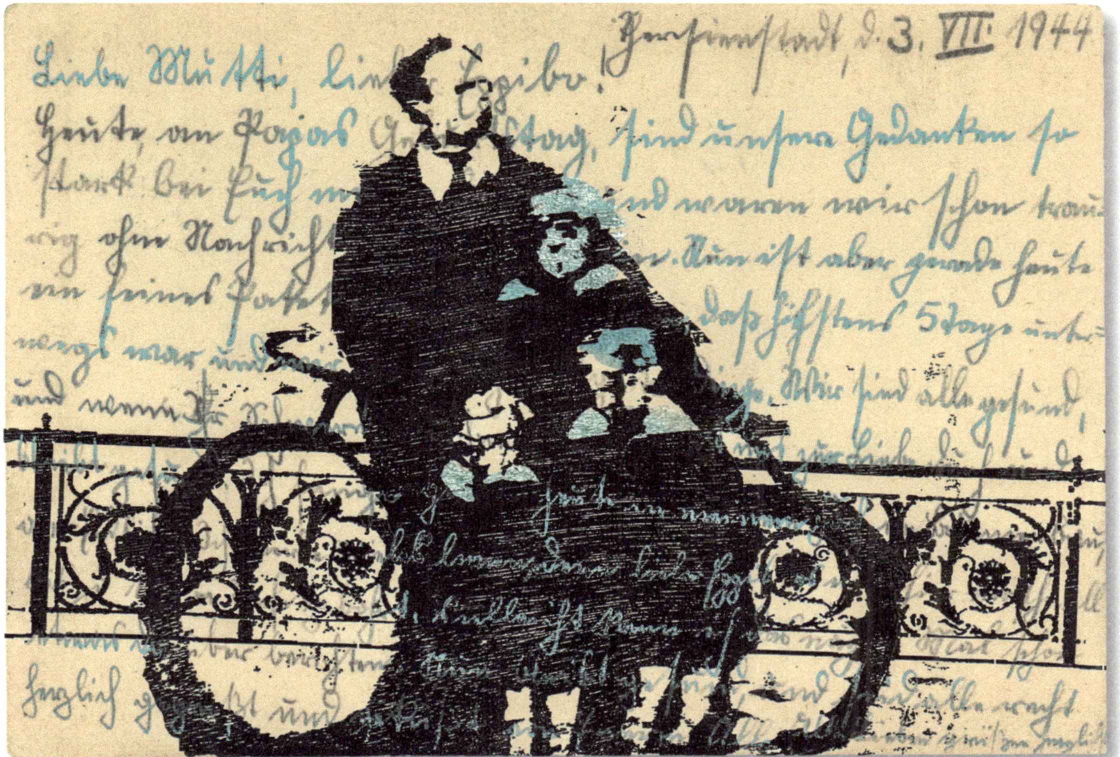

Heidelberger Platz, 2021

Woodcut and digital editing

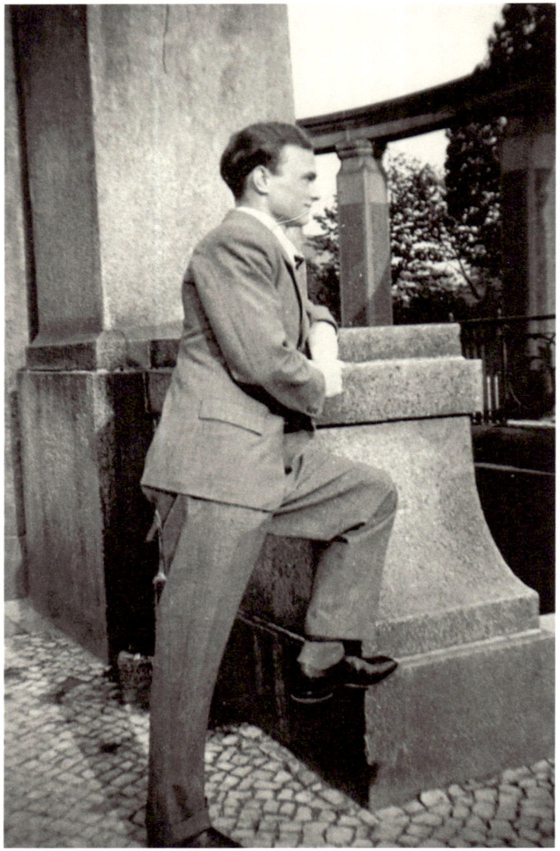

Bubi at Heidelberger Platz, photo caption in album: 'me', probably early 1930s, from Bubi's photo album (1923/24–1936)

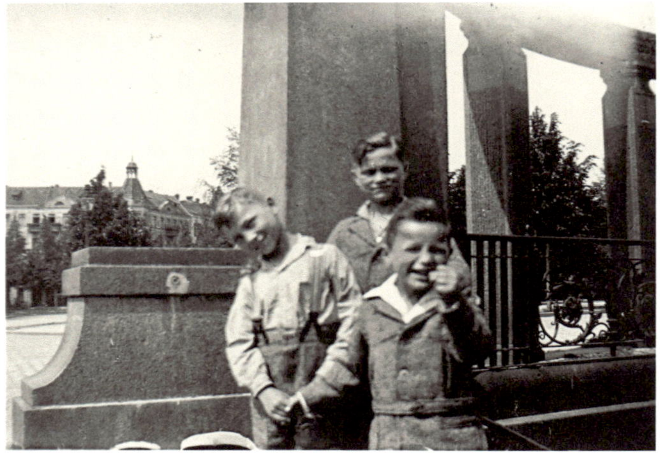

Erich, Bubi and Ulli at Heidelberger Platz, 1920s, from Bubi's photo album (1923/24–1936)

INBAR CHOTZEN

Another favourite location for taking family photos was in the park next to the Heidelberger Platz 'U-Bahn' station, situated only a few minutes' walk from the Chotzen's home. Over the years, all the boys were photographed there 'showing off' their bikes and, later, their tailored suits.
For the postcard 'Heidelberger Platz', I did not have to conduct any research, as the station has remained unchanged. The same decorative fence, the same stone sidewalks and concrete columns are all still there. It is my family that is missing.

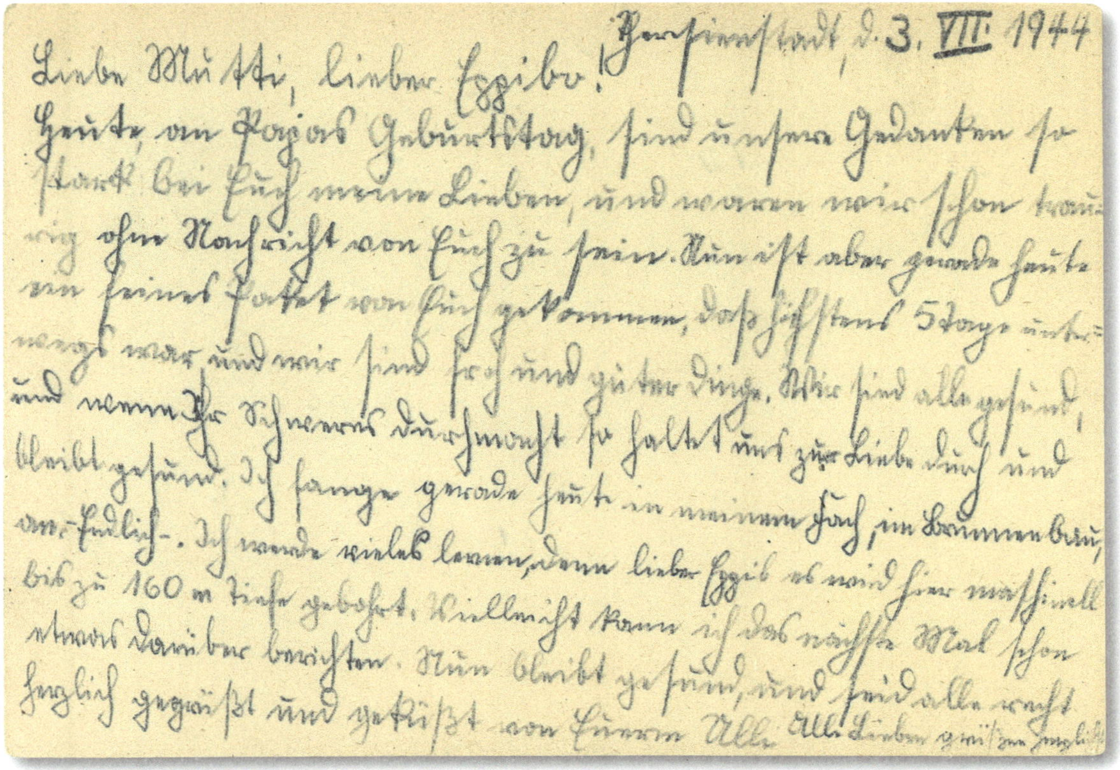

Fifty-second postcard from Ulli, 3 July 1944
postmark: 31 August 1944, Berlin-Charlottenburg

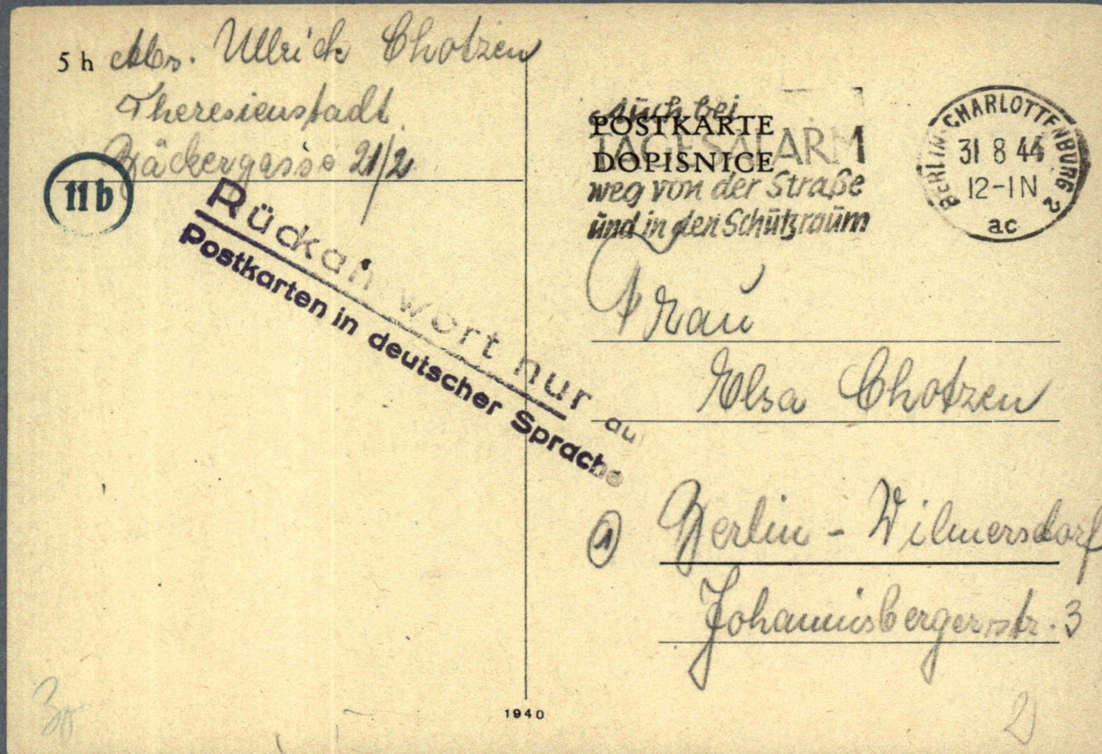

5 h Mr. Ullrich Chotzen
Theresienstadt
Bäckergasse 21/2

11 b

Rückantwort nur auf Postkarten in deutscher Sprache

POSTKARTE
DOPISNICE

Auch bei TAGESALARM weg von der Straße und in den Schutzraum

BERLIN-CHARLOTTENBURG 2
31 8 44
12-1 N
ac

Frau
Elsa Chotzen
Berlin-Wilmersdorf
Johannisbergerstr. 3

1940

About postal traffic

After this card, Ulli was only able to send three more cards with personal messages. His wife, Ruth, and his brother Bubi sent postcards to Berlin four more times. Seven more postcards arrived from Lisa. The day that this card was stamped in Berlin-Charlottenburg, more cards arrived: another one from Ulli, two from Bubi, one from Bubi under the name Gertrud Narewczewitz, two from Ruth and two from Lisa. Nine postcards on a single day.
Ruth filled out the address side of this card, too.

EPPI CHOTZEN

Many of those who returned from Theresienstadt have written about what it was like there, what took place there. [But] we could tell from their messages, (and had already suspected, even without these confirmations) that their 'hopeful' tone was meant to reassure us – especially my mother. But undoubtedly, they also wanted to reassure themselves again and again.
Bit by bit, each of them realized that they would not survive everything together,
but they all held on to some hope until the bitter end. That is natural and understandable, despite the fact that they were confronted with the reality of Theresienstadt very quickly and must have recognised that the touted 'benefits' were only lies and deception designed to mislead foreigners.

Theresienstadt, 3. VII.1944

Dear Mum, dear **Eppibo**!

Today, on **Papa's birthday**, our thoughts are so strongly with you, my dears, and we were very sad to be without a message from you. But today we received a fine parcel from you, it was at least 5 days in transit, and we are very happy and we are heartened. We are all healthy, and even though you have difficulties, please persevere for our sake, and stay healthy. I am just starting work in my field, **well construction.** Finally. I'm going to learn a lot because, dear **Eppib**,the drilling here is done mechanically to a depth of 160 metres. Perhaps I can report something about it next time. Now stay healthy, and warm greetings and kisses to all from your Ulli Best wishes from all your loved ones.

Eppibo / Eppib: Once again, Ulli combined the nickname of his brother Eppi with that of his brother's girlfriend Božka.

Papa's birthday: Josef Chotzen would have turned 61 on 3 July 1944. He died on 27 January 1942 as a result of forced labour.

Well construction: In the first postcard he sent home, Ulli had written that he hoped to be deployed in well construction. Nearly a year passed before he was transferred to that work detail. He wanted to report on this new job, but he never did. The town suffered from a permanent water shortage due to overpopulation. As a consequence, water was rationed. Ulli probably had to work on Well IV, which was located on the right side of the road leading to Deutsch-Kopist (now the district of Nové Kopisty). The well, which was 169 metres deep, was not completed until 1944.

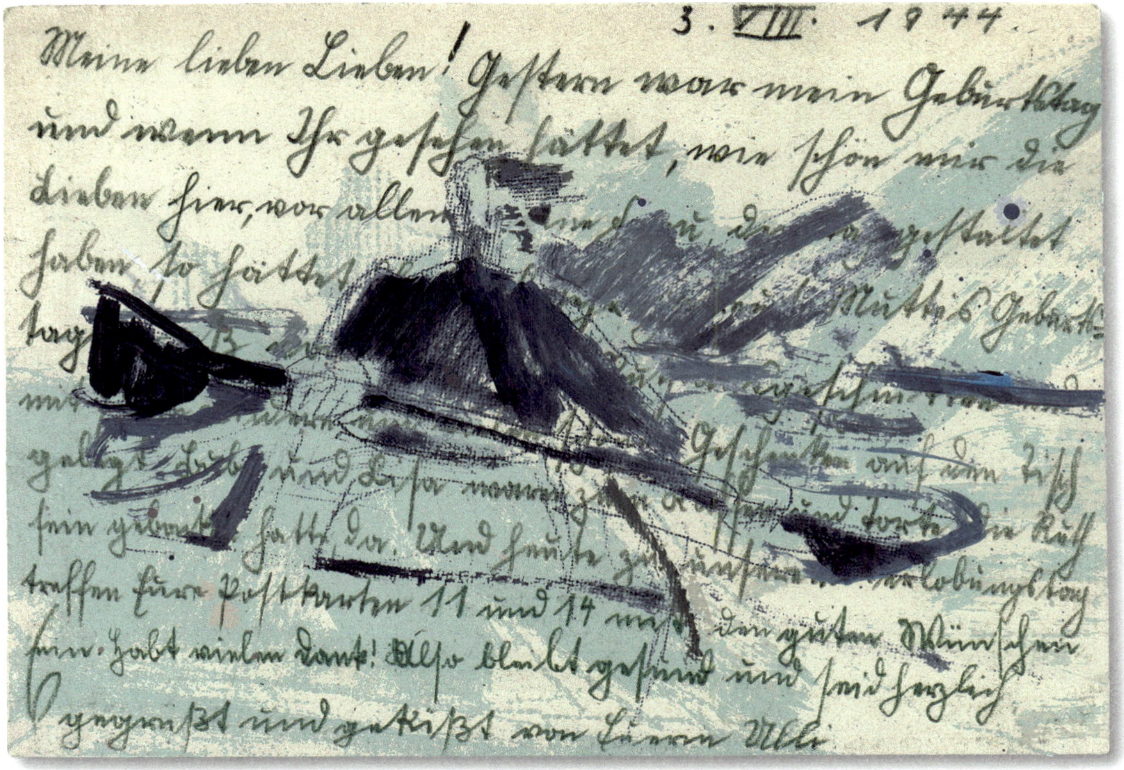

Canoe, 2021

Multimedia and digital editing

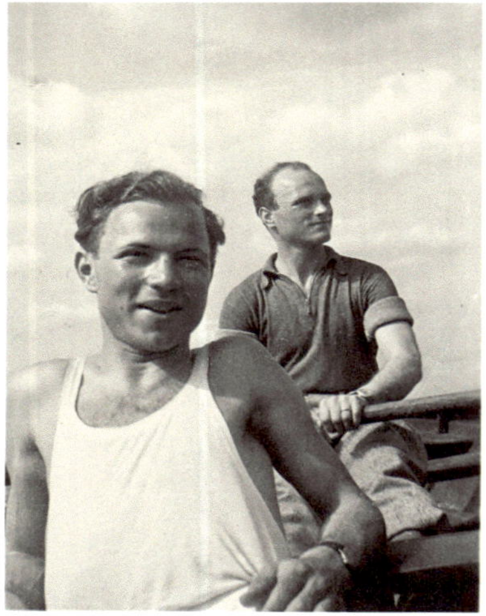

Erich and Bubi in their boat, late 1930s, from Bubi's photo album (1936–1941)

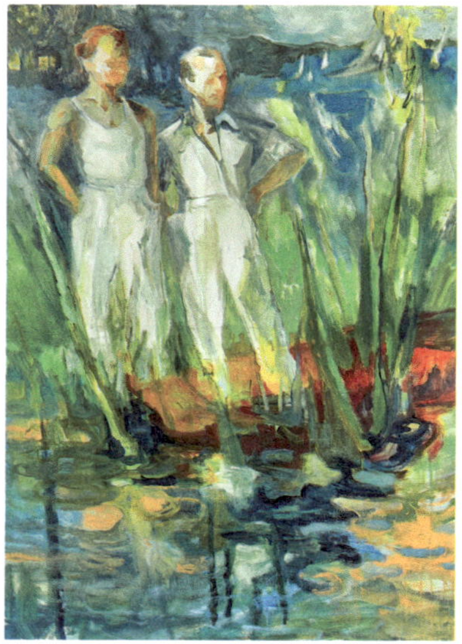

Inbar Chotzen: *Two Sailors*, oil on canvas, 2021

INBAR CHOTZEN

Eppi, Bubi, Erich and Ulli often spent their weekends during summertime on Krossinsee, navigating the lake in the canoe-paddle boat. In 2020, Barbara Schieb told me the story of the boat that "survived." The story stirred my imagination during the Covid lockdown.
In my imagination the boat was found after all these years, submerged in the lake flora, tangled in the thicket of mud and vegetation. The boat had survived but the boys did not.
This boat was stored by Eppi in a boathouse in Wernsdorf and apparently remained there for many years, even after the end of the war. Eppi never returned there. The boat was discovered in its place around 2003 by an historian who was researching the family's history. Since then, unfortunately, the boat has again disappeared and only the wooden paddle remains.

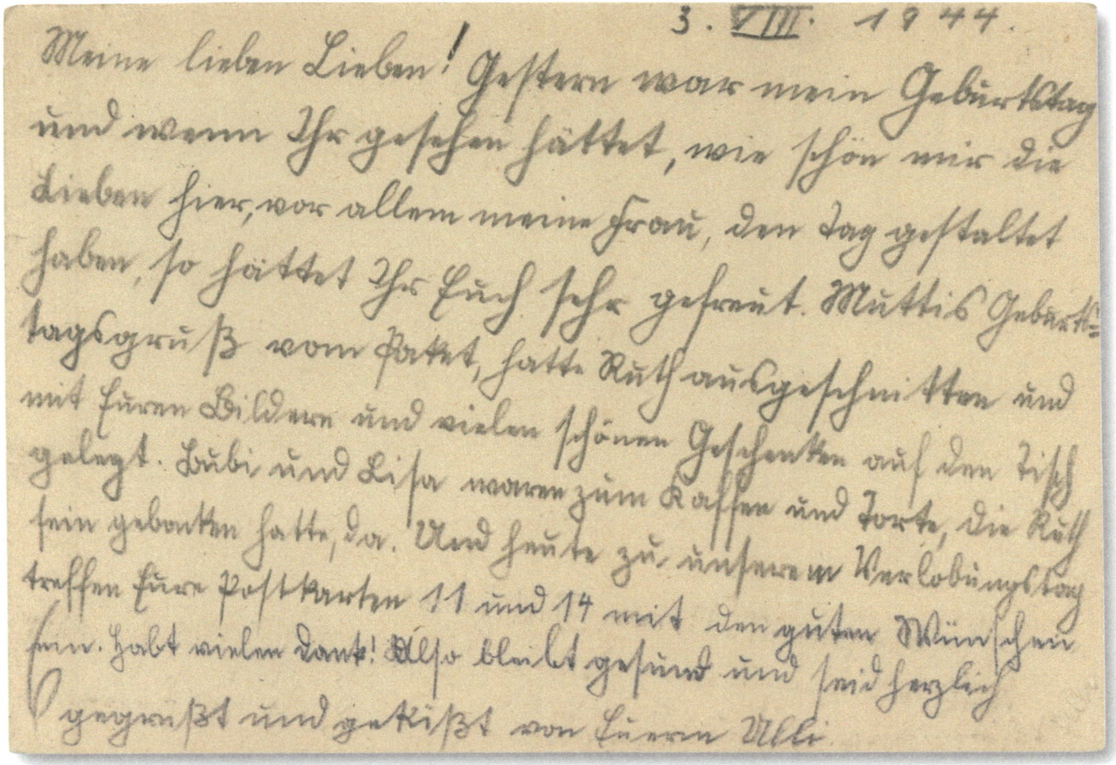

3. VIII. 1944.
Meine lieben Lieben! Gestern war mein Geburtstag
und wenn Ihr gesehen hättet, wie schön mir die
Lieben hier, vor allem meine Frau, den Tag gestaltet
haben, so hättet Ihr Euch sehr gefreut. Muttis Geburts=
tagsgruß vom Vatti, hatte Ruth ausgeschnitten und
mit Euren Bildern und vielen schönen Geschenken auf den Tisch
gelegt. Bubi und Liese waren zum Kaffee und Torte, die Ruth
fein gebacken hatte, da. Und heute zu unserem Verlobungstag
trafen Eure Postkarten 11 und 14 mit den guten Wünschen
ein. Habt vielen Dank! Also bleibt gesund und seid herzlich
gegrüßt und geküsst von Eurem Ulli

Fifty-ninth postcard from Ulli, 3 August 1944
postmark: 31 August 1944, Berlin-Charlottenburg

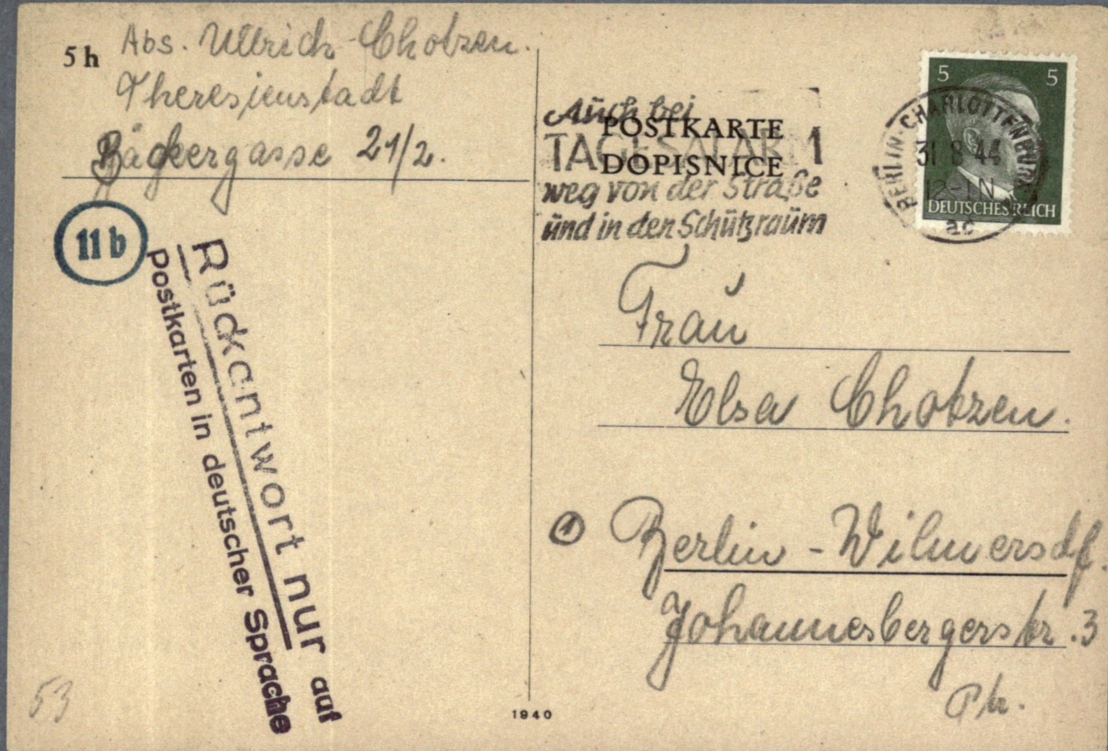
5 h Abs. Ulrich Chotzen.
Theresienstadt
Bäckergasse 21/2.

11 b

Rückantwort nur auf
Postkarten in deutscher Sprache

53

Auch bei
TAGESALARM
weg von der Straße
und in den Schutzraum

POSTKARTE
DOPISNICE

5 DEUTSCHES REICH 5
BERLIN-CHARLOTTENBURG 31.8.44 12-1 N ac

Frau
Elsa Chotzen.
① Berlin - Wilmersdf.
Johannesbergerstr. 3
Pk.

1940

About postal traffic

After this one, only two more postcards from Ulli with personal messages can be found in the Family Archive. Before his last message arrived on 10 October 1944, only parcel confirmations reached Berlin.
Although this card was written a month after Ulli's last postcard with a personal text, both cards arrived on the same day: On 31 August 1944, nine postcards were delivered to Berlin on a single day. This time too, Ruth filled out the front side.

Situation in Theresienstadt

'Notices from the Jewish Self-Administration No. 33' of 3 August 1944 addressed the issue of admission stamps for parcels sent from the Protektorat to people who had arrived in Theresienstadt before 31 December 1942. The most recent court judgements were announced (mainly concerning food theft). It stated that sales staff were needed for dishes and textiles – goods that people had brought with them were put on sale. It announced that the blackout period ran from 9.30 pm to 5 am.

3. VIII 1944

My dearest dears! Yesterday was **my birthday** and if you had seen how beautifully my dears here, especially my wife, planned my day, you would have been very happy. Ruth cut out Mum's birthday greeting from the parcel and put it on the table with your pictures and many lovely presents. Bubi and Lisa came for **coffee and cake**, which Ruth baked beautifully. And today, on our engagement day, your postcards 11 and 14 arrived with good wishes. Thank you very much! Stay healthy and accept warm greetings and kisses from your Ulli

My birthday: Ulli's birthday was 2 August. He celebrated his last one in Theresienstadt in 1944. He was 24 years old.

Coffee and cake: Thanks to the supply packages from Berlin, the Chotzens did not have to rely solely on food from the canteens. They were able to cook and bake for themselves from time to time. Elsa sent the ingredients so that Ruth could bake a cake for her husband on his birthday. He probably wrote in such an upbeat tone so that the card would get through the censor while also reassuring his mother.

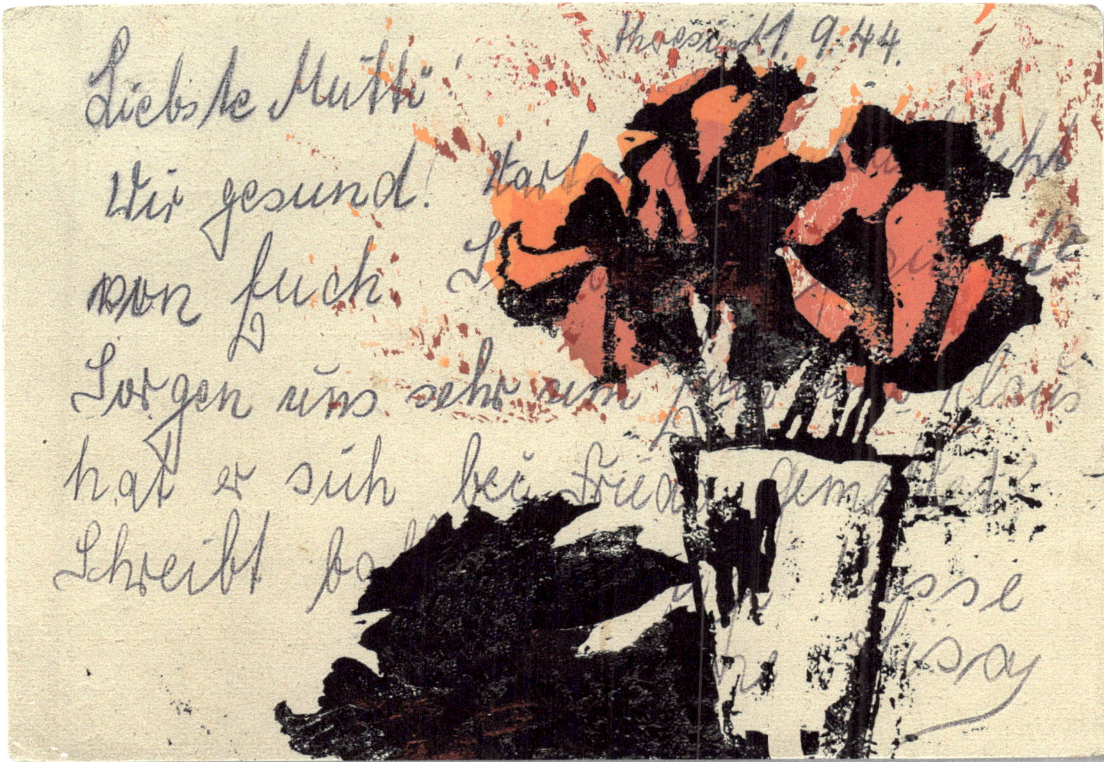

Elsa's Flowers, 2019

Woodcut and digital editing

INBAR CHOTZEN

For the postcard 'Elsa's Flowers' I chose the wood carving print technique, based on the vase of flowers in most of the photos depicting the Chotzen's apartment. One can only admire Elsa for her efforts to maintain a warm and welcoming home even in very hard times. The wood carving technique allows one to create hard edges and high-contrast lines that also connect with Lisa's short message, which conveys a feeling of urgency.

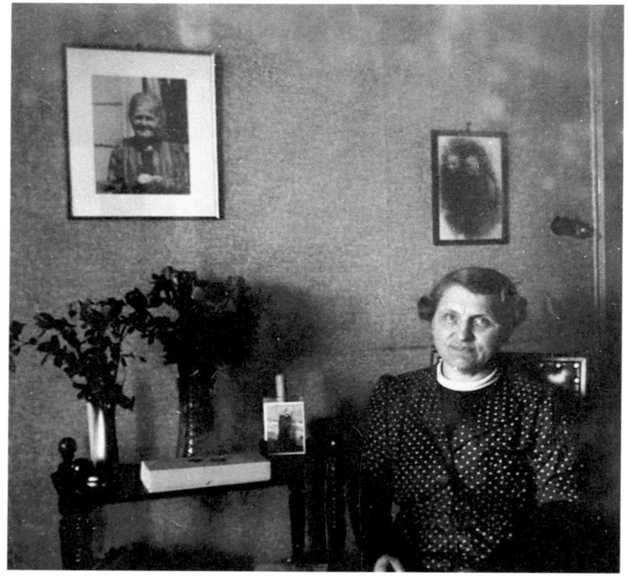

Photo caption 'Mum. My children should have such a good mother, too. Then I will also be well off!' From Bubi's photo album (1936–1941)

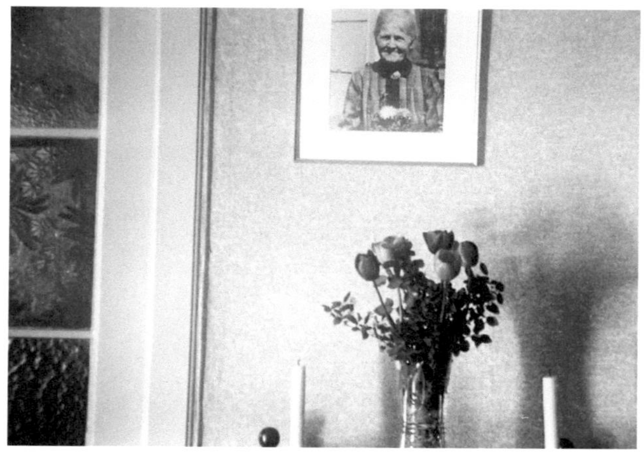

A portrait photograph on a wall, probably in the living room, of Elsa's mother, Maria Arndt, with flowers in front. Photo album of the family, undated.

Although the family's financial situation was strained, the ledger that Elsa used to track household expenses sometimes listed 'flowers'. In 1942, the ledger contained a listing for 'Flowers Papa' – these were brought to the cemetery.

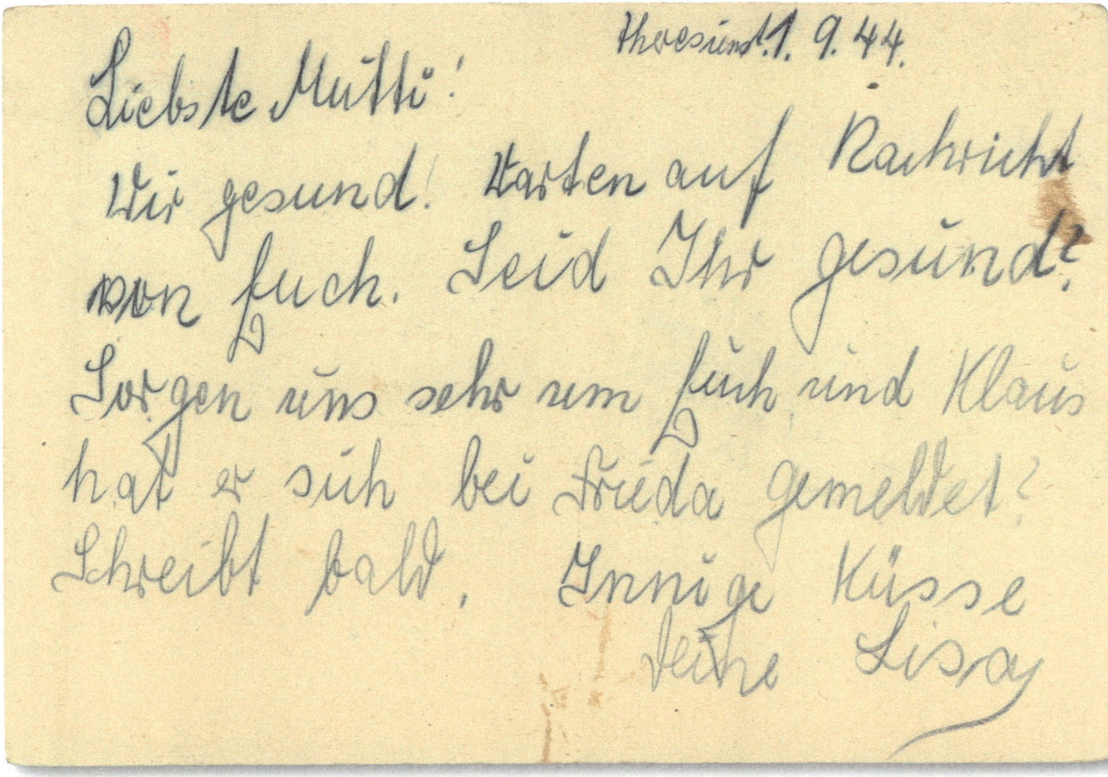

Theresienstadt 1. 9. 44.

Liebste Mutti!

Wir gesund! Warten auf Nachricht von Euch. Seid Ihr gesund? Sorgen uns sehr um Euch und Klaus hat er sich bei Frieda gemeldet? Schreibt bald. Innige Küsse Deine Lisa

Fifty-second postcard from Lisa, 1 September 1944
postmark: 30 October 1944, Berlin W62

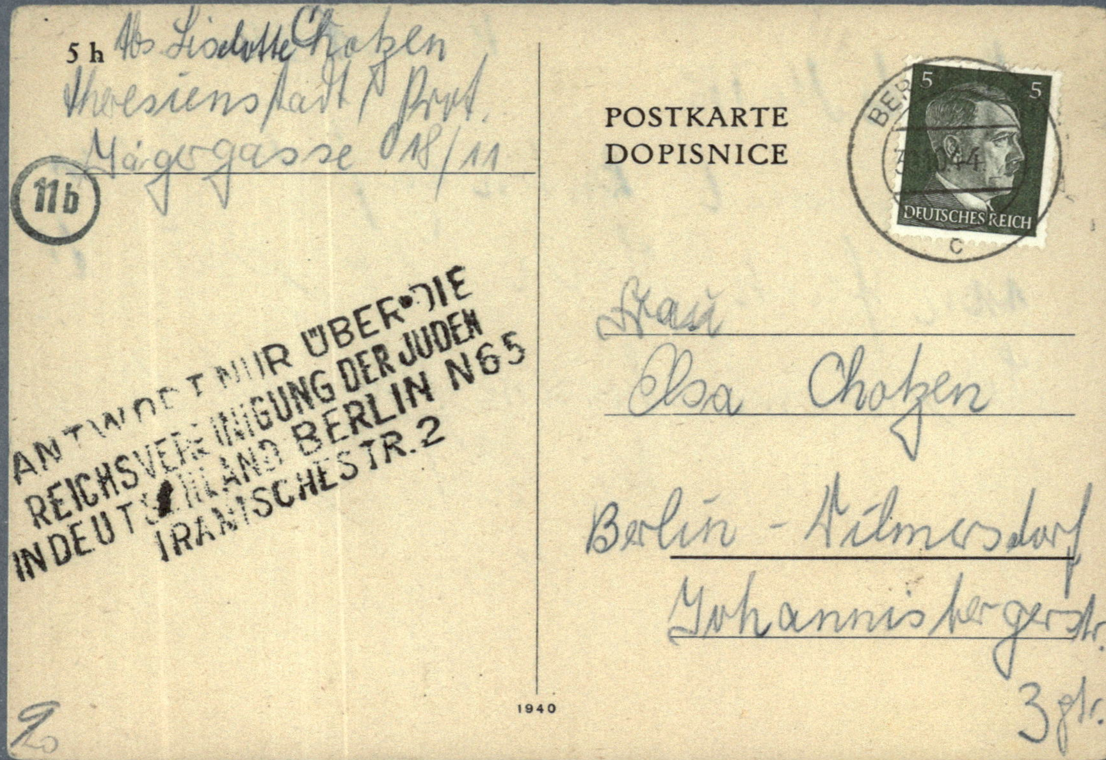
5 h
Abs. Liselotte Chotzen
Theresienstadt Prot.
Jägergasse 18/11
11b
POSTKARTE
DOPISNICE
5 DEUTSCHES REICH 5
ANTWORT NUR ÜBER DIE
REICHSVEREINIGUNG DER JUDEN
IN DEUTSCHLAND BERLIN N65
IRANISCHESTR. 2
Frau
Elsa Chotzen
Berlin - Wilmersdorf
Johannisbergerstr.
3
1940

About postal traffic

Something must have changed in early September 1944 regarding postcard correspondence: Lisa had sent her mother-in-law a postcard with personal text already six days earlier. The message she sent here is remarkably brief. Bubi and Ulli also wrote unusually short texts that same day, and the following day Ruth sent a brief thank you for food. Her message was only a few lines long. Lisa wrote again on 4 September, again quite tersely. Perhaps permission to write postcards was erratic; perhaps the change had to do with their imminent deportation. The five postcards were stamped and delivered in Berlin on the same day: 30 October 1944.

Situation in Theresienstadt

During this time, a propaganda film was being shot in Theresienstadt; it was meant to show the world that Jews had a good situation there. The atmosphere that had been created for the International Red Cross's visit was maintained. The SS forced the famous actor and current prisoner, Kurt Gerron, to direct the film, which was shot between 16 August and 11 September. Lisa's brother Klaus Scheurenberg remembered the film shoot:
To conceal the true nature of our concentration camp, a film was made about Theresienstadt, in which I was forced to take part twice as an extra. Kurt Gerron was the director. He had played the role of theatre director in 'The Blue Angel' with Marlene Dietrich. This tall, fat man was given the perverse task of creating the illusion of a friendly village in Theresienstadt that was given to the Jews by Hitler. […] The first time I was filmed pulling a cart with others that was packed full of bread. The next time I was filmed in the carpentry workshop. I was also filmed in the SS' outdoor swimming pool on the Eger. Of course, this was not on the camp grounds. It was made to look like we had our own bathing facility. […] All the fuss over the film went on for a few weeks. One day it was over.[1]

1 Klaus Scheurenberg: Ich will leben, ib d., pp. 151–153

Theresienst., 1.9.44

Dearest Mum!

We are healthy. Waiting for news from you. Are you healthy?

Worry about you a lot, and **Klaus.**

Did he contact **Frieda**?

Write soon. Warm kisses

Your Lisa

Klaus: This refers to her brother Klaus Scheurenberg, who was transferred from Theresienstadt to the Wulkow camp near Neuhardenberg to perform forced labour there in August 1944. Contact between him and the others was severed as a result of his transfer. Lisa hoped that he had written to Berlin.

Frieda: Frieda, who had been the Scheurenbergs' maid, also sent parcels to Theresienstadt. Elsa and Eppi were in contact with her. Several of the Scheurenbergs' parcel confirmations contained greetings for Frieda.

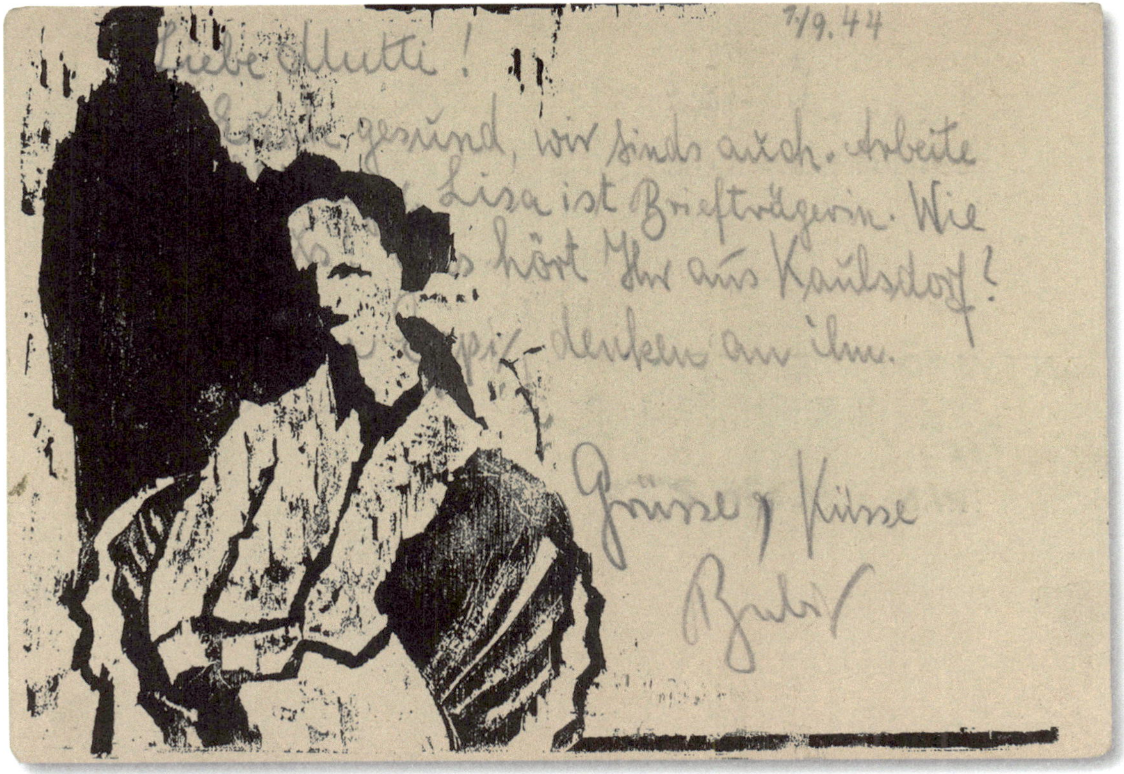

Lisa, Sitting, 2019

Woodcut and digital editing

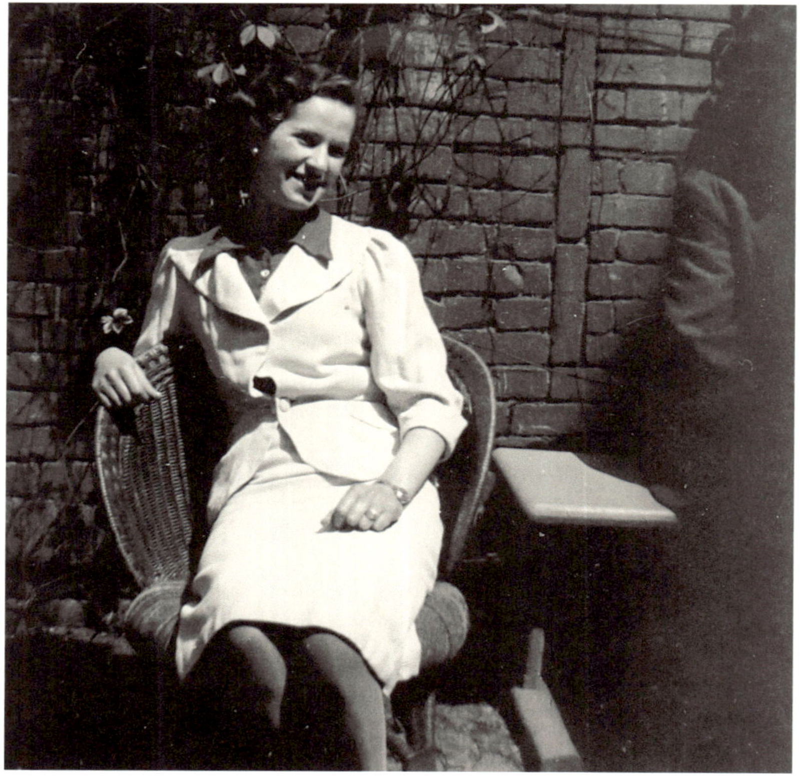

Lisa, probably 1940/41, from Bubi's photo album (1936–1941)

Lisa Scheurenberg began an apprenticeship in a corsetry shop in 1934. In 1937 or 1938, she met Bubi at the Jewish Sports Association (JSG). They became engaged in September 1940 and married on 18 November 1941. She lost her job around this time and later worked as an assistant to a Jewish dentist.

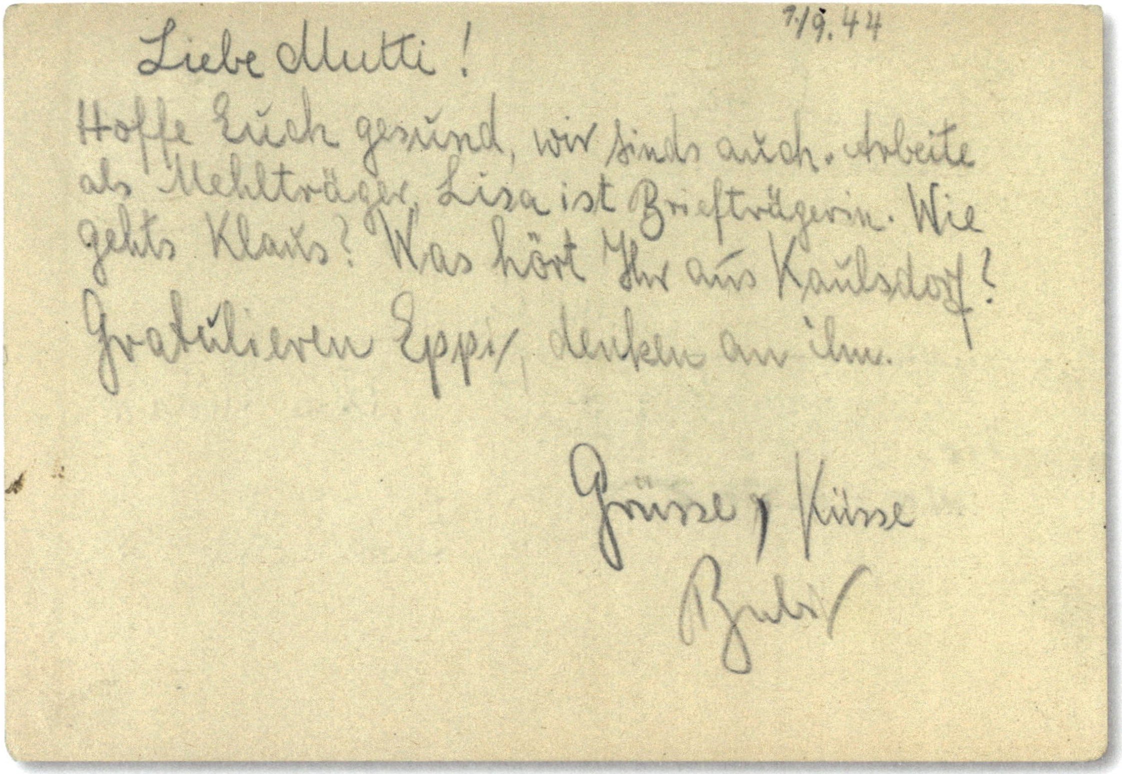

1/9.44

Liebe Mutti!

Hoffe Euch gesund, wir sinds auch. Arbeite als Mehlträger, Lisa ist Briefträgerin. Wie gehts Klaus? Was hört Ihr aus Kaulsdorf? Gratulieren Eppi, denken an ihn.

Grüsse u. Küsse
Bubi

Sixty-fifth postcard from Bubi, 1 September 1944
postmark: 30 October 1944, Berlin W62

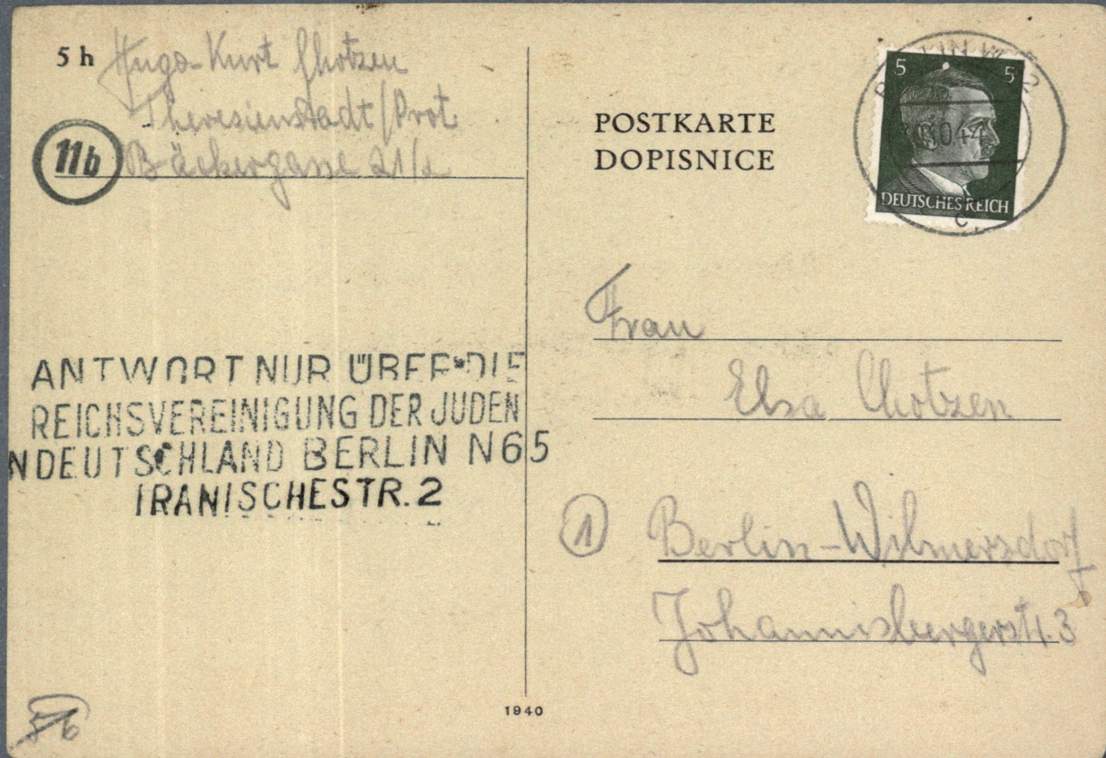
5 h Hugo-Kurt Chotzen
Theresienstadt/Prot
11b Bäckergasse 21/a

POSTKARTE
DOPISNICE

5 DEUTSCHES REICH 5

ANTWORT NUR ÜBER DIE
REICHSVEREINIGUNG DER JUDEN
IN DEUTSCHLAND BERLIN N65
IRANISCHESTR. 2

Frau
Elsa Chotzen
(1) Berlin-Wilmersdorf
Johannisbergerstr. 43

1940

About postal traffic

Another very short postcard came from Bubi. His wife and brother also wrote messages with very little text that same day. His sister-in-law Ruth wrote a day later. Permission to write may have come so erratically that they did not have enough time to write more. The four postcards with personal text were all stamped and delivered to Berlin on 30 October 1944. By then, Bubi, Ulli, Ruth and Lisa had all left Theresienstadt in three different transports bound for Auschwitz.

Situation in Theresienstadt

In his book, H. G. Adler wrote about the pseudo-documentary titled 'Theresienstadt' that engaged prisoners as actors and was filmed in the 'Jewish settlement area' until 11 September 1944:

The participation of the prisoners, insofar as it was not voluntary, was summarily enforced. The workers in the factories were given time off for rehearsals and shootings and they were sent summonses from the 'recreation office' to appear at such and such a time in the 'coffee house', the 'community house' or in other places. To the prisoners' credit, it must be said that there was strong opposition to the filming, but anyone who did not come willingly received warnings openly threatening that he would be summoned and punished if he did not appear.[1]

1 H. G. Adler: Theresienstadt 1941–1945, ibid., p. 182f.

1./9.44

Dear Mum!

Hope you are well, we are too. Working as **flour transporter**, Lisa as letter carrier. How is **Klaus**? What do you hear from **Kaulsdorf**? Congratulations to **Eppi**, thinking of him.

Greetings, Kisses
Bubi

Flour transporter, letter carrier: We don't know whether his new job as a flour transporter was better or worse for Bubi. The bakery and the central food store, at least, were located close to their residence. He never described his work in detail – the censor would not have allowed it. Lisa evidently changed jobs, too. The number of people employed at the post office rose sharply during the period when Theresienstadt functioned as a transit camp. During this time, the volume of postcards and parcels arriving from the outside and the number of messages sent within the town continued to increase.

Klaus: In August 1944, Klaus Scheurenberg was deported from Theresienstadt to the Wulkow subcamp near Neuhardenberg to perform forced labour. There was no way for him to send messages from there. He returned to Theresienstadt in February 1945 where he was reunited with his parents. His sister Lisa had meanwhile been deported to Auschwitz.

Kaulsdorf: The Raschinskis were friendly, helpful neighbours from Johannisberger Straße who had a house in Kaulsdorf. The family albums contain photos of the family's visits there.

Eppi's birthday was on 27 September. Bubi probably thought this card would arrive around that time. It actually took more than a month longer.

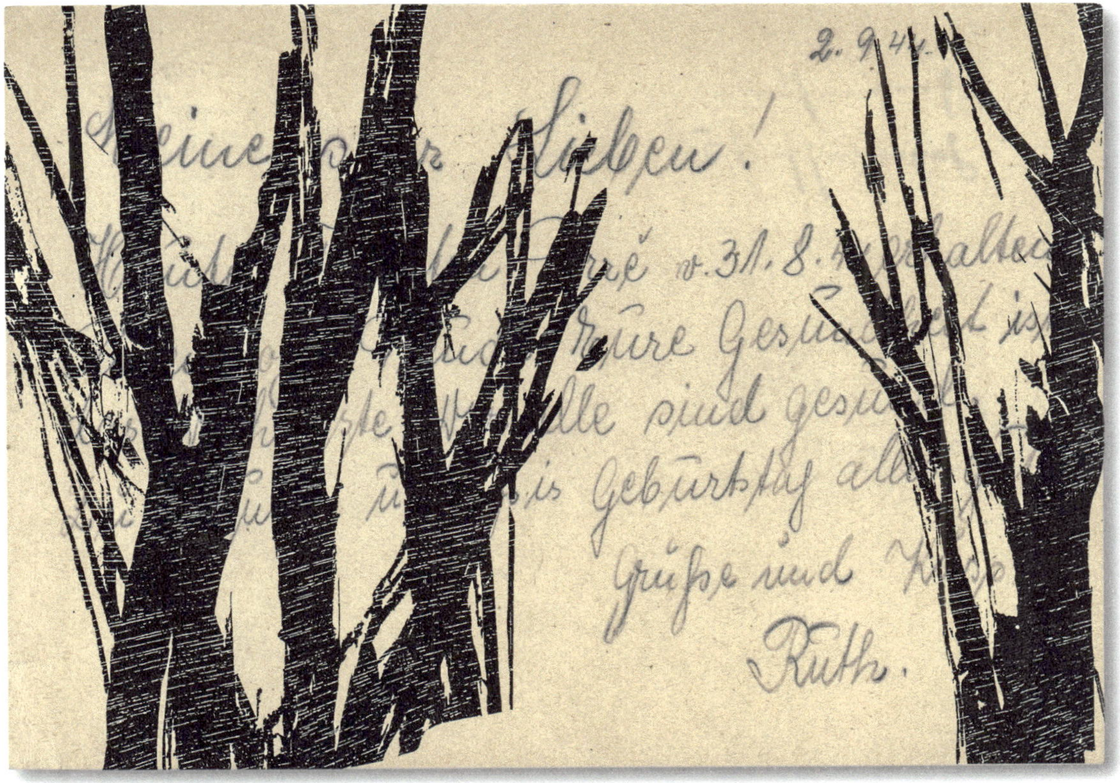

Ruth's March from Dachau to Berlin, 2025

Woodcut and digital editing

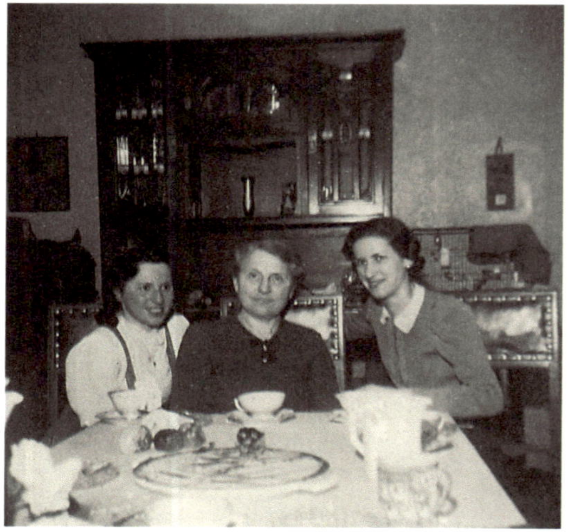

Ruth, Elsa and Lisa, ca. 1940, from: Pieken/ Kruse: The household book of Elsa Chotzen, ibid., p. 161

The historian Barbara Schieb visited Ruth in New York in 1998 and spoke with her about her experiences after the separation from Ulli. After she arrived in Auschwitz, she was sent to the so-called Theresienstadt family camp where she stayed for about three weeks. The conditions there were so terrible that she volunteered to join a group of a hundred women who left the camp on another transport. The SS sent her to Merzdorf in Silesia, a subcamp of Groß-Rosen, where she was forced to work in a fabric factory. Ruth remained there until early May 1945 and witnessed the liberation of the camp by the Soviet army. During these months, she was violently attacked several times by her guards.

After liberation, she walked with four other women to Landeshut, the next largest town. When they arrived there, the mayor allocated them a flat that had previously been occupied by an SS man and his family. This is when they finally began to feel human again. They removed their prisoner clothes and ate from porcelain plates.

Ruth had befriended another woman and the two of them set off on foot to Berlin that same month. They arrived at Elsa's home in Johannisberger Straße on 1 June. Elsa took both women in. Later that month, Ruth's mother and sisters returned from Theresienstadt and moved into a flat in the building next door. Ruth stayed with Elsa until she learned that her husband was dead, after which she decided to leave Germany.

She says about the Chotzen family in the 2004 documentary film:

'The great bond that existed between everyone was immediately noticeable. I've never experienced it again with such intensity; they literally lived for one another. There was never a loud word, never a serious argument. As young as I was at the time, that caught my attention and shaped me for the rest of my life.'[1]

1 Quoted in: Pieken/ Kruse: Das Haushaltsbuch der Elsa Chotzen. Schicksal einer jüdischen Familie 1937–1946. Berlin 2008, p. 75.

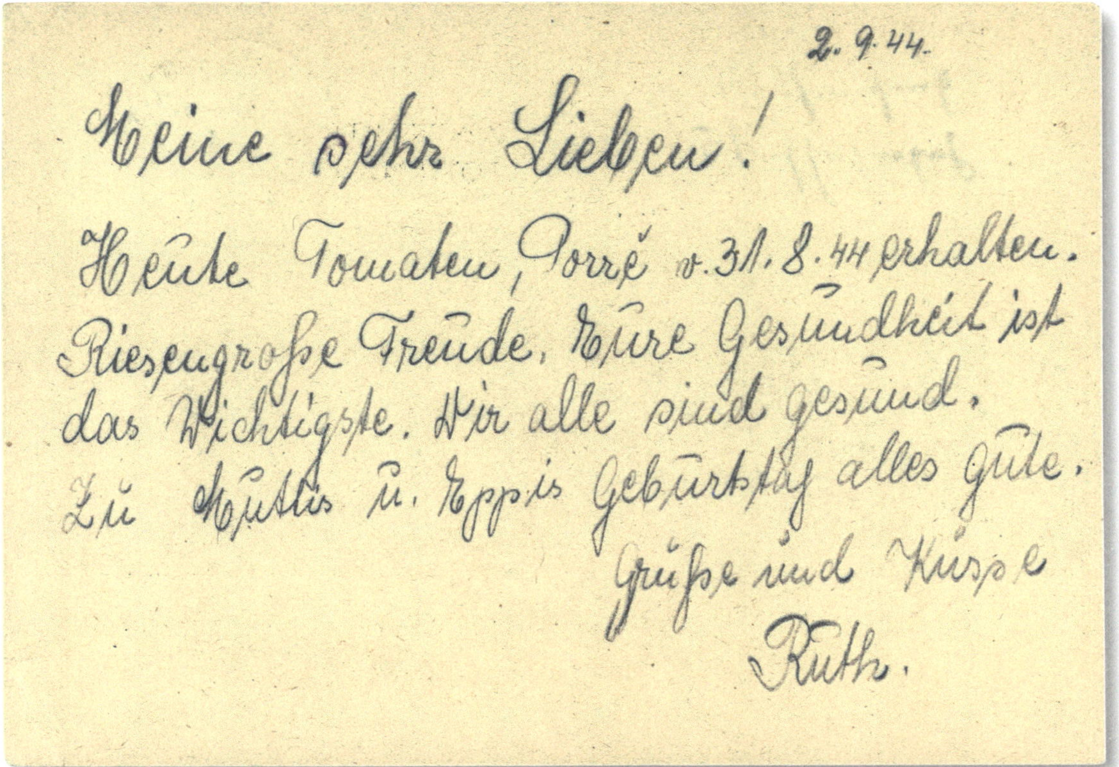

2.9.44.

Meine sehr Lieben!

Heute Tomaten, Porré v. 31.8.44 erhalten. Riesengroße Freude. Eure Gesundheit ist das Wichtigste. Wir alle sind gesund. Zu Muttis u. Eppis Geburtstag alles Gute.

Grüße und Küsse

Ruth.

Fifty-first postcard from Ruth, 2 September 1944

postmark: 30 October 1944, Berlin W62

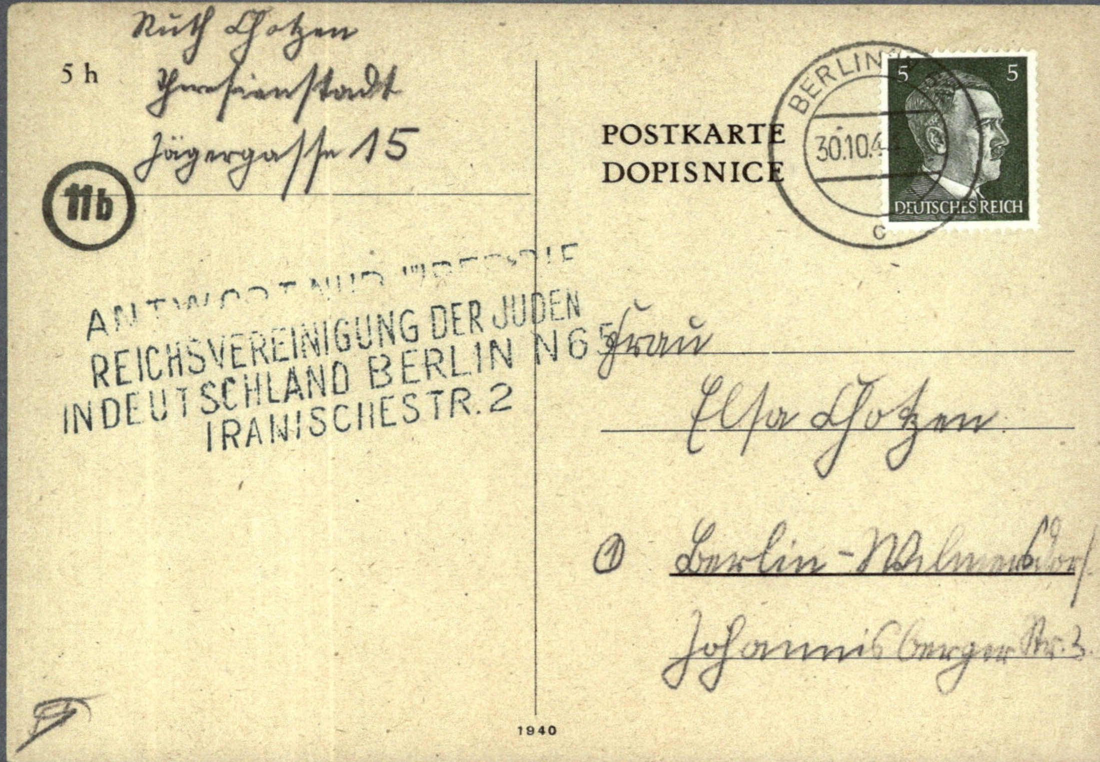
Ruth [illegible]
5 h
Theresienstadt
Jägergasse 15

11b

POSTKARTE
DOPISNICE

BERLIN
30.10.4
C

5 5
DEUTSCHES REICH

ANTWORT NUR ÜBER DIE
REICHSVEREINIGUNG DER JUDEN
IN DEUTSCHLAND BERLIN N 65
IRANISCHESTR. 2

Frau
Elsa [illegible]
1 Berlin-Wilmersdorf
Johannisberger Str. 3

1940

About postal traffic

One day after Bubi, Lisa and Ulli sent cards, Ruth sent this card to Berlin with a message that was so short it could have been included on a parcel confirmation card: She was clearly pressed for time. Ulli filled out the front. This way both left a small token for their loved ones. The four postcards with personal texts were all postmarked in Berlin on 30 October 1944, one day before Elsa's 57th birthday. By this time, the two sons had already left Theresienstadt for Auschwitz. Ruth volunteered to leave on a transport that departed on 6 October. She left believing she would meet up with her husband there.

Situation in Theresienstadt

In that day's 'Notices from the Jewish Self-Administration No. 41' it was pointed out, among other things, that these notices were now being hung in various places and that it was in the interest of every 'resident' to remain informed. One notice board stood at Bäckergasse 2, Bubi and Ulli's address.

It was also announced that the International Red Cross had sent cheese and that everyone would receive a 40 g 'triangular cheese' that evening.

The propaganda film was still being shot at that time. We know from Ruth that she watched footage of the film after the war, perhaps to see if she or her relatives were in it, but with no success. Tens of thousands of prisoners were used as extras in the film.

2.9.44

My very dears!

Received tomatoes, leeks from **31.8.44** today. Huge delight. Your health is what matters most. We are all healthy. **Happy birthday** to Mum and Eppi.

Greetings and kisses
Ruth.

31.8.44: The food was apparently only in transit for two days – the 'huge delight' was also because the food arrived fresh. In the past food had often spoiled by the time it arrived in Theresienstadt. In his memoirs, Eppi frequently stressed his mother's pragmatism:

My mother kept sending coffee substitutes in the parcels and it was only after this horrible smelly stuff was constantly being praised that she explained the whole thing to me: she had poured out part of the tobacco-brown coarse powder, put cigarettes in it and then poured the whole thing back in again; it was an ongoing success! 'You'd be amazed what you can do with this coffee substitute...' they wrote and: 'Tell Frieda, too...,' which of course we did.

Happy birthday: Eppi's birthday was on 27 September; Elsa's on 31 October. Ruth correctly calculated that her card was more likely to arrive at the end of October than in September.
Like Erich's wife Ilse, Ruth also received a necklace from Elsa with a pendant containing photographs. It is likely that Lisa, her third daughter-in-law, received a similar piece of jewelry. Ruth wore hers until she arrived in Auschwitz. She later said that that she threw the necklace away when they tried to take it from her there. It got caught in the electric fence and thus didn't fall into the hands of the SS, which gave her pleasure every day when she walked past the fence.

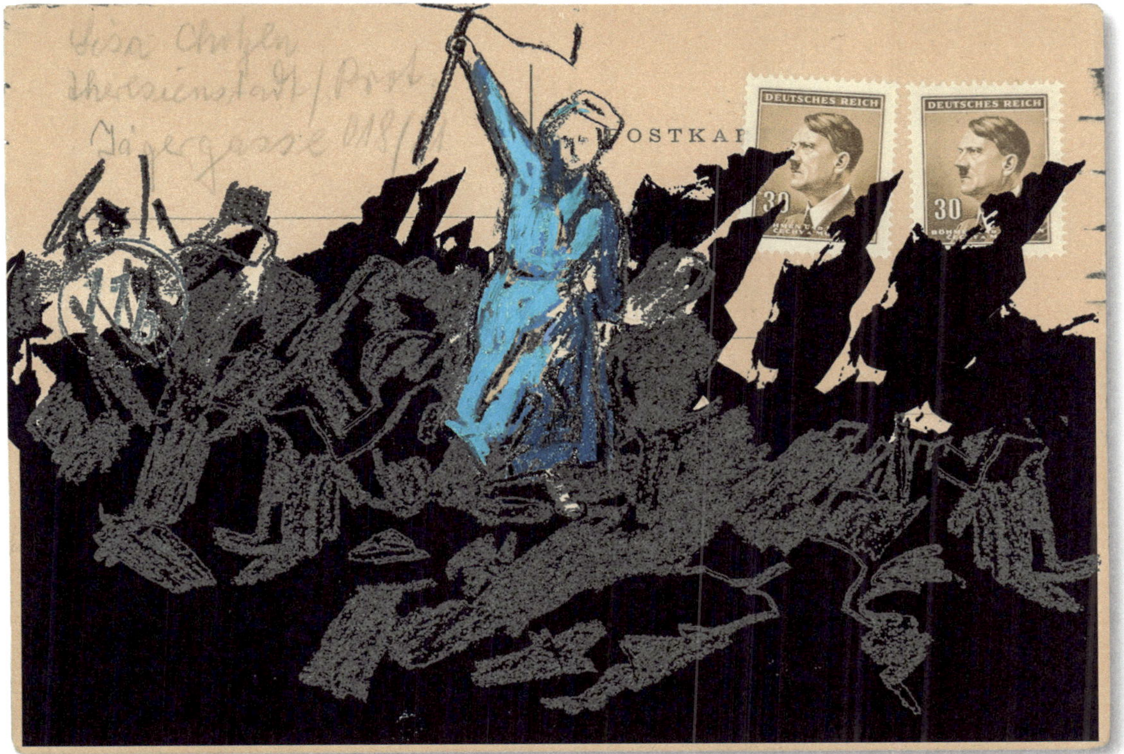

Elsa as Liberty, 2021

Multimedia and digital editing

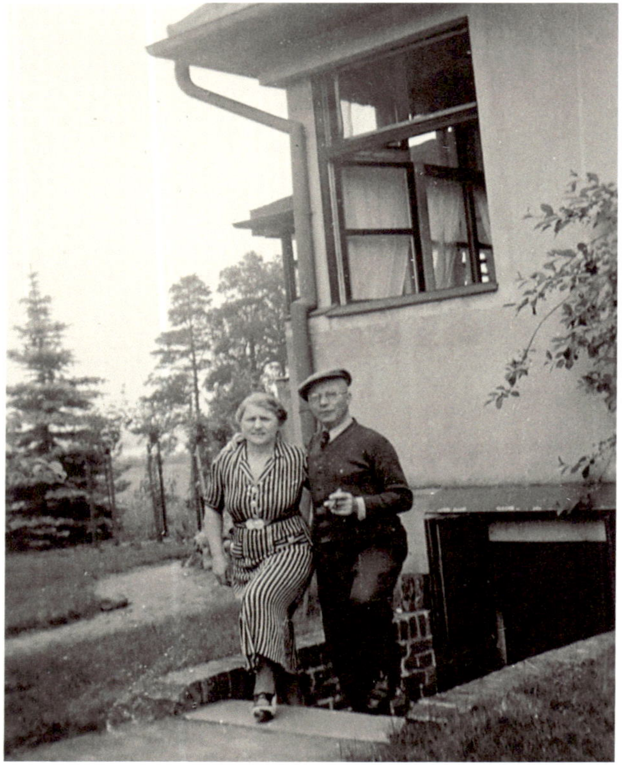

Elsa and Josef on a family holiday in Teupitz 1940, from Eppi's pocket album

INBAR CHOTZEN

In the postcard titled 'Elsa as Liberty', Elsa is portrayed as Liberty from Delacroix's painting , 'Liberty Leading the People.' Yet, Elsa was not a symbol; she fought for the release of her sons and she also took part in the Rosenstrasse demonstrations in February 1943. Together with Eppi's girlfriend Božka, who later became his wife, they kept sending small parcels of food to Theresienstadt; these parcels of hope helped the family survive in Theresienstadt. Furthermore, at great personal risk, Elsa and Eppi helped some friends who went into hiding to avoid deportation.
The black silhouette in the postcard was created by using a photo of my parents, taking part in the "black flags protest" in Israel in 2021. Elsa's struggle and Eppi's political commitment, as well as that of his cousin and his son, i.e., my grandfather and my father, are directly related to each other. It is the invisible thread linking our families.
I deeply regret not having met Elsa while I still could have.

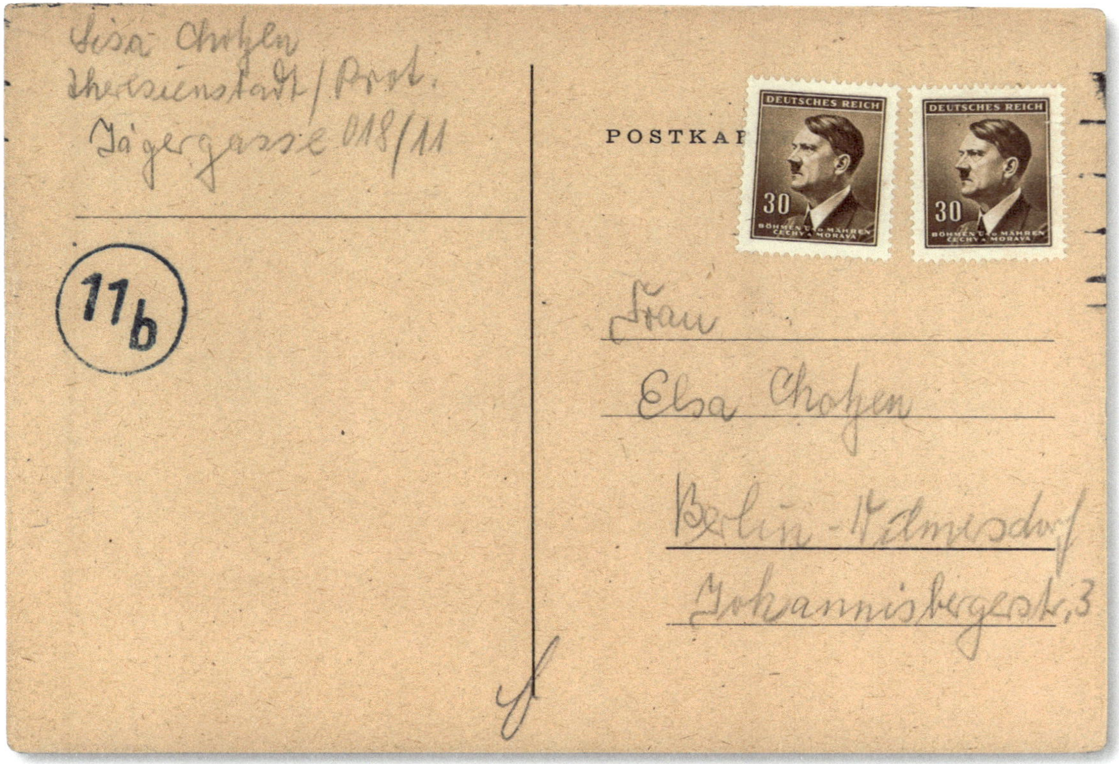

Fifty-fifth postcard from Lisa, 5 September 1944
no postmark

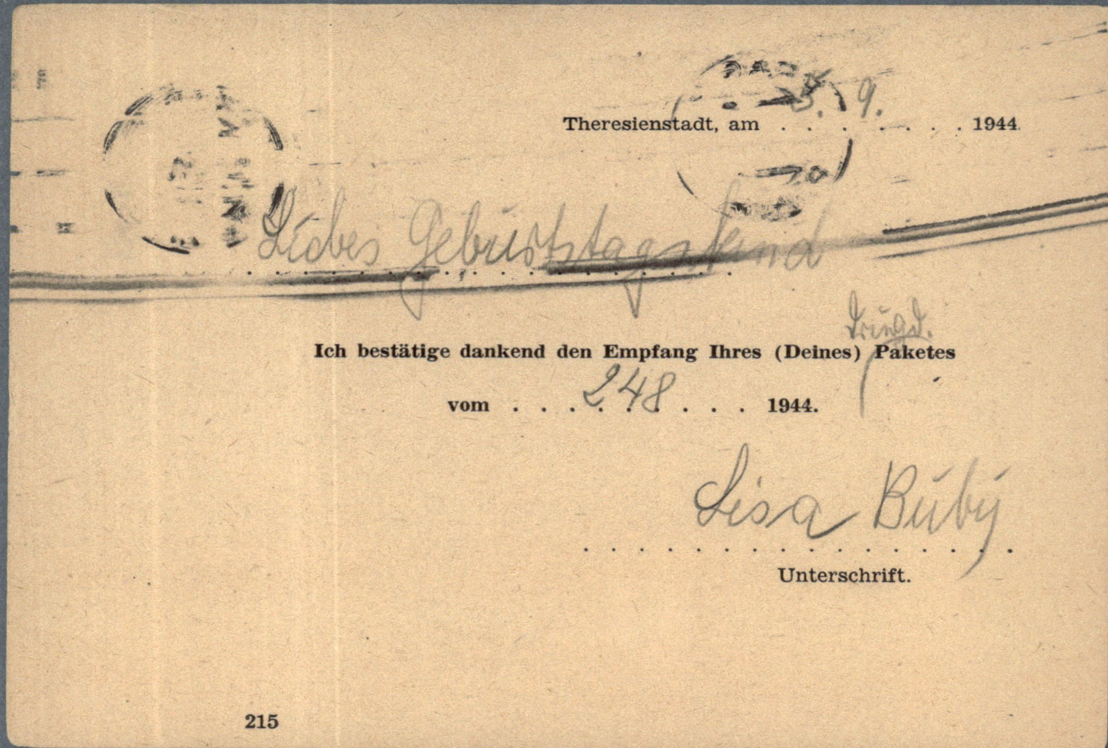
Theresienstadt, am 5. 9. 1944.

Liebes Geburtstagskind

Ich bestätige dankend den Empfang Ihres (Deines) Paketes

vom 24.8. 1944.

Lisa Buby

Unterschrift.

215

About postal traffic

In addition to this parcel confirmation postcard, which Lisa and her husband signed together, seven more pre-printed postcards from Lisa have survived. The dates of the last two raise questions, however. According to the deportation list, Lisa left Theresienstadt for Auschwitz on 9 October, but there are cards dated 10 and 14 October. It is unclear whether she left on a later transport or perhaps pre-dated the cards. Her last postcard arrived on 8 November 1944, with a final message from Bubi.

Another undated postcard with a personal text exists that was sent by Lisa in September. In it, she thanks for sending potatoes and fruit on 30 August 1944. The postal service in this direction appeared to be operating well at this time.

EPPI CHOTZEN

Various letters illustrate how important it was for them to maintain contact with everyone for as long as possible.

For example, Lucie, Klaus Scheurenberg's mother, wrote on 23 January 1944: 'We are always very happy to receive your parcels, which do indeed arrive... But we never hear from anyone else. Why is there no news from my sister-in-law?'

Another one from Paul and Lucie Scheurenberg on 4 May 44: 'I want to offer our heartfelt thanks for your kind parcels, which contribute greatly to our well-being...'

And over and over again: many thanks...along with the parcel confirmations without [text] which, like the parcels we sent, were always received.

Theresienstadt, on 5. 9. 1944

Dear Birthday Child!

I gratefully confirm having received your urgent **parcel**

vom 248 *1944.*

Lisa Bubi

Signatur

Dear Birthday Child: Eppi's birthday was on 27 September, Elsa's on 31 October. It is not clear to whom Lisa and Bubi were referring, as both birthdays were mentioned in the previous messages: They knew that the delivery took a long time. It should be noted here that, as with Ruth's last message, the parcel was not in transit for very long – from 24 August to 5 September.

Urgent parcel: Lisa added an unusually direct detail here. Never before had they indicated with such clarity that food was urgently needed. She must have felt some ambivalence about writing this since they were all concerned about the food situation in Berlin. Lisa wrote in September 1944: *'We were very happy about the potatoes and fruit. We just wonder how you do it. We would hate to think that you are depriving yourselves on our behalf.'*

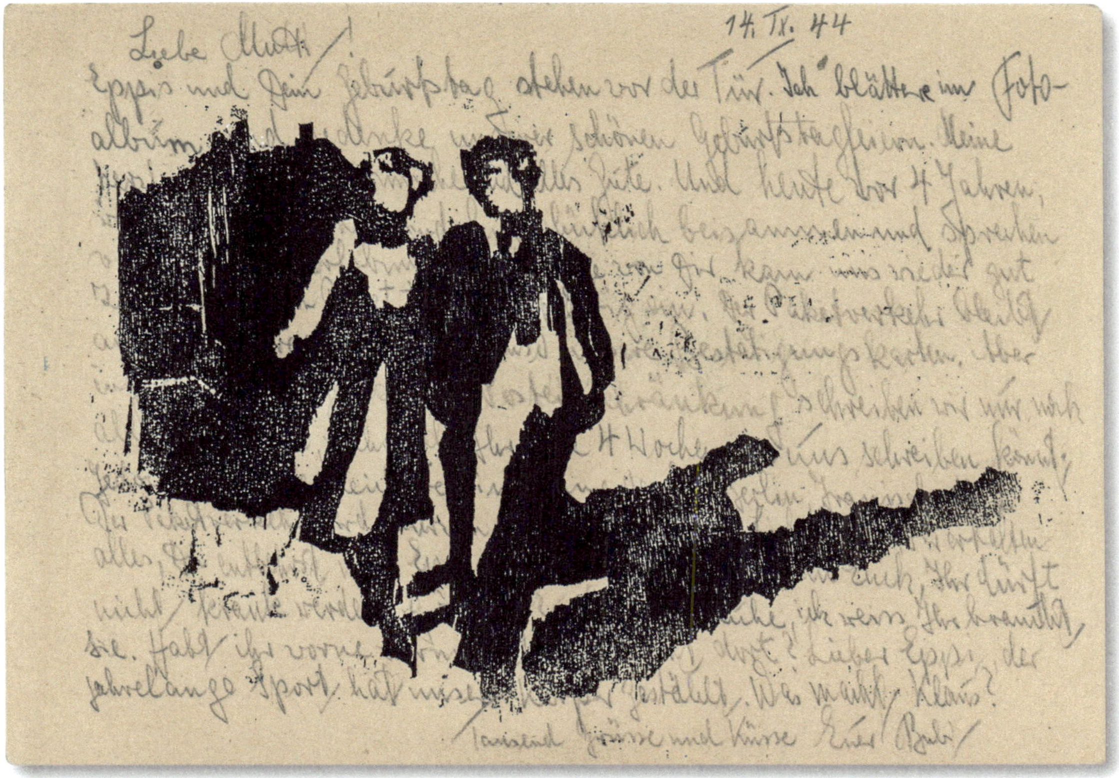

The Movies Stars, 2019

Woodcut and digital editing

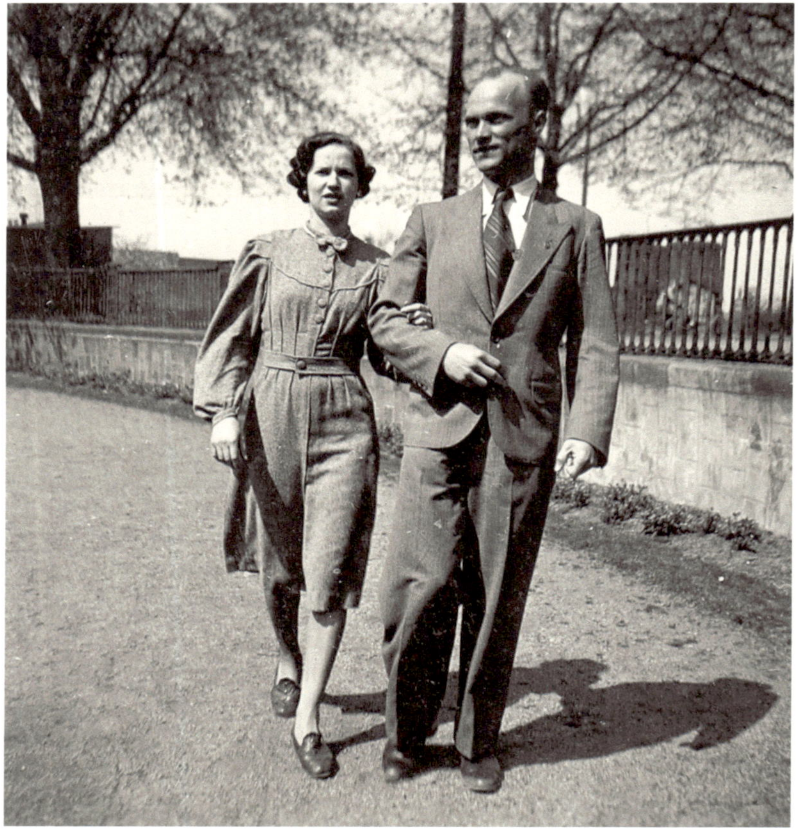

Bubi and Lisa, probably 1940/41, from Eppi's pocket album

INBAR CHOTZEN

When I looked more closely at the photograph of this young couple (Lisa und Bubi), I noticed how thin Lisa had become during the time that she did forced labour. Still, to me they looked like movie stars.

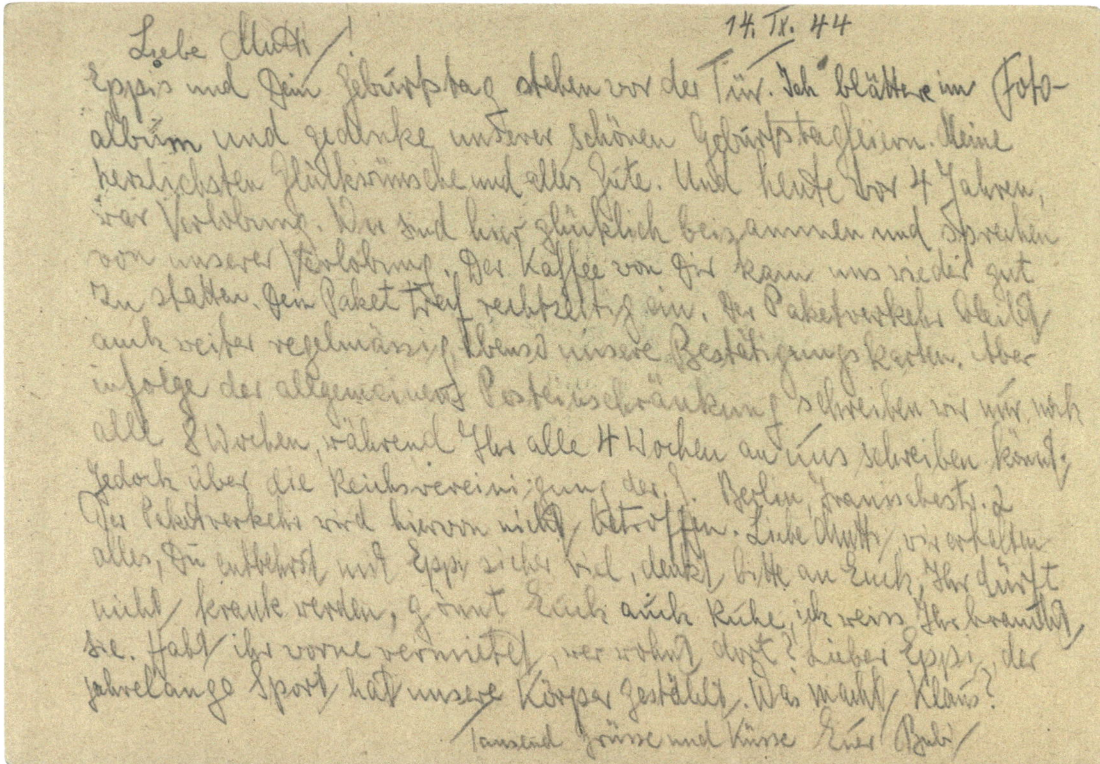

Liebe Mutti! 14. IX. 44

Eppis und Dein Geburtstag stehen vor der Tür. Ich blättere im Fotoalbum und gedenke unserer schönen Geburtstagsfeiern. Meine herzlichsten Glückwünsche und alles Gute. Und heute vor 4 Jahren war Verlobung. Wir sind hier glücklich beisammen und sprechen von unserer Verlobung. Der Kaffee von Dir kam uns wieder gut zu statten. Dein Paket traf rechtzeitig ein. Der Paketverkehr bleibt auch weiter regelmässig, ebenso unsere Bestätigungskarten. Aber infolge der allgemeinen Postbeschränkung schreiben wir nur noch alle 8 Wochen, während Ihr alle 4 Wochen an uns schreiben könnt, jedoch über die Reichsvereinigung der J. Berlin, Iranischestr. 2. Der Paketverkehr wird hiervon nicht betroffen. Liebe Mutti, wir erhalten alles, Du entbehrst mit Eppi sicher viel, denkt bitte an Euch, Ihr dürft nicht krank werden, gönnt Euch auch Ruhe, ich weiss Ihr braucht sie. Habt ihr vorne vermietet, wer wohnt dort? Lieber Eppi, der jahrelange Sport hat unsere Körper gestählt. Was macht Klaus?

Tausend Grüsse und Küsse Euer Bubi

Sixty-eighth postcard from Bubi, 14 September 1944

postmark: 4 November 1944, Berlin-Charlottenburg

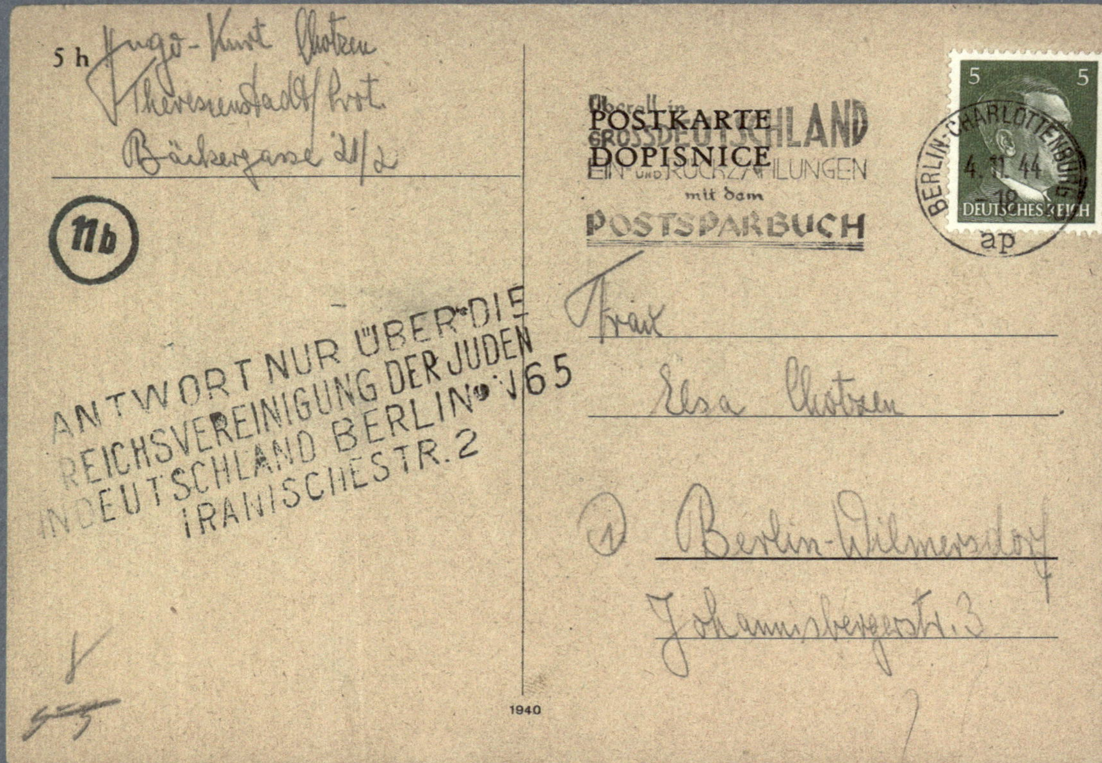
5 h Hugo-Kurt Chotzen
Theresienstadt/Prot.
Bäckergasse 21/2
11b
ANTWORT NUR ÜBER DIE
REICHSVEREINIGUNG DER JUDEN
IN DEUTSCHLAND BERLIN N 65
IRANISCHESTR. 2
POSTKARTE
DOPISNICE
Überall in
GROSSDEUTSCHLAND
EIN- UND RÜCKZAHLUNGEN
mit dem
POSTSPARBUCH
BERLIN-CHARLOTTENBURG
4.11.44
ap
5 5
DEUTSCHES REICH
Frau
Elsa Chotzen
Berlin-Wilmersdorf
Johannisbergerstr. 3
1940

About postal traffic

This was the last postcard containing a personal text that Bubi sent home before he was deported to Auschwitz with his brother Ulli. Over the past 15 months, he had managed to send eleven postcards with long texts. In these, Bubi repeatedly expressed his longing and concern for his mother and brother while also reassuring them that they were holding up well in Theresienstadt. In this postcard, too, he mentions how sports had strengthened their bodies.

This postcard reached Berlin at the same time as a Lisa's final message. Elsa and Eppi never heard from any of their loved ones again after that.

Situation in Theresienstadt

On this day, the 'Notices from the Jewish Self-Administration No. 44' announced the laundry delivery schedule, the procedure for registration stamps for parcels from the Protektorat, and provided instructions on how to operate the ovens properly. The siren warning signals were again explained:

'Air warning without traffic restriction: Siren sounds rising and falling three times in one minute.

Air alert: Siren sounds rising and falling several times in one minute.

All-clear: ongoing siren sound for one minute.'

The war was also omnipresent in Theresienstadt.

14.IX.44

Dear Mum!

Eppi's and your birthdays are just around the corner. I've been browsing through the **photo album** and recalling our wonderful birthday celebrations. My warmest congratulations and wishing all the best. Our engagement was four years ago today. We are happy together here and speak about our engagement. The coffee you sent again came in handy. The parcel arrived on time. Parcel delivery remains regular, as do our confirmation postcards. But due to **general postal restrictions**, we will only be writing every eight weeks, whereas you can write to us every four weeks. Send [the postcards], however, via the Reich Association of J. Berlin, Iranische Str. 2. This does not affect parcel delivery. Dear Mum, we receive everything;
you and Eppi are no doubt doing without so much. Please think of yourselves, don't fall ill, get some rest, I know you need it. Have you rented out the front rooms, who lives there now? Dear Eppi, the years of playing sports have toned our bodies. What's **Klaus** doing?

A thousand greetings and kisses, Your Bubi

Eppi's and your birthdays: Eppi's birthday was on 27 September; Elsa's on 31 October.

Photo album: Bubi may have had personal photos with him since his deportation or Elsa may have included photos in the parcels. Restrictions on keeping personal items were more relaxed in Theresienstadt than in other concentration camps.

General postal restrictions: This pre-formulated sentence apparently follows a current regulation. The same or similar sentences also appear in postcards from Ulli (10 September 1944), Ruth (13 September 1944) and Lisa (undated, from September 1944).

Klaus: Bubi was referring here to his brother-in-law Klaus Scheurenberg. He did not know where Klaus was or how he was doing. When Klaus returned to Theresienstadt in February 1945, he found only his parents there. His sister Lisa and his brother-in-law Bubi had left on the 'autumn transports'. They had no more contact after that.

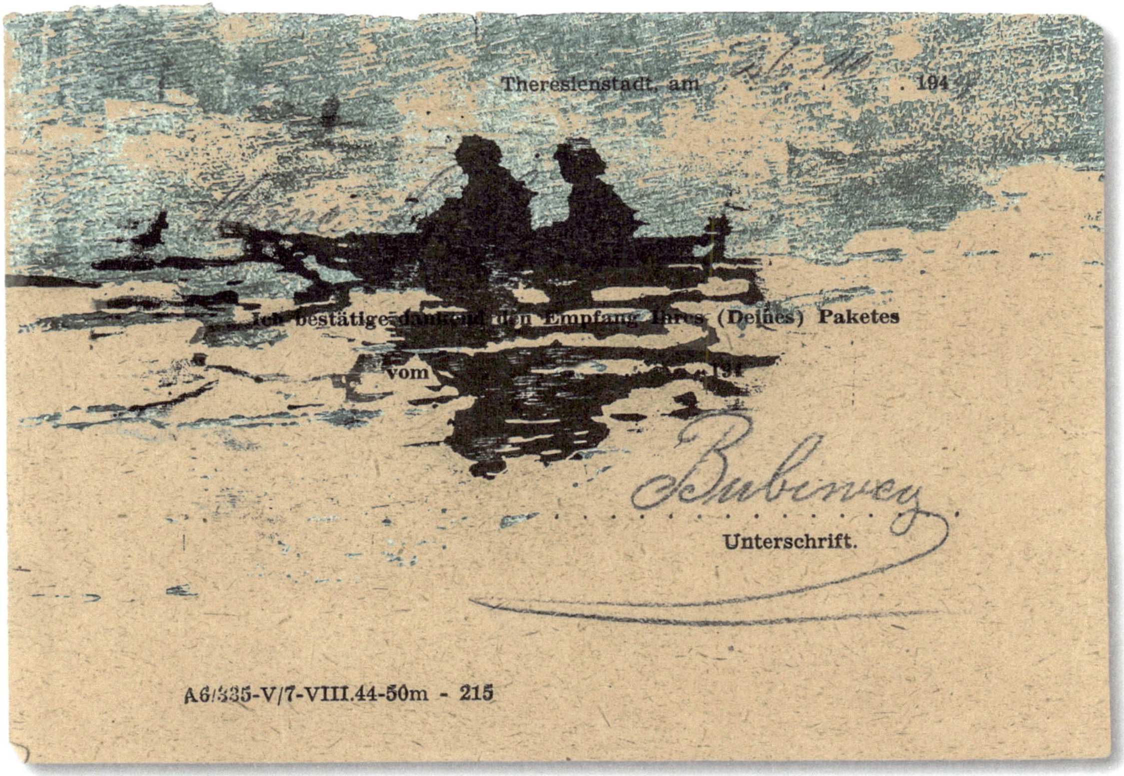

The Last Postcard, 2021

Woodcut and digital editing

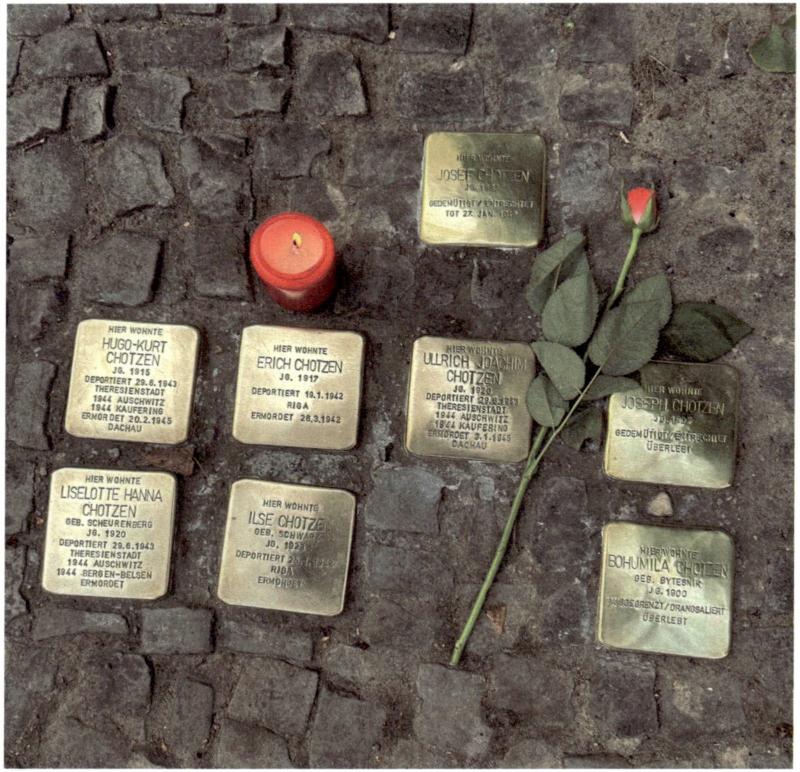

Stumbling stones for the family in front of the building at Johannisberger Straße 3 in Berlin-Wilmersdorf. Photo: Sharon McMullen-Ansorge

INBAR CHOTZEN

For 'The Last Postcard', containing the devastating coded news about Bubi's deportation from Theresienstadt, I used the motif of a couple sailing a small boat, like one might see in a romantic scene at the end of a movie in which the two sail off into the sunset.

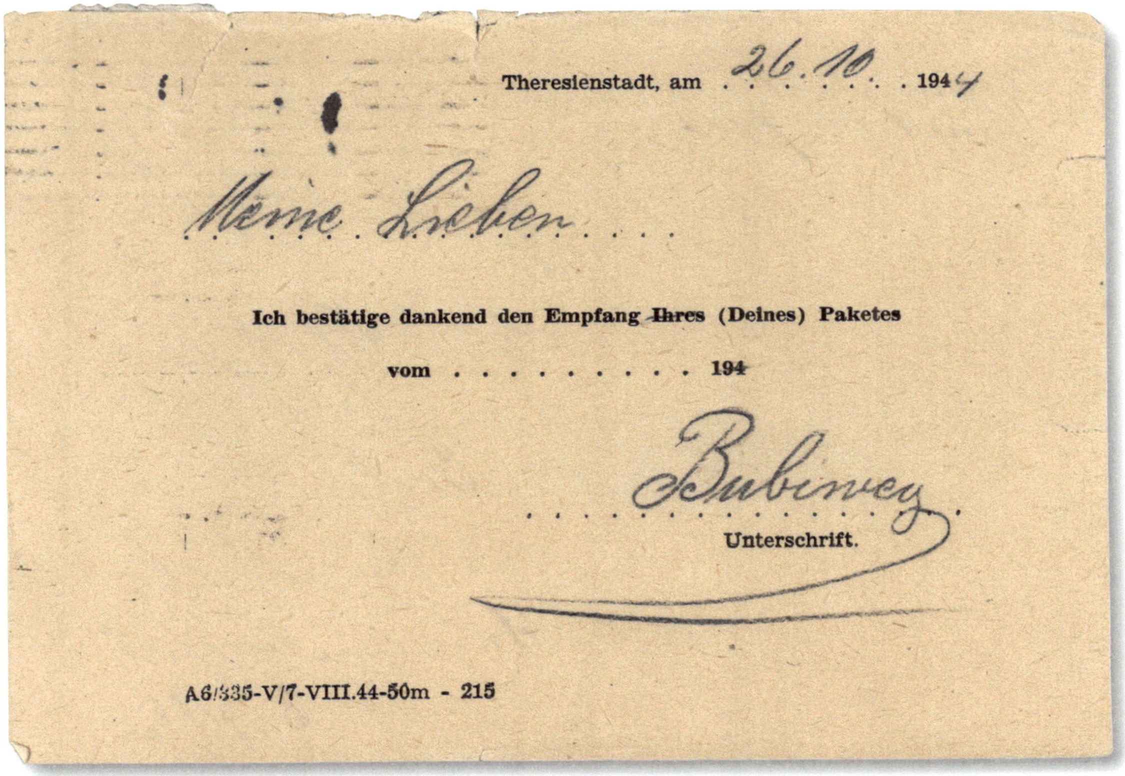

Theresienstadt, am 26.10. 1944

Meine Lieben . . . . . .

Ich bestätige dankend den Empfang ~~Ihres~~ (Deines) Paketes

vom 194

Bubinez

Unterschrift.

A6/335-V/7-VIII.44-50m - 215

Twenty-fourth postcard from Lucie and Paul Scheurenberg, 26 October 1944

postmark: 3 November 1944, Prag

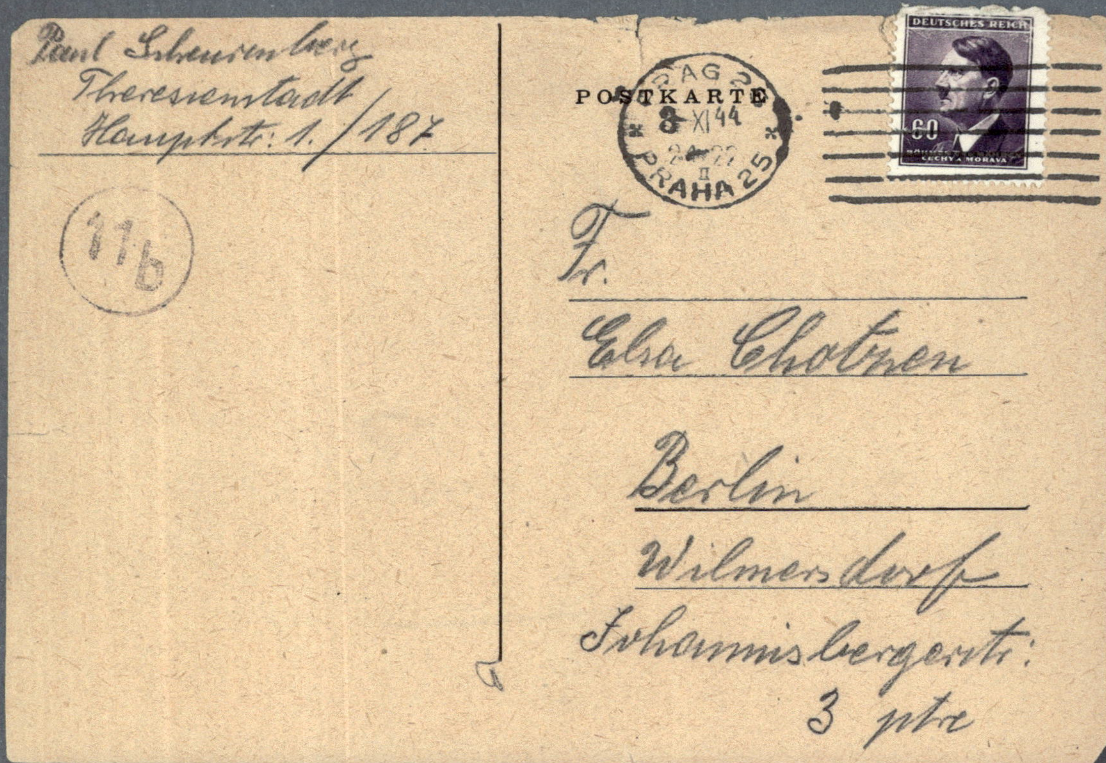

Paul Schreuenberg
Theresienstadt
Hauptstr. 1./187

11b

POSTKARTE

PRAG 3 · 3.XI.44 · 2–22 · PRAHA 25

DEUTSCHES REICH · 60 · ČECHY A MORAVA

Fr.
Elsa Chotzen
Berlin
Wilmersdorf
Johannisbergerstr.
3 ptr

About postal traffic

This postcard was not sent to confirm receipt of a parcel; it was meant to deliver a message. Bubi and Ulli had been sent on a transport to Auschwitz on September 29. One day after this card reached Berlin, Elsa and Eppi received messages from Bubi and Lisa that had been sent before they left Theresienstadt.

EPPI CHOTZEN

Before me lie 365 yellowed postcards that were
written four decades ago in Theresienstadt!
In the postcards, on which they were allowed to
write more than the pre-printed text, they send
my – our – mother encouragement and comfort,
expressing thanks for her for parcels and
repeatedly offered assurances:
'We are fine'! Yet each one also contains a great
longing, a growing sense of insecurity and fear!
These are the last cards from:
Bubi ---- Lisa ---- Ulli! ----
According to the 'Certificates of Death:'
No. 201 for Bubi –
No. 183 for Ulli –
They both arrived in the Dachau concentration
camp on 10 October 1944.
Bubi's date of death was recorded on
20 February 1945
Ulli's on 3 January 1945.[1]
The final solution had caught up with them!

1 The date of Ulli's death was corrected after further research; he died on December 23, 1944.

Theresienstadt, on 26.10. *1944*

My dears!

I gratefully confirm receipt of your parcel

from ……………… *1944.*

Bubigone

Unterschrift

This postcard was sent by Lucie and Paul Scheurenberg, Bubi's in-laws. To get around the censor, they concealed an important message to Bubi's mother, Elsa, in the signature: Bubi was no longer in Theresienstadt.

APPENDIX

BIOGRAPHIES

Inbar Chotzen-Tselniker is an Israeli artist. She received both her bachelor's degree in art communication and M.E. in 1992 from NB Haifa School of design. She was lecturer at the Avni Institute for art and design and art director in commercial advertising campaigns. As an independent artist she presented solo exhibitions and various group exhibitions in Israel and Berlin.
www.inbarchotzen.com

Klaus Hillenbrand is a journalist and author. He worked for "die tageszeitung" (taz) for many years, most recently as a senior editor for special interest pages. His books deal with the National Socialist persecution of Jews and the Nazi regime. The subject of three of his books is the situation of Jews in Berlin during the Nazi era.

Dr. Ruth Preusse is a literary scholar and historian. She has been a research assistant at the House of the Wannsee Conference Memorial and Educational Site since 2015, where she is responsible for special exhibitions and publications. Together with Inbar Chotzen, she already developed an exhibition on the Chotzen family history in 2022, in which paintings and parts of the historical estate were shown together.

LITERATURE (Selection)

H. G. Adler: Theresienstadt 1941–1945. Das Antlitz einer Zwangsgemeinschaft. Göttingen 2005 [Reprint of the second edition 1960]

Frantisek Benes / Patricia Tosnerová: Posta v ghettu Terezín: 1941–1945 [Czech, German, English]. Prag 1996

Wolfgang Benz: Theresienstadt. Eine Geschichte von Täuschung und Vernichtung. Munich 2013

Vojtěch Blodig: Theresienstadt in der „Endlösung der Judenfrage" 1941–1945. Führer durch die Dauerausstellung des Ghetto-Museums in Theresienstadt. Theresienstadt 2003

Gorch Pieken: Das Haushaltsbuch der Elsa Chotzen. Schicksal einer jüdischen Familie 1937–1946. Berlin 2008

Klaus Scheurenberg: Ich will leben. Ein autobiografischer Bericht. Berlin 1982

Barbara Schieb: Nachricht von Chotzen. Berlin 2000 [out of print]

Heinz Wewer: Postalische Zeugnisse zur deutschen Besatzungsherrschaft im Protektorat Böhmen und Mähren. Berlin 2018

THANKS

The archive of the Chotzen family is kept at the House of the Wannsee Conference Memorial and Educational Site. All photographs, postcards and letters shown here, as well as Eppi Chotzen's memoirs, are part of this collection unless otherwise indicated.

Thanks to
Evemarie and Andreas Baumstark, Daniel Berger, Roja Binder, Kay Danley, the Berlin Stumbling Stone Initiative, Dr. Lina Dedert (GHWK), Luzie Diekmann (Deutscher Kunstverlag), Michaela Dostálová (Terezin Memorial), Dr. Tomáš Fedorovič (Terezin Memorial), Svea Hammerle, Deborah Hartmann (GHWK), Jennifer Heidtke (GHWK), Kathleen Herfurth (Deutscher Kunstverlag), Carolin Hess, Viktoria Krieger (Villa Liebermann), Sharon and Bernd McMullen-Ansorge (Stolperstein-Initiative Friedenau/Stierstraße), Robert Müller-Stahl, Eva Oelze, Dr. Diana Schulle, Monika Sommerer (Jüdisches Museum Berlin), Eike Stegen (GHWK), Jana Sumičová (Terezin Memorial), Barbara Thumm (GHWK), Dr. Evelyn Wöldicke (Villa Liebermann)

In grateful memory
Barbara Schieb (1958–2023)

IMPRINT

Liebe Mutti!

POSTCARDS FROM THERESIENSTADT 1943–1944

with artworks by Inbar Chotzen

Published by
the House of the Wannsee Conference
Memorial and Educational Site

Texts
Klaus Hillenbrand, Dr. Ruth Preusse, Inbar Chotzen

Research
Dr. Ruth Preusse

Translation
Miriamne Fields

English proofreading
Marie Frohling

Design
e o t . Berlin, Lilla Hinrichs + Anna Sartorius

Printing
Grafisches Centrum Cuno GmbH & Co. KG

Paper
Munken Lynx 150gr

Publisher
Deutscher Kunstverlag
Genthiner Straße 13
10785 Berlin (Germany)
www.deutscherkunstverlag.de
An Imprint of Walter de Gruyter GmbH
Berlin/Boston
www.degruyter.com

Questions about general product safety
productsafety@degruyterbrill.com

The German National Library lists this publication in the German National Bibliography; detailed bibliographic information is available on the Internet at http://dnb.d-nb.de.

Library of Congress Control Number: 2025940437

ISBN 978-3-422-80306-0